RANJIT SINGH

Encyclopaedic History of Indian Freedom Movement Series

RANJIT SINGH

Administration and British Policy

Edited by

OM PRAKASH

ANMOL PUBLICATIONS PVT. LTD.

NEW DELHI - 110 002 (INDIA)

ANMOL PUBLICATIONS PVT. LTD.
4374/4B, Ansari Road, Daryaganj
New Delhi - 110 002
Ph.: 23261597, 23278000
Visit us at: www.anmolpublications.com

Ranjit Singh: Administration and British Policy

First Edition, 2004

ISBN 81-261-1516-5

PRINTED IN INDIA

Published by J.L. Kumar for Anmol Publications Pvt. Ltd., New Delhi - 110 002 and Printed at Mehra Offset Press, Delhi.

Contents

Preface

'Golden bird' as India was known in yore days, rich in natural resources and well-developed cottage industries it was considered an affluent country. Indian spices, fabrics and other handicrafts were in great demand the world over. In the lure of having these goods and riches, many European powers made adventurous voyages to locate India.

The story of European expansions in Asia forms one of the great epics of modern times. India was the cornerstone of European imperialism in Asia. It was the lure of the lucrative 'Indian trade' which incited European adventurers to seek a new route to India, thus inaugurating a new era of contact between these two distant lands. Among the European empires in Asia, the British empire was the most enduring and prosperous one. And India was the finest jewel of the British dominion. It is worthwhile to remember that European exploration and adventure in the east were encouraged by the great demand in Europe for the products from Malabar like spices and calicoe cloth. Symbolically, the European age in Indian and indeed Asian history began with the landing of Vasco-de-Gama at Calicut on the 27th of May 1498. During this period, there was a continuous struggle between European traders and their native rivals and among the Europeans themselves. By the end of the eighteenth century this struggle for supremacy had been resolved in favour of the English.

The European traders were originally in the position of supplicants before the native rulers in India. For example, when William Hawkins arrived at the court of Jehangir with a letter from King James I asking for trade facilities, he had brought with him, a gift of 25,000 Gold pieces. As Lane Poole observes,

"There was nothing to suggest the most distant dream that in two centuries and a half the slight introduction Hawkins was then effecting between England and India would culminate in the sovereignty of a British Queen over the whole empire."

But unlike their European rivals like the Portuguese and the Dutch, the English made their bid for power in India only when the powerful Mughal empire had begun to decline. In any case the Portuguese and the Dutch had only small coastal settlements in India even at the height of their power and influence in this country.

By the end of the seventh Century, the Portuguese had been displaced by their Dutch rivals in Malabar and in the islands, of the East Indies. As for the Dutch, they were compelled by force of circumstances to regard the factories "which they established on the main land merely as marketing points for the products of an Empire which had its capital at Batavia in the East Indies."

Moreover, the Dutch power in India was largely jeopardised on European battle fields.

The wars with England and France drained the resources of this nation. Thus, it was left to the French to provide real opposition to the English in India.

The same pattern can be detected in the story of European activity in Malabar. Here the intensity of their rivalry was greater because of three main reasons. Malabar with its many fine harbours and backwaters was more accessible from the sea, increasing the scope for European interference.

Thus, European powers who came to India with the intention of trade snatched the political power and sovereignty from the local states, principalities and feudal lords. And established complete control over India. After over hundred years colonial rule, the feeling of national integration and freedom from the clutches of foreign power developed among the Indians. Thus, began the saga of freedom movement.

This encyclopaedic study is phased into two most significant and historic diversions having deep bearing on varied kinds of events which moulded the destiny of millions of people of Indian sub-continent. These events having complete political overtones, became a glaring phenomenon with the downfall of the Mughal Empire almost with the commencement of the 18th century. The ambitious piercing eyes of four European powers — the British, the French, the Portuguese and the Dutch—did cast upon several gainful economic successes in India.

Of these powers, the East India Company's government, with well organised force, bureaucracy and diplomats achieved phenomenal successes against their adversaries. The first phase,—therefore has been marked from Plassey to the Mutiny of 1857 (The First War of Independence) when the Company's role came to an end.

The second phase, naturally, came very much in the hands of the British Government functioning under the Whitehall and ended with the dawn of Swaraj on 15 August 1947.

This multi-volumes study would take up several themes, viz. political, socio-economic, religious, constitutional, educational, press, revolutionaries, local pioneers, legislation, revenues and judicial policy, on-going process of reaction — violent and non-violent, moderates and extremists, local and all India movements, reaction of the British.Raj, efforts for conciliation, significant Acts passed by the Central Legislature, the impact of two global wars, 1914-1919 and 1939-1945; Congress, Muslim League, Hindu Mahasabha and the British Policy, a significant change in Britain soon after 1945, the Labour Government of Clement Attlee and Partition of India in August 1947.

In the first lot eleven volumes have appeared while in the present second lot ten volumes are being brought out namely the Marathas and their administration; Lord William Bentinck and Metcalf era of reforms; Raja Rammohun Roy: the reformer; Mutiny and its aftermath; History of Anglo-Sikh wars;

Emergence of Maharaja Ranjit Singh; Lord Hastings and his administrative measures; Ranjit Singh administration and British policy; British policy of intervention and expansion; and Lord Wellesley and policy of expansion.

This prestigious project is arranged, managed and looked after by a team of most dedicated and long experienced scholars of modern Indian history.

In gathering the authentic information, we have taken liberty to draw the material from the learned works of many great scholars in the field. We are deeply beholden to all those whose works are partially cited or substantially made use of in the project. I am indebted to Mr. J.L. Kumar, Managing Director, Anmol Publications Pvt. Ltd., New Delhi for his constant inspiration and moral support and finally to bring out this work. Last but not the least I am thankful to all those who have assisted me one way or other while preparing the manuscript.

—**Om Prakash**

1
Danger from Without

The British had never viewed the rise of Ranjit Singh with equanimity, diplomatic cordiality notwithstanding. In 1808-09 when he sought to extend his sway over the Sikh areas of the Sutlej-Yamuna divide, two powerful British armies[1] were forthwith despatched to drive him back to the north of the Sutlej and the solemn statutory obligation of non-intervention as incorporated in the Pitt's India Act, 1784 was conveniently jettisoned. It may even be admitted that had Ranjit Singh on this occasion declined to accede to the terms offered, the British might have ventured to subvert his authority on the other side of the river as well. Capt. Murray, at one time British Political Agent at Ludhiana, expressed the typical British reaction to Ranjit Singh's meteoric rise when he made the observation[2] that "the approximation to British boundary of an ambitious prince was an object of sufficient importance". It was felt that Ranjit Singh had become master of the Punjab almost unheeded[3] by the English and that his further expansionist activities should be strictly watched and if possible, curbed. As a first step towards that object Capt. Murray with the support of the higher British authorities started disputing the claims, though legitimate, of the Maharaja to many of his territorial possessions lying south of the Sutlej. International pressures[4] subsequently compelled the British to admit a slight modification in this policy, agreeing to accommodate the Sikh ruler on minor issues so that he might be persuaded to accommodate the British on matters of major importance, such as British attempts at penetration into Sind and Afghanistan, and navigation of the Indus.[5] But mental reservations continued as before, and when the self-styled Khalifa Sayyed Ahmad of Bareilly was waging a *jihad* against the Sikhs (1827-1831), most of the sinews required for the *jihad* were mobilised in the British held Hindustan. Though fully cognizant of this, the British did little to stop these objectionable activities, their covert object being to keep Ranjit Singh bogged down on the north-west frontier.[6] The years 1831-38 witnessed a determined attempt on the part of the British to bring Sindh and Afghanistan into their sphere of influence, which tended to complete the encirclement of the Lahore kingdom on all sides excepting the north. In 1837 when negotiations with Amir Dost Muhammad Khan of Afghanistan were in progress, attempts were even made, though in a carefully guarded manner, to urge upon Ranjit Singh to agree to transfer the Peshawar valley to the Barakzais.[7] But nothing came out of these efforts as the failure of the parleys with the Afghan ruler gave a completely new orientation to the situation. In keeping with this trend of British thinking, the British Commander-in-Chief Sir Henry Fane, while attending the marriage of Kanwar Nau Nihal Singh in 1837 as a state guest, exploited the opportunity to estimate the armed strength of his host and to calculate how much of British force would be needed if Punjab was to be conquered.[8] Almost simultaneously with this, one Major Leech[9] was conducting, under his government's special instructions, a survey of the Jamwal Rajas' resources—their forts, their revenues, their forces and their dependencies.

All this is understandable because no imperial power, whether British or any other, would take a complacent view of an ambitious neighbouring state making long strides to power. But howsoever unpalatable, the state edifice of Ranjit Singh was tolerated so long as he was at the helm of affairs. In the earlier period the British hands were full of wars with

Marathas, Pindaris, Gurkhas and Burma so that even if they so desired they could take but scant notice of what was happening across the Sutlej. By the time they had done away with these elements, Ranjit Singh had built up a mighty power which they had to recognise and respect. Ranjit Singh's continued maintenance of friendly relations with the British was another great saving grace. For this reason, the British could not get any valid excuse for aggression against the state of Punjab. Still later when under threats of Russian penetration into Iran and Afghanistan the British awakened to "new lines of policy",[10] they humoured him so as to reconcile him to the fresh curbs which they now intended to place on his ambition to enhance his power or territory any further. When the British negotiations with Dost Muhammad broke down and it was decided to replace him with Shah Shuja, they even cajoled him for signing the Tripartite Treaty (1838) and accepted his terms, though not in full sincerity, because they needed his help.[11]

The situation in which Ranjit Singh left his state at the time of his death in 1839 was fraught with grave danger to its security. The Afghan War was in full swing when he died. Though the Maharaja had refused to allow the invading British armies to pass through his territories, yet it was in the logic of things that as time passed, the British would exert greater and greater pressure upon the Khalsa Darbar for the passage of their troops and military stores *via* Punjab. Punjab being the shorter route held great temptation for them and it was clear that if they could have the facility of using this route, they would be spared much of the botheration and expense which would be the inevitable consequence if they were compelled to take the much longer and circuitous Sindh route. Ranjit Singh no doubt had agreed, though not in writing, that the British troops after the accomplishment of their task in Afghanistan would be permitted to take the Punjab route for their return. However, this concession was intended to be no more than a one-time exception.[12] But things did not prove as simple as that. The British involvement in the land of the Afghans necessitated a continuing communication and traffic between the two countries concerned. Troops from Afghanistan were to be withdrawn in several lots rather than in a single one. Convoys of supplies had to be sent from time to time. Foodgrains had to be purchased and despatched now and again, and occasionally reinforcements or replacements had to be conveyed. For all such purposes concessions after concessions were demanded by the British from the Lahore Darbar. In such a situation even the great Maharaja Ranjit Singh would have found it difficult to resist the pressure at all times and completely. But for his son and successor Maharaja Kharak Singh the difficulty was all the greater. One thing, he did not possess even a modicum of the commanding genius of his father. Secondly, he had a strong rival in the person of Kanwar Sher Singh and thus was not in a position to take a strong line against the British pressures.[13] The result was that all that was asked for was readily conceded, even at the cost of personal popularity.

II

Although there was no genuine ground for any grouse against the Lahore government, yet the British at this time deemed it proper to exploit the weakness of the new Maharaja to promote their selfish ends. Once they felt that their feet were securely planted at Kabul, they started thinking in terms of tempering with the Tripartite Treaty, which marked a substantial shift in their Punjab policy. They attempted now to interpret this treaty in favour of their nominee, Shah Shuja. Macnaghten, British Envoy to the Afghan King, was the prime mover in this respect. The line suggested by him was pursued further by Col. Wade and Lt. Mackeson, then posted at Peshawar as British liaison officers. Macnaghten asserted that the Chiefs of Swat and Buner were subject to the authority of the King of Kabul. The Lahore Darbar refuted this claim and Kanwar Nau Nihal Singh on behalf of the Darbar despatched Sardar Pir Muhammad Khan, Gul Badshah and Bhai Amir Baksh to

Swat and Buner with valuable gifts of *shawls, chogas* and Peshawar *lungis* for Inayatullah Khan and his son to keep them attached to the Sikhs. Wade and Mackeson went ahead of Macnaghten by asserting that the Yusaffzais and other tribals towards the west of Peshawar were under the authority of Kabul. This was contrary to the Persian version of the Treaty lying in the custody of the Lahore Darbar. The words *hadd-i-Khyber,*[14] meaning up to the boundary of Khyber, were clearly mentioned therein, on which ground the Darbar refused to accept the British contention. Fakir Azizuddin was especially sent to Ludhiana to meet Mr. Clerk, the British Political Agent, and to discuss the whole matter with him. Mr. Clerk was convinced of the validity of the Darbar's case and even advised his government to admit the Sikh point of view.[15] This sound advice, however, did not produce its effect immediately. The major hindrance was that about this time Macnaghten at Kabul was accusing the Lahore Darbar of extending secret support to the Ghilzais and the ex-Amir Dost Muhammad, all enemies of Shah Shuja. On that basis he was even pleading that the Tripartite Treaty should be repudiated and the region of Peshawar, in full or partly, annexed to the Shah's dominion. The Governor-General, Lord Auckland, was so much carried away by this logic of Macnaghten that in his Minute of 20 August 1839[16] he went to the extent of proposing the establishment of a permanent British mission at Peshawar and a magazine at Rawalpindi.

The situation, though very serious from the security standpoint of the Lahore kingdom, was dealt with by Kanwar Nau Nihal Singh with great diplomatic skill. He accepted all legitimate demands of the British.[17] He agreed to surrender the rebel Bhilzai chiefs to the British and remove their Barakzai protectors, Sultan Muhammad Khan and Pir Muhammad Khan, from the north-west frontier to Lahore, though he did not agree to confiscate their *jagirs,* as desired by the British. Thereby he removed the British suspicions regarding the attitude of the Lahore Darbar. In return he insisted that the British should abandon their attempts to twist the meaning of the Tripartite Treaty favourably to Shah Shuja. The British had to concede the point and thus the immediate danger to the integrity of the frontier territories of the Darbar was warded off. Another demand of the Kanwar that Col. Wade should not be allowed to return to his post of Political Agent at Ludhiana had also to be accepted became the Kanwar insisted on it and was not willing to compromise on that.

After the death of the Kanwar on November 5, 1840, Rani Chand Kaur held the reins of the government until January 17, 1841. She was succeeded by Maharaja Sher Singh on January 18, 1841. The new reign opened in extremely difficult circumstances. A wide-spread mutiny broke out in the ranks of the Khalsa army, which lasted nearly 6 months. Two principal Sandhanwalia chiefs, Attar Singh and Ajit Singh, fled the country and took shelter across the Sutlej in British territories. They had supported Rani Chand Kaur, as against Sher Singh and were afraid that they might be arrested and imprisoned if they did not escape well in time. They also wanted to seek British help against Sher Singh. The British did not agree to help them directly but granted them political asylum which was, indeed, against the spirit of friendship subsisting between the two governments. Furthermore, they were allowed to carry on their anti-Sher Singh activities unchecked inspite of repeated protests from the Maharaja.[18] Still worse, British themselves began to hatch plots for military intervention in the Punjab in the name of restoring law and order. This is very clear from a private letter of Mrs. Henry Lawrence written to Mrs. Cameron from Subathu on May 26, 1841:[19] "Wars and rumours of wars are on every side and there seems no doubt that next cold weather will decide the long-suspended question of occupying the Punjab...". Ten days later she wrote another letter to Mrs. Haye to the same effect. The fact is also evident from the letter of Henry Lawrence dated 29 October 1841, in which he offered his services to Mr. Clerk in the event of any military intervention in the Punjab.[20] But the British needed some kind of a pretext for this purpose. While they were in search of one, they met a terrible disaster in Afghanistan in November 1841. This changed the whole spectre and upset their plans, at least for the time being. They were also driven to the necessity of seeking help from the Khalsa Darbar and therefore thought it prudent to play it down. Still suspicions had been aroused in the minds of the Sikhs regarding their secret designs on the kingdom. For this reason they were not promptly ready to extend their help to the British. Seeing this attitude of the Sikh soldiery, the British again thought of making a military intervention, and the Governor-General *vide* T.H. Maddock's letter to Clerk dated 10 February 1842 empowered[21] the Political Agent, Ludhiana to hold a force of 12000 men in readiness for the purpose. The force was to enter the Punjab sometime in the month of March and would have done so but for the sharp reaction to it of Maharaja Sher Singh.[22] At the eleventh hour the British hesitated and then gave up the idea. At least they had realized the great risk involved in it. Surely the critical situation facing them was not the opportune time for the kind of adventure they had planned.

But the British fears proved wrong. The Sikhs rendered far more assistance than they were required under the terms of the agreement during the second British invasion of Afghanistan. They were "only bound to employ a contingent of 6000 men," wrote Henry Lawrence[23] to Mr. J.C. Marshman on April 11, 1842, "but they did the work with not less than 15000, leaving the stipulated number in position and withdrawing the rest to Jamrood and Peshawar, where they remain ready to support those in the pass, if necessary". The help rendered by the Sikhs was thankfully acknowledged by the Governor-General Lord Ellenborough in his notification of April 19, 1842. He also appreciated it in his letter of April 21, 1842 to Queen Victoria in these terms:[24] "The Sikh Army cooperated with that of India by a second pass leading to Ali Masjid, and there is no reason to doubt the good faith of the Sikh Government".

But this expression of gratitude was more of an act of formality or courtesy than of genuine sincerity because it did not prevent Ellenborough to assemble a huge army at Ferozepur, one object of his being to strike awe in the minds of the Sikhs. A reference to this is available in one of his letters to the Duke of Wellington, where he writes:[25] "If the Sikhs accept Jellalabad, they will be obliged to keep their principal force in the area, and the plains of Lahore and Amritsar will remain with insufficient garrison, within a few marches of the Sutlej on which I shall in twelve days at any time be able to assemble three European and eleven native battalions, one European regiment of cavalry, two irregular cavalry and 24 guns. The state of Punjab will be under my foot". Nor was the Duke of Wellington prepared to attach much importance to "the good faith of the Sikh Government". Writing to Ellenborough on April 6, 1842 he states in plain words[26]: "But this I must say, if we are to maintain our positions in Afghanistan we ought to have Peshawar, the Khyber Pass, Jellalabad and the passes between that post and Kabul". It may be noted that he was not unaware of the fact that Peshawar was a Sikh possession.

Still the fact that the Lahore Darbar had given full cooperation to the British in the reconquest of Afghanistan had its wholesome effect on Anglo-Sikh relations. There was now no major pretext or ground left with the British for any immediate military intervention in the Punjab and hence there was no talk of this for about a year at least. The basic policy of the British, however, was not changed. Only the mode of pursuing it was altered. The new mode was based on underground activities conducted with the object of undermining the position of the Sikh government. This fact comes out clearly from what Ellenborough wrote to the Duke on October 18, 1842:[27] "The conflict of parties in the Punjab will render it more dependent every year, and, indeed, he who knows it best does not think the Government can last a year. I intend to be most courteous and liberal to both parties, and to wait till I am called in". It is not difficult to read the real intentions of the British government in this statement of the Governor-General. The British were not mere spectators of the internal feuds of the Lahore Darbar, they played an active role in furthering these conflicts. Knowing that the relations between Maharaja Sher Singh and his Minister Raja Dhian Singh were getting strained, the British Political Agent at Ludhiana, with the consent of the higher authorities, took a special opportunity during his visit to Lahore to intercede with the Maharaja on behalf of the Sandhanwalia chiefs. The Maharaja accepted the advice not caring to understand why the British were so keen on this rapproachement. The result was that within less than a year of their reinstatement the Sandhanwalias finished the Maharaja, the Heir-Apparent and the Minister, thereby plunging the kingdom into complete chaos. It is not without significance that the British government was all the time aware of the impending tragedies. For example, note the following statement of the Governor-General:[28] "The Maharaja of Lahore is pulling his house down upon his head; the catastrophe was very nearly taking place three weeks ago, but it is deferred".

Referring to the Lahore murders the *British Friend of India* published in London wrote in December 1843:[29]

> "We have no proof that Company instigated all the king-killing which has been perpetrated in the Punjab since Ranjit died...we must say we smell a rat".

However, Ellenborough's prognostication that the murders would lead to the break-up of the Lahore kingdom did not come true. The murderers, Ajit Singh and Lehna Singh Sandhanwalias, were immediately cornered and despatched by the Khalsa troops in response to the passionate appeals of Rajas Hira Singh and Sochet Singh for assistance. A new government was formed with Raja Hira Singh as Minister and Pandit Jalla, his mentor, as Deputy Minister. The new rulers succeeded in establishing a reasonable stable government and thus saved the state from immediate disintegration. The army too played a decisive role in this direction through its system of regimental *panchayats*. The British were disappointed because in such circumstances as these there was no possibility for them to make a military intervention in the Punjab. However, they were shrewd enough to put a gloss over their secret intentions and tried to maintain cordial relations with the Lahore Darbar. They even argued among themselves that the continuance of a stable Sikh government in the Punjab was in their best interest.[30]

In reality the British did not have much faith in what they outwardly professed. They were convinced that the internal party feuds in the Punjab government would not cease and the situation there would progressively deteriorate to their great advantage. Their eyes were, therefore, all the time rivetted on Punjab happenings. Their policy now was: 'wait and see'.[31] Every dispute which took place during the ministry of Raja Hira Singh—whether it related to the *jagirs* of the Kanwars Kashmira Singh and Peshaura Singh, or to the dissatisfaction and intrigues of Raja Sochet Singh, or to the unauthorised march of an army regiment from Peshawar to Lahore, or to the demands of army *panchayats* for redress of grievances—was watched vigilantly by the British. Instead of helping the Lahore Darbar by diplomatic support, they attempted to accentuate its difficulties by affording asylum to its enemies. A most striking example of this tendency is provided by the manner in which Sardar Attar Singh Sandhanwalia was allowed to recross the river Sutlej and take shelter in the British territories, as also to mobilise support to be used against the government of Raja Hira Singh. The British took keen interest in Bhai Bir Singh of Naurangabad who in the name of the slogan that Khalsa *raj* must be saved from the Dogras had become the rallying centre of all disgruntled Sikh elements in the state. Welcoming this development the British quietly allowed Sardar Attar Singh Sandhanwalia to join Bhai Bir Singh with a contingent of his own. A military action soon followed in which the Lahore troops of Raja Hira Singh killed Bhai Bir Singh, Attar Singh and Kanwar Kashmira Singh besides hundreds of ordinary people. The movement of Bhai Bir Singh thus came to naught.

The result was a sore disappointment to the British government. To satisfy the Lahore Darbar that the British had no hand in the affair, Col. Richmond, the Political Agent at Ludhiana, as penalized for his negligence and transferred from his position there. A few months later a terrible family dispute developed between Raja Gulab Singh and his nephew Raja Hira Singh. The quarrel took a serious turn when Hira Singh despairing of a peaceful solution to the problem decided to order the march of a big army upon Jammu. The dispute was ultimately settled amicably.

Ellenborough derived much satisfaction from the defiance of Raja Hira Singh's authority first by Raja Sochet Singh and later by Raja Gulab Singh. For example after the death of Sochet Singh he wrote a letter to the Duke on May 9, 1844, in which he plainly observed:[32] "The destruction of Soocheyt Singh has had the effect of entirely separating the Hills, under Gulab Singh, from the Plains, still ruled in a manner by Heera Singh. Everything is going on there as we could desire if we looked forward to the ultimate possession of the Punjab".

A clear hint about the Governor-General's Punjab policy at this time is contained in a letter of his addressed to the Queen dated April 21, 1844. "Lord Ellenborough cannot but feel that the termination of the present state of things in the Punjab is essential to the security of the British power in India; but he will wait, cautiously preparing our strength for a contest he would willingly defer, but which he considers inevitable".[33] He even went to the extent of suggesting a date by which he would be in a position to attack the Punjab. About this he wrote to the Secret Committee on February 11, 1844:[34] "I must frankly confess that when I look at the whole condition of our army I have rather, if the contest cannot be further postponed, that it were at least postponed to November 1845". This was 22 months before the actual war took place. Obviously, he wanted to use the intervening period for "unostentatious but vigilant preparation". This implies that but for the urgent necessity of adequate military preparations, he would not have hesitated to start the invasion immediately.

Unfortunately for him, before he could realize his dream, he was replaced in July 1844 by Henry Hardinge. The new Governor-General, however, continued the policy of his predecessor. He had been selected for this post mainly for his long military experience because the Home Government was convinced of the speedy approach of a war with the Lahore government.[35] The views of the new Governor-General regarding his Punjab policy have been discussed at length in and need not be repeated here except to remark that he ruled out any policy which sought to maintain the Sikh state as a buffer or as a protectorate. His argument in its ultimate analysis was in favour of complete annexation rather than any solution short of that.

III

The war preparations begun under Ellenborough were not only continued but also intensified under Hardinge. The military stations on or near the Punjab frontier were considerably strengthened. Taking the frontier as a whole (exclusive of hill stations) the number of men was raised from 17,612 at the end of Ellenborough's period to 40,523 and of guns from 66 to 94. At Ferozepur the increase in the number of men was from 4,596 to 10,472 and in the case of guns from 12 to 24. Ludhiana had an increase of men from 3,030 to 7,235. The number of guns there, however, remained unchanged at 12. In the case of Ambala and Meerut, two major bases in the rear, men increased from 4,113 to 12,972 and from 5,873 to 9,844 respectively. In the case of guns the increase was from 20 to 32 in respect of Ambala and from 18 to 26 in respect of Meerut.

(ii) Not only big additions were made to the numerical strength of troops and guns at the military stations of Ferozepur, Ludhiana, Ambala and Meerut, a large number of pontoons were also collected at Ferozepur to be used for putting up a bridge across the Sutlej for the troops to cross over into the Punjab when the time for such a forward movement would arrive. The idea had been first suggested by the Duke of Wellington in a letter to Ellenborough.[36] The Governor-General acted promptly on the suggestion and was in a position to write back to the Duke on May 9, 1844:[37]

"I expect that by the end of December there will be on the Sutlej seventy boats of about thirty-five tons each, all exactly similar, and each containing everything necessary for its equipment as a pontoon. These will bridge the Sutlej anywhere and when not used they will convey troops up and down, and save us an enormous charge for the hire of boats".

What was left undone in this direction was completed by Lord Hardinge. He brought up to Ferozepur 56 pontoons as part of the equipment of the assembling army. But instructions were issued that this fact should be kept hidden from the Lahore government. To this effect Major Broadfoot, Company's new Political Agent at Ludhiana was told in a confidential letter of February 20, 1845:[38]

"It is not desirable that the purpose to which these boats can be applied should unnecessarily transpire. But if an inquiry should be made hereafter, your answer will be that this flotilla of boats is not at present required on the lower Indus, that our commissariat arrangements do require the employment of boats between Ferozepur and Sukkur for the supply of the latter place with grain and that these are purposely adapted for military as well as trading purposes......"

(iii) While the British troops were being collected on the Sutlej frontier, a supply depot was established at Basian, 10 miles to the south-east of Jagraon and about 4 miles to the north-west of Raikot. This was a clear indication that the British purpose of assembling their troops in this area was no less than to prepare for a war with the Punjab government which they thought was in the offing. Otherwise, there was no point in dumping supplies at a place which was neither a grain market nor a military station.

(iv) The appointment of Broadfoot as Political Agent at Ludhiana was also a calculated move made with an eye on the fast approaching war with the Punjab. He was a man who felt happier in war-like atmosphere than where there was peace and no action. He had written to Ellenborough in December 1843 that his health had been impaired by the peaceful atmosphere of Tennaserim (Burma) and that he eagerly wanted "a change to military service with the climate of northern India". Ellenborough had assured him in reply on February 1, 1844 that:[39] "If there should be at any future time a prospect of our having more important operations to carry on, I will if possible, have you with me".

Before his departure Ellenborough recommended Broadfoot to Henry Hardinge, the new Governor-General who was one of his close friends. Hardinge soon replaced Col. Richmond with Major Broadfoot who, true to his promises, threw himself, head and shoulders, into the task of war preparations.

On his arrival in the Punjab, Broadfoot straightway started interfering with the territories of the Lahore kingdom. "He not only acted," says Campbell,[40] "as if the Lahore territories, cis-Sutlej, were entirely under his control, but as I now learn for the first time from his biography, he seems to have set up a formal claim to such control and asserted that this Lahore territory was just as much under his jurisdiction, as he called it, as any of the small protected states". This was clearly against the terms and spirit of the Treaty of 1809. Campbell also admits it: "I can only say that I cannot find a word in the treaties or agreements of any kind to support it, and in all my connection with the office never saw anything to justify it". Col. Richmond and George Clerk, both his immediate predecessors in the Ludhiana Agency, also did not accept this view of Broadfoot as legally valid.[41] But he did not care much for legalities and[42] "avoided that he had arranged to occupy the Lahore territory, cis-Sutlej in case anything should happen to Dalip Singh who was ill. And he forbade the Durbar to send any troops over for any purpose whatever".

This fact is further confirmed by J.D. Cunningham in his *History of the Sikhs* (pp. 295-96):

> "One of Major Broadfoot's first acts was to declare the cis-Sutlej possessions of Lahore to be under British protection equally with Puteeala and other chiefs and also to be liable to escheat on the death or deposition of Maharaja Dalip Singh. This view was not formally announced to the Sikh Government, but it was notorious and Major Broadfoot acted on it when he proceeded to interfere authoritatively, and by a display of force in the affairs of the priests like Sodhies of Anundpoor Makhowal".

A typical example of his conduct towards the Lahore government on this particular issue is provided by the case of Lal Singh Adalti. When he was appointed for judicial duty in the cis-Sutlej Lahore territories, he crossed the Sutlej at Talwandi to assume charge of his new assignment. On learning this Broadfoot roughly and very peremptorily ordered the Sikh party back over the river. Lal Singh, not wanting to risk a collision, obeyed and returned to the river. But Broadfoot, not satisfied with this, followed him in person and his party. One shot was also fired. The Sikh leaders were captured and detained.[43] Campbell describes this act of Broadfoot as "wholly unjustifiable". Robert Cust, the assistant and companion of Broadfoot, calls it "the first shot of the great Sikh war".[44]

(v) Raja Sochet Singh, the youngest of the three Dogra brothers, had secretly deposited at Ferozepur a large amount of coin and bullion worth about 15 laksh of rupees. After his death the Lahore Darbar claimed the treasure both as escheated property of a feudatory of the Sikh government and as confiscated property of a rebel killed fighting against his sovereign. On both legal and moral grounds the property belonged to the Lahore government. But the British government refused to hand it over to the Sikhs. The Lahore government made many protests against this unfriendly posture of the British and repeatedly demanded the money back but in vain, as the British paid heed neither to their protests nor to their requests. The controversy regarding this matter started during the Ministry of Raja Hira Singh and continued through the periods of Jawahar Singh and Lal Singh. It was only after the war of 1845-46 that Raja Gulab Singh was recognised as the legitimate heir to the property and the amount was duly adjusted against the British claim of dues from him.

(vi) The issue of the village Moron, though a minor one, was a matter of great prestige for the Lahore Darbar. Many years back it had been acquired by Maharaja Ranjit Singh from Raja Jaswant Singh of Nabha and then had given it to one of his people Dhanna Singh in *jagir*. Twenty-five years later, Jaswant Singh's son, Raja Devinder Singh got offended with Dhanna Singh and resumed the control of the village without the sanction of the Lahore government. The action of the Nabha ruler was greatly resented by Lahore and was considered a calculated affront to its authority. The British government being the paramount authority of the states of the region was approached to intervene and get the place restored to the Lahore government. The British authorities, however, decided the matter in favour of the Raja of Nabha and no heed was paid to the protests of the Lahore Darbar. Obviously, this attitude on the part of the British government was considered in the Punjab as unfriendly to the Lahore Darbar.

(vii) There was a small island in the river Sutlej, near Ferozepur. Legally it belonged to the Lahore kingdom but it was occupied by the British by force. This was another act of high-handedness on the part of the British government. This fact has been plainly brought out by contemporary British writer, Major Carmichael Smyth, in his *History of the Reigning Family of Lahore*. "The year before the war broke out," he writes,[45] "we kept the island between Ferozepur and the Punjab, though it belonged to the Sikhs, owing to the deep water being between us and the island. And I only ask, had we not departed from the rules of friendship first?" He has also quoted from Prinsep's *Ranjit Singh* in support of his opinion that the island belonged to the Sikhs and its occupation by the British was a breach of the rules of friendship.

(viii) It will be seen from some of the cases noted above that the British government was not merely making war preparations and strengthening their various military stations, but also was giving deliberately one provocation after another to the Lahore kingdom to bring about an early out-break of hostilities between the two powers. This fact is further confirmed by an entry in the confidential Persian Office diary of George Broadfoot at Ludhiana. The entry is dated 26th March 1845 and reads as follows:[46]

"Having been sent for, Genda Singh, the *Mu'tamad* of the Raja of Nabha, came to the presence of the Exalted Gentleman (Major George Broadfoot). During the interview the Sahib said to him, "You go to Lahore as the *Mu'tamad* of the Raja, stay there and inform us in detail about the state of affairs there, spread hatred and discord in that state in whatever way it can be done and suggest the entry of the British government and also send us a genealogical table of the Sarkar of Lahore. The Sarkar (British Government) shall bestow favours upon you and consider it as an act of great loyalty of the Raja of Nabha.

"Genda Singh wrote out the genealogical table, but he refused to go to Lahore and stay there. At last the Exalted Gentleman being very much displeased, wrote to the Raja of Nabha that Genda Singh had been dismissed with a robe. The Sahib complained against him for disobedience and desired him to be punished; and informed him (the Raja) of the order issued and disobeyed and desired him (the Raja) to prepare for the purpose his (Genda Singh's) son, who is a shrewd person".

This was reported to the Lahore Sarkar by their *vakil* at Ludhiana and they felt much disturbed over the secret activities of their British neighbours for the subversion of their state.

This is only example but this should be enough to indicate how the British Agent, Broadfoot, was actively engaged in sending spies and provocateurs to the Punjab territories with the sinister object of sowing seeds of discord in the ranks of the Sikhs and provoking the Sikhs to hostilities.

(ix) When the relations between the two powers were thus increasingly getting stramed, many British officials and the Anglo-Indian press in particular were carrying on a regular propaganda against the Sikhs, perhaps with a view to preparing the people of India and England psychologically for the news of the forthcoming Anglo-Sikh War and covering up their warlike preparations. What Carmichael Smyth

> writes in this context is not without significance. He says:[47] "With the Sikhs for several years past, in fact ever since the death of Ranjit Singh, we have been playing the fable of the Shepherd Boy and the Wolf. The papers and the politicals have constantly been crying out: "The Sikhs are coming", until at last we would not believe them".

Smyth also refers to a speech of Sir Charles Napier published in the *Delhi Gazette* stating that the British were going to war with the Sikhs, and says:[48]

> "The Sikhs had translations of Sir Charles Napier's speech stating that we are going to war with them (the Sikhs)".

Such statements coming from high British officials served to confirm the suspicion that what was being published in the Anglo-Indian newspapers was not based on imagination but had the secret support of his British authorities.

(x) Cunningham has drawn attention to yet another source of concern to the Sikhs in the Punjab. He writes:[49] "Nor did the Sikhs seem to be menaced by their (British) allies on one (Sutlej) side only". In the summer of 1845 some horsemen from Multan crossed a few miles into the Sindh territory in pursuit of certain marauders. The boundary between the Punjab and Sindh being not clearly defined then, the action of the Sikh horsemen was so serious offence. Still the military governor of Sindh, Charles Napier, reacted sharply and immediately ordered a regiment to Kushmor, a few miles below Rojhan. Apparently it was a measure to preserve the integrity of his frontier from violation by the Sikhs, but in reality it was a stern warning to the Sikhs who "looked upon the prompt measure of the conqueror of the Sindh as one more proof of the British desire to bring about a war with the Punjab".[50]

All such factors as have been briefly touched upon in the foregoing pages had by the year 1845, rather much earlier, created a firm belief in the minds of the Sikhs that their country was seriously threatened by the expansionist designs of British imperialism. In the words of J.D. Cunningham they had begun to consider that the fixed policy of the English was territorial aggrandisement, and that the immediate object of their ambition was the conquest of Lahore".[51] In the then prevailing situation no inference other than the one formed by the Sikh *panchayats* was possible. The selfish chiefs of the Lahore Darbar, blinded by the dread of the Khalsa army, got a golden opportunity to play upon the fears of their soldiery and deliberately endeavoured to accentuate their wrath and excitement. But "had the shrewd committees of the armies observed no military preparations on the part of the English, they would not have needed the insidious exhortations of such mercenary men as Lal Singh and Tej Singh".[52]

Carmichael Smyth corroborates Cunningham by saying that British provocations were too glaring to be overlooked by the Sikhs. He writes:[53] "Regarding the Punjab war, I am neither of opinion that the Seiks made an *unprovoked attack,* nor that we have acted towards them with great forbearance......; for if the Seiks were to be considered an independent state, in no way answerable to us, we should not have provoked them!—for to assert that the bridge of boats brought from Bombay, was not a *causa belli,* but merely a defensive measure is absurd". He even goes further and observes that it was the British who had "departed from the rules of friendship first".

The subsequent chain of events lends further confirmation to the above inference of Smyth. On about the 20th of November 1845 British troops of Ambala were instructed to hold themselves in readiness and between the 2nd and 10th of December they were actually on the move towards Ferozepur. Meanwhile Brigadier Wheeler, with about

5,000 infantry, two regiments of cavalry and twelve field guns, had left Ludhiana to converge on the same point. Hardinge himself arrived at Ambala on 2nd December. The very next day he severed diplomatic relations with the Darbar by dismissing its *vakil* from his camp on the plea that the Darbar had not cared to explain the reason for the movement of its troops. The *vakil* had in fact sought explanations for Broadfoot's actions and for British military activities on the Punjab borders. On 6th December Hardinge set out in company with Lord Gough, British Commander-in-Chief, at the head of a large British army for the Sutlej border.[54] While all this was happening on the British side, the Sikh soldiers were still encamped at Lahore. Not a single soldier of the Sikh army had crossed the Sutlej up to the 11th of December. Even when they made the crossing on that day, they continued to stay in their own territory. Yet this was made a pretext by the Governor-General for issuing a proclamation declaring war on December 13.

How far Hardinge was convinced of the justification of his proclamation is revealed from the following entry occurring in the Journal of Robert Cust:[55]

> December 18th—I rode behind the Governor-General and we sat under a tree to await the infantry. The Governor-General remarked: "Will the people of England consider this an actual invasion of our frontier and a justification of war?"

The inescapable conclusion from all this evidence is that it was the British and not the Sikhs who were responsible for the war.

REFERENCES

1. The two armies were commanded respectively by Col. Ochterlony and St. Leger.
2. *Foreign Political Proceedings*, 16 August 1828, No. 3.
3. J.D. Cunningham, *History of the Sikhs* (1915), p. 163.
4. *Punjab Government Records*, Vol. II, p. 46.

5. *Foreign Political Proceedings,* 5 October 1836, No. 27; N.K. Sinha, *Ranjit Singh,* p. 78.
6. Sinha, *op. cit.,* p. 80; *Foreign Political Proceedings,* 17 June 1831, No. 41. For detailed information on the Khalifa's activities see Ganesh Das Vadera, *Char Bagh-i-Punjab,* pp. 317-18; Diwan Amar Nath, *Zafar Nama-i-Ranjit Singh,* Chapters XXX and XXXI.
7. Wade to Macnaghten, 7 November and 21 December 1837, and 7 January 1838.
8. Quoted by Cunningham in his book on the Sikhs, p. 193.
9. *Foreign Secret Cons.,* 18 November, 1843, Nos. 18, 19.
10. N. K. Sinha, *op. cit.,* p. 78.
11. While accepting the terms demanded by Ranjit Singh, the British had it always at the back of their minds that the Maharaja was not going to live long and that after his death they would have the option for suitable manoeuvres in accordance with their interests.
12. *Umdat-ut-Twarikh,* Daftar III, Part V, pp. 62, 86-87.
13. Sohan Lal, *op. cit.,* Daftar IV, Part I; S.R. Kohli, *op. cit.,* p. 23.

    The British exploited this factor for their selfish motives. For instance, when Mr. Clerk went to Lahore in September 1839 to felicitate the new Maharaja and to ask for confirmation of Ranjit Singh's concession regarding the passage of British troops through the Punjab, this was at first refused. But the British Agent did not give up his hope of achieving the point. While continuing to persuade the Darbar, he went out of his way to pay a courtesy call on Prince Sher Singh, hoping that the sense of insecurity resulting from this action might make the Darbar more amenable to his cause. This manoeuvre succeeded in its purpose, became when the subject was reopened a few days later, the Darbar agreed to the demand.
14. Fauja Singh and M.L. Ahluwalia (ed.), *Maharaja Kharak Singh* (Delhi 1977), Intro., pp. XLVII-XLVIII.
15. *Ibid.,* Introduction, pp. XLVI-XLVII.
16. *Ibid.,* S.R. Kohli, *Sunset of the Sikh Empire* (Delhi 1967), p. 21.
17. That the kingdom was in grave danger from the British is also clear from the following remark of Auckland contained in his private letter to Hobhouse:' If the Lahore Darbar refuses permission for the march of the British Brigade through their territories to reach Kabul, it must be absolutely insisted on and we are collecting

a force in consequence.' *For. Secret Cons.* dated 9 November 1840, Nos. 53-55 and 23 November 1840, Nos. 55-56.

18. *Foreign Dept. Sec. Cons.*, 17 January 1842, No. 68 and 29 July 1842, No. 34.

19. Edwardes and Merivale, *Henry Lawrence,* Vol. I, pp. 216-17.

20. The letters of Ellenborough to the Duke of Wellington, dated 15 and 26 October 1841 further confirm this fact. In these letters the Duke is requested to give his opinion "as to the best mode of attacking the Punjab". See Ganda Singh (ed.) *Private Correspondence Relating to the Anglo-Sikh Wars* (Amritsar-Patiala, 1955), pp. 451-52—henceforth to be referred to as *Private Correspondence.*

    The relevant extracts from these letters read as follows:

    Letter dated October 15, 1841: "I shall probably have as one of my aides-de-camp Lieutenant Durand of the Bengal Engineers, one of those who flew open the gates of Ghuzni. He was recommended to me by Lord Fitzroy, and if he should accept the proposal I have made to him, I have requested Lord Fitzroy to employ him at once in obtaining all the information he can with respect to the Punjab, and making a military memorandum upon the country for your consideration. I am most anxious to have your opinion as to the general principles at least upon which a campaign against that country should be conducted..."

    This letter was written while he was in England and was yet to take charge of the Governor-General's post in India. Another letter, also written while in England, dated October 26, 1841 contains the following lines:

    "What I desired, therefore, was your opinion, founded as far as it could be upon the imperfect geographical information which can be given to you, as to the best mode of attacking the Punjab".

21. *Foreign Dept. Sec. Cons,* 14 February 1842, No. 64. Earlier on 29 January 1842 Henry Lawrence from Peshawar had proposed "that on the terms of efficient support we assist Raja Goolab Singh to get possession of Jellalabad and endeavour to make some arrangement to secure it and Peshawar to his family". Edwardes and Merivale, *op. cit.*, Vol. I, pp. 326-27.

22. Cunningham writes that when Sher Singh became aware of it, he is said to have drawn his finger across his throat, meaning that the Sikhs would at once take his life if he assented to Clerk's proposals. *History of the Sikhs,* p. 214.

23. Edwardes and Merivale, *op. cit.*, Vol. I, p. 363.

24. *Private Correspondence,* Appendix A-7, p. 455.
25. S.R. Kohli, *op. cit.,* p. 60—Ellenborough to the Duke, 18 October 1842. Also see *Private Correspondence,* p. 457.
26. *Private Correspondence,* p. 454.
27. *Ibid.,* p. 457.
28. *Ibid.,* p. 461. Ellenborough to the Duke of Wellington, September 20, 1843. Many months earlier, on May 11, 1843 the same British authority had informed the Duke as thus: "General Ventura is with the Maharaja Sher Singh, and it is clear to me that, relying on his support the Maharaja will take the first occasion of cutting off his Minister Dhian Singh. This Dhian Singh knows, and is prepared for. The break-up of the Punjab will probably begin with the murder". *Private Correspondence,* p. 52. Introduction. On August 12 he wrote: "The affairs of the Punjab will probably receive their denouement from the death of Sher Singh".
29. *Ibid.,* p. 53—Introduction.
30. *Private Correspondence,* p. 454—Duke of Wellington to Ellenborough, April 6, 1842; Ellenborough to the Secret Committee, 20 January 1843.
31. On October 20, 1843 Ellenborough writing to the Queen observed: "...but it is impossible not to perceive that the ultimate tendency of the late events at Lahore is, without any effort on our part, to bring the plains fist, and at a somewhat later period, the hills under our direct protection or control". On the same day he said in a letter to the Duke: "We adhere to the policy pursued for so many years; and for my own part I desire the continuance of a government in the Punjab like that of Ranjit Singh. The thing, however, will not be and the time cannot be very distant when the Punjab will fall into our management and the question will be what we shall do as respects the Hills. Probably the Hills will be very much divided under a separate government and I look to the protection of our Government being ultimately extended to the Sikhs of the Plains and the Rajpoots of the Hills and Mussulmans of Mooltan, precisely as it is now to the Sikh chiefs on the left of the Sutlej.... I do not look to this state of things as likely to occur next year, but as being ultimately inevitable, if we do not bring on union against ourselves and indisposition to our rule by some precipitate interference. I should tell you, however, that there is, as there long has been, a great disposition even in quarters not military, to disturb the game". *Private Correspondence,* pp. 462-63.

32. *Ibid.*, p. 468.
33. *Ibid.*
34. *Ibid.*, Introduction, p. 58.
35. "Without doubt", writes his son, "the selection of a distinguished soldier, who also possessed the experience of a cabinet minister, pointed to the anticipation of war". *Ibid.*, Introduction. p. 62
36. The letter as mentioned in *Private Correspondence*, p. 454 bears the date April 2, 1842. The relevant extract reads as follows: "This position would be an excellent defensive one from which you could with facility move on an offensive plan. I would recommend you to add to the equipment of the army pontoons for the formation of a bridge. I see that when the armies were lately on the Sutlej there was a difficulty in procuring boats, particularly for the formation of bridges at the island of Bukkur. It might be desirable to avoid the delay of collecting boats to form a bridge".
37. *Ibid.*, p. 468.
38. *Ibid.*, Introduction, p. 65; *Career of Major Broadfoot*, p. 284.
39. *Career of Major Broadfoot*, pp. 202-03.
40. *Memoirs of my Indian Career*, edited by C.E. Bernard (London, 1893), 2 vols., p. 75.

    According Dr. S.S. Bal this idea was given to him by Hardinge. Hardinge had discussed it with Lord Rippon in England and taken him into his confidence. Rippon in turn had discussed it with Mr. Clerk. Somehow the news leaked out to the Lahore Darbar and its armed forces, confirming their suspicions about the *mala fides* of the British. In the words of Dr. Bal, the intention of the British leaked out to the Sikh army through the indiscretion of Clerk. Hardinge believed that Mohan Lal had heard it from Clerk and passed it on to his brother-in-law Hodges in India, and that the latter passed it to the Darbar".

    British Policy towards the Punjab, 1844-49, p. 242.
41. Clerk's view was that from the legal point of view the proposal was wrong because the cis-Sutlej territories of the Lahore Darbar were not the personal property of Maharaja Dalip Singh. But on practical grounds he was not averse to the British taking over the administration of these territories. Bal, *op. cit.*, p. 242.
42. *Ibid.*, p. 76.
43. Campbell, *Memoirs*, pp. 76-77.

44. *Oriental and Linguistic Essays*, Part, V, pp. 43-44. Written from 1840 to 1903.
45. *A History of the Reigning Family of Lahore*, Introduction, p. XXII (first published in 1847. Reprinted in 1970).
46. Quoted in *Private Correspondence*, Introduction, pp. 78-79.
47. *A History of the Reigning Family of Lahore*—Introduction, p. XXIII.
48. *Ibid.*, p. XXII.
49. *History of the Sikhs*, pp. 297-98.
50. *Ibid.*
51. *Ibid.*, p. 252.
52. *Ibid.*, p. 257.
53. *Op. cit.*, p. 22—Introduction.
54. *Private Correspondence*, pp. 83-85; also see Hardinge's letter to Secret Committee, 21 December 1845 where he makes a significant observation: "On the 13th I first received precise information that the Sikh army had crossed the Sutlej, and was concentrating in great force on the left bank of the river. The Ambala force at that time had been in movement three days".

    According to Robert Cust who accompanied the British force from Ambala, the army left Ambala on December 6 and had been in movement for a week when the Proclamation was issued. Also see Charles Macfarlane, *History of British India*, p. 592.
55. Cust, R, *Linguistic and Oriental Essay*, Part V, pp. 46-47.

2

Foreign Aggression and National Resistance

I

It will be seen from the preceding three chapters that towards the end of 1845 things were fast heading towards a cataclysm. The British had amassed large numbers of troops at their military stations on the frontier, Ferozepur and Ludhiana. They had strengthened their positions in the rear, at Ambala and Meerut. They had collected pontoons for throwing a bridge across the Sutlej, to be used when the eventuality arose. A large supply depot had been established at Basian, near Raikot. On top of this both the Governor-General and the Commander-in-Chief were personally advancing towards the Punjab. The Lahore Darbar and the Khalsa army were not unaware of what was happening on the other side of the Sutlej. Their spies, intelligences and sympathisers were keeping them adequately informed of these developments. There was no doubt left in their minds that the British were determined and well set for the invasion. All that they needed was some kind of an excuse which could enable them to say that they were not the aggressors but had to take up the sword because a war had been imposed on them. The reactions of the Lahore Darbar and the Khalsa army to this situation, expectedly, were not united. To the Khalsa army it appeared a great challenge. They felt that the time for patriotic duty had come and were prepared to stake their all in defence of their beloved country. The Lahore Darbar thought differently. To them the coming war was most welcome, for two reasons: (i) The Khalsa army would get entangled in a deadly war with the mighty British and be crushed; (ii) the Darbar would be able to get British protection and be permanently rid of danger from their own army.[1] True to their interests, they did not want just to be spectators but wanted to play a "positive" role. On the one hand they approached the troops, apprised them of the imminent danger of British invasion and appealed to their patriotic instinct in order to put them in a state of excitement. On the other, they got in touch with the British and assured them of their full cooperation in the event of hostilities breaking out between the two powers. They were even prepared to oblige the British by furnishing them with the kind of pretext they were in need of to start the war.

Major G.C. Smyth refers to several occasions on which "Lal Singh in open Darbar produced and read papers purporting to be letters from Kardars of the country beyond the river, and in which it was stated that the British army was already advancing gradually and was creating disturbances and annoyance in the Sikh States". This intelligence, he adds, created considerable excitement among the troops and the people at Lahore, and "soon formed almost the only topic of discussion and remark".[2] Smyth also speaks of two important meetings, one held in the Shalimar Gardens in the beginning of November 1845 and the other some days after during the same month at the *smadh* of Maharaja Ranjit Singh. At the first meeting Diwan Dina Nath on behalf of the Rani read out a letter which he said had been sent to the Darbar by the *kardars* of the states beyond the Sutlej intimating that "the British[3] authorities really meant to seize that part of the country, that they were causing great annoyance to the servants of the Darbar, and had actually given orders to the people of several villages to pay no tribute but to the British Government, to whom as they now formally declared, the country belonged". The other assembly, held at Ranjit Singh's *smadh,* witnessed a solemn oath of allegiance to the state and its defence against the apprehended invasion. The people who participated in the ceremony included chiefs, officers and *panchas.*[4] A glimpse of the spirit animating the army at this time is provided by Cunningham. "...and when the men were tauntingly asked whether they would quietly look on while the limits of the Khalsa dominion were being reduced, and the plains of Lahore occupied by the remote strangers of Europe," he writes, "they answered that they would defend with their lives all belonging to the commonwealth of Gobind, and that they would march and give battle to the invaders on their ground. The men would assemble in groups and talk of the great battle they must soon wage, and they would meet round the tomb of Ranjit Singh and vow fidelity to the Khalsa".[5]

The mood of the soldiery may also be seen from the readiness with which they decided to suspend their powerful regimental *panchayats* and submit themselves thoroughly to the authority of the Rani. Also, without any hesitation they accepted Raja Lal Singh and Misr Tej Singh, appointed respectively as *Wazir* and Commander-in-Chief by her.[6]

As compared with the men, the chiefs and the higher officers were insincere, devoid of patriotism and bent upon treachery. Cunningham calls them[7] "basemen", "mercenary men", and "unworthy men". Still if they had succeeded in arousing great enthusiasm among the men for the war against the British, it was because the latter were convinced of the imminence of a British invasion upon their country. "Had the shrewd committees of the armies observed no military preparations on the part of the English, they would not have heeded the insidious exhortations of such mercenary men as Lal Singh and Tej Singh".[8]

When the troops were finally ordered to march towards the Sutlej, they executed the tasks assigned to them with surprising vigour and zeal. "Every Sikh considered the cause as his own, and he would work as a labourer as well as carry a musket; he would drag guns, drive bullocks, lead camels and load and unload boats with a cheerful alacrity, which contrasted strongly with the inept and sluggish obedience of mercenaries, drilled, indeed, and fed with skill and care, but unwarmed by one generous feeling for their country or their foreign employers. The youthful Khalsa was active and strong of heart..."[9] As against this, their commanders Lal Singh and Tej Singh shirked responsibility and were much reluctant to lead the troops personally in the battles to come.[10] Or it may be said that in this they were motivated to delay the march deliberately for the benefit of the British.

II

As was to be expected, the Darbar did not pay much attention to the proper planning and organisation of the operations to be undertaken. The men at the helm of affairs were interested in losing rather than winning the war. Their whole endeavour therefore was somehow to commit the Khalsa army to a war with the British[11] and then watch for the result. About war preparations they felt the least concerned. Whatever was done was done just to put a veil upon their real intentions. They were "indifferent from their firm persuasion that if victorious they will find new means of power and wealth and if beaten they will be what most of them desire, the heads of a subsidiary instead of an independent state".[12] Otherwise, too, Lal Singh and Tej Singh lacked the requisite competence. Lal Singh had never seen war before and Tej Singh was just a mediocrity who owed his rise more to Ranjit Singh's affection for his uncle Jamadar Khushal Singh than to his own merit.[13]

A plan of war was drawn up on the night of 17th November, according to which the army was to be divided into seven divisions, one to remain at Lahore, one to proceed to Peshawar and the rest to march against Ropar and the hills nearby, Ludhiana, Hurrike, Ferozepur and Sindh. Each division was to be 8000 to 12000 strong. Sham Singh Attariwala, Lal Singh, Tej Singh and Ranjodh Singh were to be the commanders of the Ferozepur, Ludhiana and Ropar divisions, respectively. Under the same plan[14] Raja Gulab

Singh was assigned the duty of guarding Attock with his own army. Either because there was no proper security arrangement or for the reason that the authors of the plan were not much interested in secrecy, the plan was communicated to Broadfoot, the British Agent at Ludhiana, the very next day.[15] This plan, however, did not work and was soon altered under the pressure of disturbances breaking out in certain parts of the kingdom. One brigade had to be sent to Dera Ismail Khan for the suppression of the rebel Fateh Khan Tiwana, and a similar force had to be despatched to keep peace in Poonch and Hazara. On certain uprising taking place at the instigation of the British in Kulu and the neighbouring hills, despatch of troops in that direction also became imperative. However, this difficulty was got over by raising local levies which were charged, besides this function, with guarding of the passages of the upper ranges of the Sutlej. As a result of all of these developments a few necessary adjustments were made in the strength of the divisions intended to march against the different places, the main emphasis being laid on the Ferozepur-Hurrike front. Further, Ranjodh Singh was now put in charge of the Ludhiana front, and the command of the Ropar force was transferred from him to Col. Chet Singh. When the various disturbances had broken out, it was feared that they would, by enhancing the commitments, adversely affect the principles of economy of force and concentration, but thanks to the large size of the Khalsa army, the Sikh effort was not affected in any serious manner and they were able to bring into the war a force 35,000 to 40,000 strong with 150 pieces of artillery, exclusive of the force detached towards Ludhiana.[16] But though the plan of troop distribution for different fronts was sound, their supply arrangements broke down from the very outset. Even before the river Sutlej was crossed, there were reports of scarcity of provisions from Lal Singh's camp[17] and several villages were plundered on the way.[18]

The Sikhs were the first to cross the river Sutlej on 12 December 1845.[19] This was done without any declaration of war. The object of doing so was not, however, to gain any initiative or surprise but it was done because the Sikh leaders were in a hurry to commit their troops to a war with the British.[20]

Whatever be the motive, the Sikhs by their act of crossing some days before the British troops had come anywhere near the Sutlej, gained an excellent opportunity to attack and reduce the garrison of Ferozepur, to isolate it from Ludhiana, and to destroy the main British depot at Basian. "Had the Sikhs pushed forward at once after crossing", says Henty,[21] "Bassein with its great stores of provisions must have fallen into their hands and a week or ten days must have elapsed before arrangements for provisioning the Umbala force could have been made. In that case the whole Sikh army would have been able to concentrate its efforts upon the capture of Ferozepur which, in the absence of any fortifications capable of withstanding a powerful artillery, could scarcely have been defended successfully". And had they won these successes in the initial stages of the war, the entire British Indian soldiery of the Bengal army and almost the whole of the people of the cis-Sutlej Sikh states would have most probably joined hands with them. The Indian sepoys of the British were greatly disaffected towards their masters and allured by the higher pays of the Sikh army, were merely waiting for a favourable opportunity to declare themselves openly.[22] Similarly, the cis-Sutlej rulers were fed up with the British treatment with them. Also, they had a genuine sympathy for their co-religionists from across the Sutlej.[23] In the event of such an eventuality taking place the events of 1857 would perhaps have been anticipated with much better chances of the British being thrown out of the country.

But nothing of the sort came to pass and a golden opportunity was lost owing to the incompetence and insincerity of Sikh leadership. Instead of taking the course which could be of advantage to the Sikhs, Raja Lal Singh put himself in secret communication with Capt. Nicolson at Ferozepur immediately after crossing the Sutlej at Hurrike, conveying that "he was helpless but he could delay the Sikh attack on Ferozepur, divide the Sikh force and induce a great part to march to Ferozshah to attack the Governor-General and recommended that the British troops at Ferozepur then should attack the remainder".[24] On hearing from Capt. Nicolson that "professions of friendship were of no value without corresponding action", Lal Singh and Tej Singh put it cunningly to their men that they wanted to leave the easy prey of a mere cantonment untouched for the time being and attack the leaders of the English and exalt the fame of the Khalsa by the captivity or death of a Governor-General. So, while Tej Singh was left to carry on operations against Ferozepur, Lal Singh marched away with the bulk of the army in the direction of the advancing British troops. A village called Ferozshah at a distance of about 10 miles from Ferozepur was selected as the site of the prospective battle with the British. It was a wise choice because the place lay across the road which alone, owing to scarcity of water, could be used for the advance of the British army towards Ferozepur.[25] But not satisfied with the division of the army already made, Lal Singh further divided it and took a small portion consisting of less than 2000 infantry, about 22 pieces of artillery and 8,000 to 10,000 horse, not to prevent the junction between the enemy's Ambala and Ludhiana armies, not even to attack the enemy depot at Basein, but foolishly enough to challenge the entire united British force. Clearly, his sinister plan was to get the Khalsa army defeated in detail and to earn the gratitude of the British.[26] Cunningham[27] supports this view when he says that Lal Singh "in accordance with his original design involved his followers in an engagement, and then left them to fight as their undirected valour might prompt". However, the battle of Mudki was regarded by the determined Khalsa as an experimental war exercise only. They had taught a lesson to the enemy and this, in spite of their heavy losses, gave them considerable encouragement,[28] which inspired them to the heroic action of Ferozshah. But they had realised the folly of having fought in the open and now quickly threw up waist-high earth works to give the next battle from an entrenched position.

Having tasted of the Sikh steel at Mudki, the British felt it imperative to effect a junction with the division of Gen. Littler at Ferozepur before engaging in another action with the Sikhs encamped in a horse-shoe form round the village of Ferozshah. So they left the main road and made a detour. At this stage the Sikhs wanted to take an offensive and fall upon the enemy, but were withheld by their officers from doing so. This made them so bitter against Lal Singh that they plotted to murder him.[29] Tej Singh, with his usual lack of vigour and vigilance, allowed Gen. Littler to slip away and join Lord Gough's force. Even then in the battle which ensued soon after this, the British might have been defeated if the Sikh leaders had not proved insincere. Lal Singh fled away in the midst of the fight and thereby revived the spirits of the enemy who were nearly defeated. When Tej Singh arrived on the battle scene next morning with a fresh host drawn up in battle order, "the worried and famished English saw before them a desperate and perhaps useless struggle".[30] He had been urged by his zealous and sincere soldiery to fall upon the English at day-break, but his object was to have "the dreaded army of the Khalsa overcome and dispersed, and he delayed until Lal Singh's force was everywhere put to flight. Even at the last moment he rather skirmished and made feints rather than led his men to a resolute attack and after a time he precipitately fled, leaving his subordinates without orders and without an object at a moment when the artillery ammunition of the English had failed, when a portion of their force was retiring upon Ferozepur and when no exertions could have prevented the remainder from retreating likewise, if the Sikhs had boldly pressed forward". Victory was practically within their grasp but Tej Singh let it slip away treacherously.[31]

The battle of Ferozshah had left both the parties shattered and disorganised. The victors were no better than the vanquished who were left unpursued to recross the Sutlej at will. The myth of the British invincibility was broken,[32] with the result that their cis-Sutlej feudatories began to show signs of indifference and occasional hostility towards their masters.[33] Realizing that without reinforcements it would be impossible for them to resume operations, the British now sent for more troops and a heavy park of artillery with ammunition from Delhi, Meerut and Kanpur and in the meantime decided to remain strongly entrenched at Sultan Khan Wala, watching the frontier.

The Sikhs after the defeat returned to the right bank of the Sutlej. They had suffered heavy losses both in men and material and were practically without guns, ammunition and food supplies. Yet their morale was high and their spirits unbroken. They did not regard their defeat as one in a fair fight but on the contrary attributed it to the treachery of their leaders. Therefore, they rallied and decided to continue the fight, preferably under new leaders. Their *panchayats* again became active which sent a deputation to wait upon the Rani and Raja Gulab Singh.[34] They made urgent appeals to the latter to assume charge of *wuzarat* at Lahore and to take over the conduct of the war from the hands of the traitorous Lal Singh and Tej Singh. The Rani was hesitant to accept the change but she was forced to agree to that. Raja Gulab Singh soon after arrived at Lahore with his army and was vested with the office of the *Wazir*.

In the meantime war preparations had been continued and were being pursued with remarkable zeal and vigour. Work on a bridge across the Sutlej and a bridgehead on its left bank had been started under persistent pressure from the men.[35] Simultaneously with this, Diwan Mul Raj and Ranjodh Singh were ordered to threaten the British flanks. The former had been indifferent from the very start of the war and had remained nearly neutral[36] as the result of which Charles Napier, the Governor of Sind, advanced into Bahawalpur and menaced the right flank of the Sikhs.[37] But unlike the Diwan, Ranjodh Singh crossed the Sutlej with a force about 8,000 strong, and threatened Ludhiana then protected only by a weak garrison. Fire was set to its cantonment[38] by one of the predatory bands of the Sikhs, which struck great terror in all the frontier military stations of the British. It was a move of great strategic value. It enabled the Sikhs not only to draw supplies from the left bank of the river and to carry them over to the right bank but also to put them in a position from where they could seriously interfere with the British reinforcements under way from Delhi and other stations.[39] From the British side Harry Smith was sent to encounter and eliminate this threat. He reduced the Sikh fort of Dharamkot without any resistance and then proceeded to make a junction with the Ludhiana force. Ranjodh Singh, like a shrewd strategist, occupied the village of Badowal which lay on the road being followed by Smith and tried to cut him off from Ludhiana. But Smith was undeterred and he made a detour. Ranjodh Singh also marched in a parallel line and isolating the enemy's rear fell upon and plundered it but he failed to bring Smith to a battle and to prevent him from joining the Ludhiana army. Had he taken the offensive boldly he might have not only destroyed the force of Smith but also upset the whole plan of Lord Gough.[40] His failure cost him and the Sikhs heavily because he was soon forced to fall back on the Sutlej under a serious threat to his line of communications with Phillaur from Smith and Godby on one side and Wheeler on the other.[41] Taking advantage of this Smith immediately occupied Badowal and prepared himself for an attack upon Ranjodh Singh on the Sutlej. The Sikh commander failed to appreciate the imminence of the danger properly and being over-confident of his strength, wanted to make a move for the relief of the fort of Gungrana or for the occupation of the neighbouring town of Jugraon, both of which were close to the British line of communications with the Jumna.[42] But he was completely outmanoeuvred and forced to fight in the open and with a river in the rear—both of them serious blunders. Moreover, he failed to maintain secrecy about his resources and intentions because Mr. Brown whom he sent as a spy to the English camp, betrayed his master's cause and passed on to the enemy much-valued information about the Sikh force. The results were bound to be disastrous.[43] He was also handicapped by non-cooperation from some of his chiefs. Of them Ajit Singh of Ladwa had been quarrelling with him all the time and the commander of the Ahluwalia contingent was insincere and secretly in league with the British.[44] The Sikhs were overpowered at Aliwal and Ranjodh Singh's force was driven back in a shattered condition across the Sutlej to Phillaur where it made a half-hearted attempt to rally, but it was no use, because it was refused all help from Lahore.[45] With this defeat all Sikh influence on the left side of the Sutlej came to an end while the British prestige was raised considerably. The people who were indifferent or hostile to the British hitherto, now convinced of their ultimate victory, deserted the Sikh cause and yielded to the British. All the forts along the Sutlej opposite Phillaur fell into the hands of the British so that the left flank of the Sikhs was completely exposed to danger. Under these circumstances the commander of the Rupar-Anandpur front, Col. Chet Singh, was also compelled to stage a retreat across the river.[46]

The effects of the Aliwal defeat on the policy of the Lahore Darbar were still more serious. Raja Gulab Singh who had been appointed *Wazir* with the specific object that he would lead the Sikhs in the war, now openly refused to undertake that responsibility. Instead, he reproached the Khalsa for rashly entering upon hostilities and opened negotiations with the English. But the English would not make any peace unless and until the formidable Lahore army was disbanded. It was not in the power of the Raja to promise that but an understanding was reached that the "Sikh army should be attacked by the English, that when beaten, it should be openly abandoned by its own government, and further that the passage of the Sutlej should be unopposed and the road to the capital laid open to the victors".[47] "It was under such circumstances of discreet policy and shameless treason that the battle of Sobraon was fought," writes Cunningham.[48]

The bulk of the Khalsa army, which had been in the meantime assembled near Sobraon for the final trial of strength with the British and which was engaged day and night on the erection of fortifications around its proposed site of battle, was also adversely affected by the tragic results of Aliwal. Their spirits were damped and the weak-hearted among them fled away to their homes. Gulab Singh Dogra put them in a state of suspense and uncertainty by issuing orders for withdrawal from the left bank of the Sutlej.[49] Lal Singh and Tej Singh who could not be replaced for want of better leaders, were thereby encouraged in their treacherous designs. On the eve of the battle, Lal Singh sent to Lord Gough a full report "on the position and nature of the entrenchments and the account and disposition of troops and guns", through his confidential agent Shamsuddin.[50] Some time earlier Tej Singh too had sent a secret agent, Ram Das, to the same gentleman conveying that he was unwilling to fight and would not fight and requesting that the reply should be sent orally and not in writing.[51] No wonder, therefore, that some valuable opportunities were lost. Mouton[52] complains that his sound advice to Tej Singh not to accept any battle with the river in the rear and either to withdraw to the right bank or to make a bold attack on the enemy before they were reinforced from Delhi or rejoined by Harry Smith, was not accepted and a course of action was adopted which was bound to lead to disasters. The British completed their preparations and chose their own time for attack. The Sikhs were surprised,[53] when the attack was made, owing to their habit of withdrawing their advance pickets during the night. All the same, they put up a gallant fight. But at a critical moment Tej Singh, the supreme commander, turned turtle and ran away from the field. Mouton says that after his flight he even sent orders to all his Generals to abandon their troops and join him but only one obeyed him. There is a strong belief that Tej Singh was also responsible for sinking the central boat in the bridge which resulted in a great slaughter of the Sikh army by the enemy.[54]

Immediately after the battle of Sobraon the British crossed the Sutlej. Nothing was done to block the passage of the river,[55] though frantic appeals were made by men like Mouton in the name of honour and fatherland. The army tried to rally but strict orders were sent from Lahore, "peremptorily[56] forbidding the troops to fight during negotiations". Strictest measures were also taken against the entry of any of the defeated troops into Lahore. Raja Gulab Singh hastened his peace parleys and concluded the Treaty of 1846. Raja Gulab Singh, Raja Lal Singh and Misr Tej Singh were fully rewarded by the grateful victors for their meritorious services rendered in bringing about the collapse of the mighty Khalsa army.[57]

III

If the leaders did nothing, the soldiers did everything possible.[58] "The soldiery were the most stubborn we ever fought in India", write Gough and Innes.[59] "Their guns were heavier and more numerous than ours, and were admirably served". At Mudki there were no entrenchments, but all the same the Sikh position was a strong one lying "in a deep belt of dense jungle and stunted trees", which while giving cover to the artillery of the Sikhs, rendered the fire and approach of the enemy difficult. The disposition of the Sikh army was in a long deployed line "extending the British line on either side"[60] and having artillery and infantry in the centre and cavalry on the right and left wings. The battle opened with a gun duel which lasted for about an hour. At the same time the great masses of Sikh horse advanced on both the flanks as if to attempt a great enveloping movement, but this attempt was soon completely foiled by the counter moves of British cavalry. The Sikhs were now themselves outflanked and their cavalry under Raja Lal Singh took to flight.[61] As a result of this, the position of the Sikh centre became very critical. For a time the Sikh artillery and infantry posted in the centre, with their blast of grape and musketry, and the Sikh sharp shooters hidden in trees, slowed down the pace of the troops advancing upon them. When the Sikhs were attacked, they met the attack resolutely. But then after some time they were forced to give way as their number was very small as compared with that of the enemy. Still their retreat was most dogged. While being pursued they several times rallied and turned back upon their pursuers.

Next was the battle of Ferozshah which was "one of the most momentous and certainly the hardest fought-out one ever engaged in by the British in India".[62] Realizing from their Mudki experience the danger of fighting in the open, the Sikhs took up here a much more difficult position which was accessible, like Mudki, only through a belt of jungle and further was entrenched on three sides, besides having a village in the midst to be used as a fortification within a fortification. The disposition of the Sikh troops was carried out in the usual deployed order, but their plan being to conduct the battle from within an entrenched area, this order was so modified that all the three arms were properly distributed along the entire length of the line.[63] The infantry and cavalry were deployed behind as well as between the guns which were mounted at all prominent points. The cavalry was dismounted to be hidden from the enemy's view. A little away to the rear but within the enclosure itself was situated their field camp surrounded by mines for security's sake. Like Mudki sharp shooters were also employed here. They were posted round the wells to shoot down all who approached them. As usual the battle was opened by a gun duel in which the Sikh guns being superior in weight and calibre, had the better of the British artillery, but instead of following it up with an offensive they waited in their trenches for a British attack. However, while the British were advancing, the Sikh guns grew fiercer and fiercer. Europeans were their special targets, for the Sikhs believed that if they were demoralised, the backbone of the enemy's opposition would be broken.[64] As a result of this, Littler's attack upon the extreme left was successfully repulsed with severe losses. Similarly the blast of the Sikh guns was turned upon the divisions of the Gilbert and Wallace which were moving forward to attack the Sikh centre. The two English divisions, continuing their march, fell upon the Sikh gunners with the bayonet. Thereupon, the infantry behind the gunners formed squares and put up a vigorous fire of musketry from the lying position. By the time these troops were beaten and driven back, the Sikh *ghorchurras* had come up and attacked the invaders. While this fight was going on, the infantry that had been pushed back, rallied and made a counter-attack upon the British troops, though only to be driven back once again. In the meantime the Sikhs on the left had made a counter-attack upon the gap opened by the retreat of Littler's division[65] and attempting to pierce through that, had threatened the left flank of Smith's division.[66] There was a furious encounter there in which the British caused the Sikhs to stage a retreat to their camp. Both Gilbert and Smith then moved forward towards the Sikh camp, but they were soon repulsed. The Sikhs continued firing upon the enemy through the night, so much so that the British despaired of success and were prepared to retreat. Some suggested a retreat to Ferozepur and some counselled an unconditional surrender. Capt. Lumley, the Officiating Adjutant General, issued a direct order to Harry Smith "to collect every soldier and march direct to Ferozepur". Robert Cust thus writes[67] in his diary for 22nd December 1845: "News came from the Governor-General that our attack of yesterday had failed, that affairs were desperate, that all state papers were to be destroyed, and that if the morning attack failed, all would be over; this was kept secret by Mr. Currie and we were concerting measures to make an unconditional surrender to save the wounded, the part of the news that grieved me the most". Another source The *Career of Major Broadfoot*[68] confirms this fact. "In case of disaster, which was far from impossible, the Governor-General sent orders to Mudki, where Mr. Currie was in charge of official papers of the Government of India, and Mr. Cust of the Records of the Agency, for the destruction of all state papers. Sir Henry's son, Charles, who was his private secretary, being a civilian, was ordered off the field".[69]

But when victory was within the grasp, Lal Singh fled away during the night with all his irregular cavalry and the gunners of 60 pieces of artillery, thereby exposing to danger the whole of the left side of the camp, which was under his charge. Yet there was a good chance of Sikh success because early next morning Tej Singh appeared with a large fresh army on the battle-scene. He was urged by his zealous and sincere soldiery to fall upon the English but he paid no heed to that. His object was "to have the dreaded army of the Khalsa overcome and dispersed".[70] Instead of making a resolute attack upon the enemy, he only skirmished and after a time precipitately fled. Thus the field was left clear for the English. All the gallantry[71] which the Sikh soldiery had shown was thus cast away due to the treachery of their commanders.

After the battle of Ferozshah, some ten thousands of the Khalsa soldiers, including many officers, dispersed and fled to their homes in a mood of great frustration. But the mood of their countrymen and kith and kin was such that everywhere they went they "received very rough usage". "Those who reached their houses had to encounter the taunts and reproaches of their friends and neighbours, and in many instances even of their wives who bitterly reviled them for their cowardice. They were robbed and abused and beaten, even the women of the villages turning out to rail at them and strike them as they hurried along".[72] This had the salutary effect of inducing the deserters to return to their posts on the banks of the Sutlej.

Ferozshah was followed by Aliwal. The battle position here was not carefully chosen. Instead of any jungle or uneven ground interventing between them and the enemy, there was an open plain which could offer the least impediment to the attackers. A few trenches were no doubt dug out but they were insignificant as compared with those of Ferozshah. Another serious flaw in this position was that the line of retreat was obstructed by the Sutlej at the back. The only redeeming feature was the inclusion of two villages, Bundri and Aliwal in the battle line at the two ends. As regards the disposition of troops, it was more or less on the lines of the battle of Mudki. The fight was as usual opened with a fierce cannonade from the whole length of their entrenchments. Smith, the British commander, decided to attack on the Sikh left and centre. A deadly struggle seemed impending for the Sikh ranks were steady and the play of their guns incessant. But the holders of the left wing of the Sikh army were hill-men who had been raised because they were sober and indifferent to the Khalsa. After firing a straggling volley they gave way and fled in confusion. The Sikh commander Ranjodh Singh also fled with them.[73] Thus the British attack on the Sikh left was met with great success. However, the Sikhs on their right were strongly entrenched in spite of the exertions of the English infantry and artillery. The reason was that there were regular Sikh infantry battalions there. When a European regiment of lancers supported by one regiment of Indian cavalry attacked the Sikh right, the Sikhs knelt[74] to receive them with a volley at short range. A little later when the Lancers broke into them, the Sikhs threw away their muskets and fought fiercely with swords and shields but they were ultimately driven back. Meanwhile, Smith had thrown some squadrons of horse against an entrenched Sikh battery. The Sikh infantry in the rear of the battery boldly advanced to meet them with sword and closed with them in a bloody and determined struggle. These Sikh battalions trained by Avitabile fought most gallantly. The British infantry advanced to second their cavalry. However, the village of Bundri on the Sikh right could not be carried until two batteries of horse artillery had been brought up. At last the Sikhs began to disperse but "not until the mass has been three times ridden through".[75] The British dashed among the fleeing soldiers until 800 to 1000 men rallied under the high bank of a *nullah* and opened a heavy but ineffectual fire from below the bank. Once again they were charged and exposed to a deadly fire of 12 guns within 300 yards. The battle was now decided in favour of the British. The Sikhs, completely hemmed in, fled in disordered masses into the ford and the boats in utter confusion. The British howitzers then began to play upon the boats, causing heavy losses. There were four main reasons for the Sikhs failing so badly in this battle: (i) The commander Ranjodh Singh showed lack of competence and courage. By running away from the left wing, he set a very bad example for his men;[76] (ii) the hill-men deployed on the left end of the Sikh line proved great cowards and fled away without offering resistance to the enemy; (iii) the Sikh cavalry gave a very poor account of themselves, being under the influence of Ranjodh Singh and other Sardars; (iv) the high aiming of the guns due to the mischief of Mr. Potter who was secretly in league with the British.[77]

Regarding the battle of Aliwal there is also a view that there was no such battle in fact. It was only a scrimmage which has been magnified into a regular battle by the imagination of Harry Smith. Dr. Andrew Adams calls it a battle of the despatch. He writes:[78] "Much has been said of Aliwal, but candid witnesses give a far different account from that written at the time. I wandered over the field with one who had been present at the engagement; he assured me, and his testimony has been corroborated by many others, that a fruitful imagination was at work when the official account was drawn up". The eye-witness account referred to by the above writers reads[79] thus:

> "Aliwal was the *battle of the despatch*, for none of us knew we had fought a battle until the particulars appeared in a document, which did more than justice to every one concerned. But the public gulped it down, and like many of our Indian battles and Indian blunders, the final issue of the struggle disarmed criticism. As an Irishman would say, 'we gained a disadvantage at Budiwal', by the baggage of the army falling into the hands of the enemy; that no exaggeration could well turn into a victory; but shortly afterwards, a few shots, and the charge of a squadron or two in pursuit of a host of retreating Sikhs, was magnified into a grand combat, and thus the plain of Aliwal has been recorded as the scene of one of India's marathons".

In view of this evidence it is difficult to accept the veracity of the description of the Aliwal battle as found in British writers' accounts. Still it seems certain[80] that the Sikhs made a hasty retreat across the Sutlej while the troops under Harry Smith's command advanced quickly and attacked their camp. They also fired on the boats carrying the Sikhs, resulting in many deaths.

Sobraon was the final battle of the war. The Sikhs put their last stake on it and defensive works of so formidable a nature were constructed that the like of them had never been seen in any of the previous battles of their war. They could only be surmounted by the aid of scaling ladders and were so arranged that they afforded complete protection to three lines of infantry, one above the other, who could thus pour a tremendous fire upon an advancing foe.[81] However, their weak point was on the right where a considerable part of the line was defended only by slight entrenchments on account of the fact that the looseness of the sand there rendered it impossible to throw up parapets.[82] The entire bridge-head occupied a perimeter of about 4000 yards, the river line being about 2750 yards, in extent. This bridge-head was joined by means of a boat-bridge to the entrenchments on the other bank of the river. As at Aliwal, the position of the Sikhs had a river close behind it, which rendered it extremely dangerous.[83] Troops were disposed in the usual deployed order. Infantry and artillery were mainly deployed on the centre and the left, whereas irregular cavalry supported by zamburaks was posted on the right. The reserve force of the Sikhs consisting of all the three arms was arranged on the right bank of the Sutlej in such a way that its batteries could play upon the flanks of any hostile force advancing on the right side of their encampment.

The defensive tactics of the Sikhs enabled the British to choose their own time for commencing the attack. However, when the British troops made the move forward, the Sikhs quickly sounded the alarm and in a few minutes they manned their batteries and opened fire on the assailants. In the gun duel which now ensued and lasted for about two hours, the enemy guns got the better of the Sikh guns, sheltered as they were behind well-constructed batteries of earth, planks and fascines.[84] "Not dismayed by this rebuff the British advanced to the attack of the rightwing of the Sikh encampment which being the weakest was the easiest to counquer.[85] The Sikh tried to arrest their advance by a terrific fire from their cannon including those across the river, wall pieces and muskets, When they saw the enemy still moving steadily forward, a rally was attempted by Mouton with a body of irregular cavalry.[86] After some initial success, these troops fled back in great disorder. The advancing troops, emboldened by this, dashed forward and stormed the entrenchments and drove the Sikhs in confusion, from their guns upon their inner entrenchments. The Sikhs recovered speedily and counter-attacked, sword in hand, with the utmost determination.[87] Lord Gough who was keenly watching the situation at once sent reinforcements, and at the same time directed Gilbert and Smith to throw out their light troops and make demonstrations on the centre and the left of the Sikhs. The Sikh troops of the battalions of Gen. Court and Gen. Mehtab Singh, who were posted in the centre, did not take the slightest notice of these feints and turned all their efforts against the invaders on the right. Gradually the British were forced back and the Sikhs recaptured their guns and batteries, thereby frustrating Lord Gough's original plan of action. Then the British Commander ordered that the feints of Gilbert and Smith be converted into real attacks. The Sikhs relieved from the pressure upon their right flew to their centre and left to take up the challenge. Gilbert's first two attempts were foiled by the Sikhs. The ramparts were too high to be ascended without scaling ladders. On the extreme left Smith was likewise frustrated by Sham Singh Attariwala. Hick's brigade which led the assault thrice was driven back with heavy losses. For full one hour the issue of the fight was in the gravest doubt.[88] It was only after the fall of Sham Singh with all his followers that the English could reach his batteries. But the diversion of the Sikhs from their right to their centre and left had enabled the English on that side to rally and renew their attack with success. In the meantime Gilberts' troops making another assault had at last penetrated into the entrenchment, the men hoisting each other up the embrasures in default of ladders. The Sikhs now pressed from three sides began to give way slowly and stubbornly and were ultimately driven back upon their bridge of boats which gave way under the weight of the retreating troops.[89] By a strange fatality the river had also risen considerably during the night. The Sikhs had therefore to wade through the water under a shower of shot and shell from the cannon of the enemy and perished in thousands and thus had to pay a heavy price for their blunder of having a river across their line of retreat.

The Sikhs lost the battle not for any lack of courage on their part but because their leaders Gulab Singh Dogra, Lal Singh and Tej Singh were hostile and insincere. As regards the demeanour of the Khalsa troops, "although assailed on either side by squadrons of horse and battalions of foot, no Sikh offered to submit and no disciple of Gobind asked for quarter. They everywhere showed a front to the victors, and stalked slowly and sullenly away, while many rushed singly forth to meet assured death by contending with a multitude. The victors looked with stolid wonderment upon the indomitable courage of the vanquished and forbore to strike where the helpless and the dying frowned unavailing hatred".[90] Lord Gough, the British Commander-in-Chief, after what he had seen at Sobraon, could not suppress his admiration of the bravery and resoluteness of Sikhs. "Policy", he wrote,[91] "prevented my publicly recording my sentiments of the splendid gallantry of a fallen foe, and I declare, were it not from a conviction that my country's good required the sacrifice, I could have wept to have witnessed the fearful slaughter of so devoted a body".

The treachery of their supreme leaders was not completely unknown to the soldiery. They often gave vent to their alarm and indignation in fierce reproaches on the treachery of their leaders, but that was all they could do. In the words of Smyth, "They were unable to extricate themselves from the position into which they had been thrown".[92] "We know", they said to their leaders, "that you have leagued with the court to send us against the British and to pen us up here like sheep for them to come and slaughter us at their convenience; but remember that in this acting you play the part not only of traitors to your country but of ruthless butchers and murderers. You destroy whole army which, whatever its faults and crimes may have been, has always been ready to obey the orders of the state and its officers. We might even now punish you as you deserve, but we will have you to answer to your Guroo and your God, while we, deserted and betrayed as we are, will do what we can to preserve the independence of our country".[93]

Taking the entire course of the Sutlej campaign, it may be said without any doubt that in spite of the great handicaps which they had to face from the outset the Khalsa acquitted themselves admirably. It was the hardest fought war that the British had ever fought in India. The British had thought low of them[94] when they commenced the war. They soon realized their blunder and though they were victorious in the end, the victory for them had been rendered possible in no small measure by their secret intrigues with the leading chiefs of the Lahore Darbar.

REFERENCES

1. Cunningham, *op. cit.*, p. 293.
   "Their (Lal Singh' and Tej Singh's) desire was to be upheld as the ministers of a dependent kingdom by grateful conquerors".
2. Smyth, *op. cit.*, p. 168; Pandit Debi Prashad, *Gulshan-i-Punjab*, p. 96 (1872).
3. *Ibid.*
4. *Ibid.*, p. 170; Thornton, *op. cit.*, p. 331.
5. Cunningham, *op. cit.*, p. 258.
6. *Ibid.*, p. 263.
7. *Ibid.*, pp. 257, 263.
8. *Ibid.*, p. 257.
9. *Ibid.*, p. 264.

10. It was on 17 November 1845 that the army was to march according to the original decision. But for 20 days no march took place, because Lal Singh and Tej Singh hung back. Two reasons may be thought of. One, they did not want to lead the troops personally against the British. Two, they wanted to delay the march as the date did not suit the British. The Commander-in-Chief, Lord Gough, who was already present at Ambala, was anxious to wait for the Governor-General to arrive. The Governor-General, Henry Hardinge, only arrived on 2nd December 1845. It cannot be said with certainty but the probability is that Lal Singh had got a hint from the British through their *vakil* at Lahore or somebody else, that the march of the Khalsa divisions towards the Sutlej should be delayed.

11. *Punjab Papers*—Governor-General to the Secret Committee, December 2, 1845.

12. *Foreign Secret Progs.*, 26 December 1846, No. 184—Broadfoot to Currie, November 20, 1845.

13. *Punjab Papers*, p. 434; *Foreign Secret Progs.*, 26 December 1846, No. 197; Smyth, *op. cit.*, p. 171.

14. *Foreign Sec., Progs.*, 26 Dec., 1846, No. 192-Broadfoot to Lord Gough, 20 Nov., 1845.

15. Gough and Innes, *Sikhs and the Sikh Wars* (1897), p. 71.

16. Cunningham, *op. cit.*, p. 262.

17. *Foreign Secret Progs.*, 26 Dec., 1846, No. 210—a news letter from Lahore.

18. *Ibid.*, No. 216.

19. Diwan Ajudhia Prashad however gives a different view. He says that the crossing was not begun till 16th December. V. Suri, *Some Original Sources of Punjab History* (English translation of some contemporary Persian *Mss.*), p. 67.

20. *Foreign Secret Progs.*, 26 Dec., 1846—No. 212—News Abstract dated 5 Dec., 1845.

21. Henty, *Through the Sikh War*, p. 196.

22. J. W. Fortescue, *History of the British Army*, Vol. XII, p. 345 (London 1923).

    Also *Foreign Secret Progs.*, 26 Dec., 1846, Nos. 199-200. Assurances of native soldiers in the British army to come over and join the Sikhs are mentioned here.

23. *Foreign Secret Progs.*, 26 December 1846, Nos. 1300 and 1309—H. Lawrence to Currie, 27 July 1846 and the Governor-General's *Minute,* dated 11 Nov., 1846.—"There can be no doubt that if we had suffered reverses, as in the case of Patiala troops at Badowal, the contingents would have joined the enemy and we should have had a grand rising of the population in our rear as far as Karnal, cutting off our supplies and our small detachments and making war upon us to the knife"
24. *Foreign Secret Progs.*, 26 December, 1846, No. 889—Mem. of Henry Lawrence; Cunningham, *op. cit.*, p. 263; M'Gregor, *op. cit.*, Vol. II, p. 81; Mouton, *Rapport*, p. 5.
25. Henty, *Through the Sikh War*, p. 157.
26. Mouton (*Rapport*, p. 5) says that this scheme was suggested to Lal Singh by Nicolson.—"The treason saved the English from a sure defeat". Malleson, *Decisive Battles of India,* (London, 1883), p. 355. According to Diwan Ajudhia Parshad, the march of the Sikhs towards Mudki was most haphazard, unplanned, disorderly and bound to end in disorder. V. Suri, *op. cit.*, p. 71.
27. Cunningham, *op. cit.*, p. 265.
28. M' Gregor, *op. cit.*, Vol. II, pp. 51-52.
29. V. Suri, *op. cit.*, p. 73.
30. Cunningham, *op. cit.*, p. 267.
31. Malleson, *op. cit.*, p. 364.
32. *Ibid.*, p. 365.
33. *Ibid.*, p. 366.
34. M' Gregor, *op. cit.*, p. 149; V. Suri, *op. cit.*, p. 82.
35. V. Suri, *op. cit.*, p. 82.
36. *Foreign Secret Progs.*, 26 December 1846, No. 302.—Cunningham to Napier, 18th & 31st Dec., 1845; Governor-General to Napier, 26, January 1846.
37. *Ibid.*, No. 304.—Governor-General to Gough, 13 January 1846.
38. Burton, *First and Second Sikh Wars* (Simla, 1911), p. 30.
39. Fortescue, *op. cit.*, Vol. XII, p. 372; Gough and Innes, *op. cit.*, p. 111.
40. Burton, *op. cit.*, p. 37; Fortescue, *op. cit.*, Vol. XII, p. 380.
41. Burton, *op. cit.*, pp. 30-32; Fortescue, *op. cit.*, Vol. XII, p. 375.
42. Cunningham, *op. cit.*, p. 275; *Foreign Secret Progs.*, 26 Dec., 1846, No. 342.—Memorandum of Intelligence, 27 January 1846.

43. Ranjodh Singh was not merely an incompetent commander but also a traitor. See Cunningham, *op. cit.*, p. 276. He says: "Ranjodh also was insincere because he headed those who fled away after firing a straggling volley only".
44. They sent a letter assuring the British of their assistance. See *Foreign Secret Progs.*, 26 Dec., 1846, Nos. 334, 368, 381.
45. *Ibid.*, Nos. 333, 370.
46. *Ibid.*, Nos., 347, 370.
47. Cunningham, *op. cit.*, p. 278; *Foreign Secret progs.*, 26 Dec., 1846 Nos. 363, 367, 370.
48. Cunningham, *op. cit.*, p. 279; Malleson, *op. cit.*, p. 368.
49. *Foreign Secret Progs.*, 26 Dec., 1846, Nos. 367, 370.—*Punjab Intelligence* for 4 Feb., 1846.
50. *Ibid.*, No. 891 V. Suri, *op. cit.*, p. 85. A little earlier Lal Singh had fled away. He had been arrested and brought back by the troops.
51. *Ibid.*, No. 321; V. Suri, *op. cit.*, pp. 83-84.
52. *Rapport,* p. 7. Mouton also mentions that at his suggestion a plan of attack on the enemy on 4 February was adopted. However, the attack could not be made because a General, who was jealous of Tej Singh, instigated the troops not to take part in the attack. According to Ajudhia Prashad there was utter confusion in planning on the eve of this battle. "Every scheme revealed their lack of intelligence, imprudence and folly". V.S. Suri, *op. cit.*, p. 86.
53. George Mac Munn, *Lure of the Indus* (London, 1934), p. 207.
54. *Rapport,* pp. 8-9; Cunningham, *op. cit.*, p. 284.
55. This happened according as it had been secretly arranged previously.
56. *Rapport,* pp. 8-9.
57. *Foreign Secret Progs.*, 26 Dec., 1846, No. 370.—Lahore, Feb., 14 & 15, 1846.
58. Cunningham, *op. cit.*, pp. 279-80.
59. Fortescue, *op. cit.*, Vol. XII, p. 351.
60. Gough & Innes, *op. cit.*, pp. 76-77; Gen. Gough to Governor-General, Dec. 19, 1845.
61. "Lal Singh headed the attack, but, in accordance with his original design, he involved his followers in an engagement, and then left them to fight as their undirected valour might prompt". Cunningham, *op. cit.*, p. 265.

62. Gordon, *The Sikhs* (London, 1904), p. 143.
63. V. Suri, *op. cit.*, p. 71.
64. R.S. Rait, *Life and Campaigns of Lord Gough,* (London, 1913), p. 31.
65. Fortescue, *op. cit.*, Vol. XII, p. 362.
66. Rait, *op. cit.*, p. 22.
67. *Linguistic and Oriental Essays,* Vol. VI, p. 48.
68. P. 395. The Governor-General even gave his sword—a present from the Duke of Wellington and which once belonged to Napoleon and the Star of the Bath to his son, with directions to proceed to Ferozepur remarking that if the day were lost, he must fall. *Life of Gen. Sir Hope Grant,* edited by H. Knollys, p. 72.
69. "On that memorable night the English were hardly masters of the ground on which they stood". Cunningham, *op. cit.*, p. 267.
70. *Ibid.*
71. Shah Muhammad in his versified account of the battle mentions the gallantry of the Khalsa in glowing terms. See *Var Shah Muhammad* edited by Sita Ram Kohli, pp. 170-71.
72. Smyth, *op. cit.*, p. 176. Also see *Var Shah Muhammad,* p. 174.
73. Cunningham, *op. cit.*, p. 276.
74. *Ibid.*
75. *Ibid.*, p. 227.
76. Cunningham has questioned the sincerity of Ranjodh Singh as well. But according to *Punjab Chiefs* (1865), p. 88, he was superior to the other leaders of the Sikh army and was no traitor. "He had no confidential agents in the British camp as Raja Lal Singh had, nor did he like the Raja pray for and labour for the triumph of the English".
77. M'Gregor, *op. cit.*, Vol. II, p. 140.
78. *Wanderings of a Naturalist in India,* pp. 60-61.
79. *Ibid.*
80. This much is mentioned even in *Var Shah Muhammad* (p. 178), edited by S.R. Kohli.
81. *Through the Sikh War*, p. 176. Construction was conducted under, the supervision of two foreign officers, Mouton (French) and Hurbon (Spanish).
82. The Sikhs proposed to Tej Singh that the *ghorchurras,* howitzers and guns should be posted on the right so as to strengthen it,

but he did not listen and left the open ground unoccupied. V. Suri, *op. cit.*, p. 84.

83. Mouton writes that he was against fighting with the enemy in this position. He held it to be untenable. He was for attacking the British immediately or withdrawing across the river. *Rapport*, p. 7.

84. Burton, *op. cit.*, p. 39.

85. It is said that Tej Singh himself had informed the British about this weak point in the Sikh defence.

86. *Rapport*, p. 8.

87. Fortescue, *op. cit.*, Vol. XII, p. 386.

88. *Ibid.*

89. Tej Singh was "the first to quit the bloody field of Sobraon". He did it quite early in the fight and thereby left his troops without any commander to coordinate the efforts of the various units. "Some even assert that having made good his own retreat, the ropes by which the bridge was held, were by the Sirdar's orders, cut or cast loose whereby it became impossible to the retreating masses". Smyth, *op. cit.*, p. 184.

90. Cunningham, *op. cit.*, pp. 284-85; also see *Var Shah Muhammad*, p. 181.

91. Gough and Innes, *op. cit.*, p. 138.

92. Major Smyth, *op. cit.*, p. 180.

93. *Ibid.*

94. Gough and Innes, *op. cit.*, p. 137.

3

Emergence of Army

I

Maharaja Ranjit Singh had left a numerous, well-trained and well-disciplined army behind. After his death many new developments occurred in its organisation, numerical strength, and power. Between 1839 and 1845 the numbers went up from 80,000 to 1,50,630 marking an increase of a little under 100%. During the same period military expenditure was raised nearly four-fold. Important as these developments were, the most notable change, however, was effected in its relationship with the state. The internal feuds of rival chiefs afforded repeated opportunities to the army to assert its presence and get involved in political issues of the time. By 1845 it had become, in respect of power, the predominant political force in the country, a veritable colossus stalking the land, of which even the highest in the state stood in awe. But its positive side was far more significant than its negative aspect. It was deeply committed to the defence of the state against the perils of foreign aggression. It was not a mere fighting machine but was a national army prepared to make any sacrifice for the cause of the country.

The reign of Maharaja Sher Singh (20 January 1841—15 September 1843) marked the beginning of the process. Immediately after his accession a terrible mutiny broke out among the troops at Lahore. There were three main causes. First, the new Maharaja proved ineffective in keeping the troops under his control. His latitude towards the predatory acts of the soldiers during the days of the siege of the Fort of Lahore encouraged the belief that the soldiers could safely indulge in such acts. Secondly, the army now had the feeling that even if the Maharaja had the necessary desire, he could not do any harm to them because it was to them that he owed the throne. Another factor which proved instrumental in the outbreak of the mutiny was the time-lag in fulfilling the promises rashly held out at the time of seeking the support of the army.[1] Shortly after, as it usually happens in such situations, some new demands emerged. They demanded, for example, that all corrupt and unpopular pay-clerks and officers should be dismissed, and to pressurise the government to accept these demands, they set up regimental *panchayats* on the pattern of village *panchayats* with which they were well familiar. The government, too, took due notice of these *panchayats* and rather than ignore them made them the medium of their talks with the army, thus recognising their representative character. A meeting was soon called to which each military *panchayat* sent its representatives. The meeting proved stormy. While the government was prepared to dispense with the services of corrupt pay-clerks, it refused to concede the demand regarding the dismissal of the officers the soldiers did not like. The failure of the meeting[2] whetted the bitterness of the troops all the more with the result that henceforth they indulged in turbulence with vengeance. For eight to ten weeks the city of Lahore was turned into a veritable hell. "The enormities[3] of which they were guilty, it is said, almost baffle belief. Property was plundered and wantonly destroyed, merchants and shopkeepers were tortured; under the pretext of seeking for obnoxious commanders and monshees, every species of violence and cruelty were perpetrated". In the words of Sita Ram Kohli,[4] "The common sepoy became so overbearing that the peaceful citizens were allowed to quarter, and people of rank were not immune. Ministers and secretaries of government were mocked and jeered at, and Sher Singh himself greeted with the refrain that unless he paid up, Rani Chand Kaur would be restored". When all efforts of the government failed to curb the disturbances at Lahore, the trouble spread to several other parts of the kingdom. In Srinagar the *nazim* of Kashmir Mehan Singh was murdered. In Mandi Commandant Foulks, in Hazara Major Ford and in Amritsar Sobha Singh, the garrison commander, were done to death. The *nazims* of Peshawar and Multan, Avitabile and Sawan Mal, narrowly escaped death. Central Court had to run away to Ferozepur to save his life while General Ventura and Jamadar Khushal Singh would have fallen dead but for the timely help provided by the Maharaja's personal guards. Col. Mouton was saved by the heroism of his wife who threw herself between him and his assassin and called upon them to kill her first.[5]

The mutiny with fits and starts lasted for a period of about six months. It practically disappeared towards the end of June 1841. Several factors had contributed towards this result. Most of the demands of the army had been met. The promised increase of one rupee in the monthly salary of the soldier had been granted along with one month's additional pay as bonus or gratuity. The corrupt pay-clerks who had escaped being killed at the hands of the mutinous sepoys had been dismissed from service. Raja Dhian Singh to whom the Maharaja had wisely left the handling of the problem had tactfully and firmly managed the delicate situation. The most turbulent elements in the army had been shunted off while the military units which had earned notoriety for indiscipline had been shifted from the capital to places where the scope for mischief by them was much less. A still more important measure was the recruitment of thousands of non-Sikh soldiers, mostly men from the hills. Between the months of June 1841 and February 1842 some 6000 of these hillmen were recruited and formed into 8 battalions of infantry and 3 units of light artillery.[6] The recruitment of such people continued even after that. Another important factor which affected the situation was the growing apprehension of British designs on the Punjab. What was the policy of the British government towards the Sikh kingdom at this time has been discussed in a separate chapter. But whatever be this policy, there were constant rumours afloat that the British would soon attack the Punjab and annex it to their empire. This is amply clear from what Mrs. Henry Lawrence wrote in a letter dated 26 May 1841, to her friend Mrs. Cameron: "Wars and rumours of wars are on every side and there seems no doubt that next cold weather will decide the long-suspended question of occupying the Punjab; Henry, both in his civil and military capacity, will probably be called upon to take part in whatever goes on". To another friend, Mrs Haye, she wrote on June 5: "Nothing yet promulgated, but H. supposes the army for the Punjab will be divided into three columns; the main body accompanied by Mr. Clark, our chief, and others by H. and Mr. Cunningham".[7] The Anglo-Indian press also had a notable part to play in the circulation of such rumours. As time passed, the Sikh apprehensions about the British intentions were further strengthened and even responsible people at the Lahore Court started believing them. For example, *the Punjab Intelligence* reported in December 1841: "The Minister (Dhian Singh) at Lahore, several of the chiefs, and in some measure the Maharaja himself are not without apprehension that the British design to invade the Punjab when a portion of the Khalsa army may have been drawn off to Peshawar".[8] The situation was so critical during the first half of the year 1842 that Mr. Maddock, Secretary to the Governor-General, had to write to Mr. Clerk, British Agent at Ludhiana, ordering him[9] "to give to the Maharaja the assurances of the Governor-General that his government entertains no wish to express or occupy any portion whatever of His Highness's Dominion and is desirous only that His Highness should long retain them all in Honour and Prosperity..." Still the fear was not wholly removed; rather it continued as before with the result that in November 1842 the people in Lahore were seen removing their property to other places or burying it.[10] Convinced of the evil designs of the British, Raja Dhian Singh on 7 December 1842 observed to the Maharaja that "the British appear to have an intention of encroaching on the Punjab territories as all news-writers in Hindustan write that the British troops are assembling from all quarters at Ferozepur".[11] Lehna Singh Majithia, in confirmation of this fear, informed the Maharaja that "since they (the British) had withdrawn from Afghanistan they have nothing else but long for Punjab".[12]

Although the mutiny was over and peace was finally restored, the events of the reign of Sher Singh left a deep mark on the shape of things to come. During the stormy days of military disorders *panchayats* had appeared and they had functioned effectively as representatives of the various military units. With the return of peace they were no longer considered necessary and were disbanded. Still a powerful precedent had been set. The soldiers had seen the utility of these army committees or soviets, and there was every likelihood that should such a situation be repeated, the soviets could be revived and made to serve the peculiar ends of the troops. This is what exactly happened in the time of Raja Hira Singh's Ministry.

Secondly, the bonds of discipline were somewhat visibly loosened. After the worst days of the mutiny were over, the army no doubt returned to its normal functioning and carried out the orders of the government. But this was not always willingly done. For instance, the Charyari *sowars* refused to march to Peshawar when they were ordered to do so on 16 December 1841.[13] A Muslim force was commissioned to accompany the British officers from Peshawar to Jallalabad but it fled away from Jamrud against orders.[14] At Peshawar a few other incidents of indiscipline happened. Attacks were made on British godowns on one or two occasions and some of the food grains stored therein were forcibly seized. There were some stray cases in which a few British officers were jeered at.[15] But there was no such thing as a state of disorganisation in the Khalsa army as some British officers like Clerk and Gen. Pollock would have us believe.[16] The dissatisfaction of the Khalsa troops assembled at Peshawar sprang chiefly from two factors: (i) There were rumours widely circulating that the British intended to occupy Peshawar.[17] Therefore the Khalsa troops had no heart in the scheme of helping the British. It was not their war or the cause for which they could be enthusiastic; (ii) the British had made bulk purchases of food grains and stored them in their godowns. By this conditions of scarcity had been created in the Peshawar region and prices had risen sharply putting the Khalsa troops to great hardships. They were very unhappy and their attitude towards the British was almost unfriendly. This fact comes out clearly from what Major Gen. Pollock wrote to Lt. Col. Luard.[18] "Our connection with the Sikh Government is properly friendly and the chiefs are as far as I have observed courteous and perhaps well-disposed towards us, but the bearing of the soldiery, one and all, is insolent, and they scruple not to express their wish that we may meet with reverses, they are a disorganised rabble but dangerous as neighbours. Our officers require escorts between camp and Peshawar, and our sepoys or camp-followers dare not move beyond the pickets after dark".

It is not without significance that there was not a single case of the Sikh troops at Peshawar misbehaving with or being rude or disobedient to their own officers. Hence, the reports of the British officers on the lack of discipline among the Sikh battalions and regiments at Peshawar are exaggerated, one-sided and misleading. Even the strong anti-British sentiment subsided when it was finally decided to force the Khyber and the Jubhagi passes. The spirit of gallantry with which the Sikh troops acquitted themselves in carrying out the assigned responsibilities, elicited admiration from the same British officers who only a short while ago were so critical of them. Gen. Pollock wrote to the Maharaja on 6 April 1842 praising the Khalsa troops' bravery in forcing the mountain pass and capturing Ali Masjid.[19] The Governor-General in a special letter dated 14 May 1842 offered thanks to Sher Singh for the assistance rendered by the Sikhs.[20] But this is not to say that there was no fault with these troops. The state of discipline was not what it should be. It was for this reason that Sikh chiefs and commanders in their heart of hearts entertained fear of the troops. Raja Gulab Singh who was sent to Peshawar to organise help for the British trusted his own hill soldiers much more than the Sikh battalions.[21] The Maharaja and Raja Dhian Singh also were not free from this fear.[22] The British, however, exaggerated this element of fear as it admirably fitted in with their sinister designs on the Lahore kingdom. For example, Clerk informed Maddock in his letter of 15 March 1842:[23] "The state of the Sikh army continues to present great difficulties to the administration. I still see not in the Punjab the means of restraining it. Crores of rupees have in vain been disbursed to it and on the other hand punishment has been inflicted on the most insubordinate with as little success". A week later the same Mr. Clerk wrote to Gen. Pollock:[24] "You are aware that a long period of disorganisation prevailing in the Sikh army has left the Lahore Government without any confidence in its zeal or efficiency in the field. Even at the capital all important duties are entrusted to Hill soldiers". The motivation behind such writings may be evident from the fact that this was the time when he was planning to sent a powerful British army into the Punjab.[25] He was actually making out a case for military intervention in the Punjab.

Yet another legacy of Maharaja Sher Singh's reign was the army's involvement in matters of political nature. So far it was just no more than the beginning. But the fact that it had started carried much significance for in the years to come it went on growing until the army became the supreme political force in the country. We have already seen that the reluctance of the troops to help the British actively was politically motivated. An equally striking instance is provided by some of the Sikh battalions conducting secret correspondence with the Sandhanwalia chiefs residing in the British-held cis-Sutlej areas.[26] Some letters pertaining to this correspondence were intercepted by the British towards the end of the year 1841. It comes out from these letters that the troops concerned were dissatisfied with Maharaja Sher Singh because he had left everything to the Dogra Raja. They favoured Rani Chand Kaur as ruler and Attar Singh Sandhanwalia as *Wazir*. The Sandhanwalia as felt greatly encouraged by this and started levying troops with the object of crossing over. On learning of their preparations, the Maharaja lodged a complaint with Mr. Clerk against the Sandhanwalias.[27] It may, however, be noted that the troops did not pursue the matter any further. There was no overt move on their part at any time during the reign of Sher Singh to remove him or his minister.

II

After the abrupt ending of the period of Maharaja Sher Singh and Raja Dhian Singh on 15 September 1843, power passed into the hands of Raja Hira Singh and his mentor Pandit Jalla. As the new Maharaja, Dalip Singh, was just a small child, the new incumbent's authority was complete and almost absolute. During the new regime (16 September 1843 to 21 December 1844), the Khalsa gained tremendously in power. Dissatisfaction increased in its ranks which threatened to disintegrate it but it was saved by the mechanism of the regimental *panchayats* which reappeared simultaneously. These *panchayats* established their firm hold on the army as a whole and not only saved it from the impending danger of disintegration but also helped maintain a strict discipline in its various units and branches. Gradually the army emerged as the predominant political force in the state. A far more significant development was its transformation into a national army.

Like Maharaja Sher Singh, Raja Hira Singh also owed his ascendancy entirely to the army. The role of the army as the king-maker gave an added sense of power to it and it began to cherish the idea that it was strong enough to dictate terms to the new government. In case the Raja refused to accept these terms, the army felt that it had the power to dislodge him from his position and put somebody else in his place. This was a serious enough matter for no government can function properly under such conditions. Being well aware of this the Raja began to think of devices to break the unity of the army. One method devised by him was to increase the number of hill soldiers by fresh recruitment. This was no new device but was a continuation of his father's policy. Naturally this was resented by the Khalsa which constituted the bulk of the soldiery. What caused still greater resentment among them was the Raja's policy of gifts and donatives. It was a selective and discriminating policy which seems to have been adopted deliberately with a view to sowing seeds of dissensions in the ranks of the armed forces. The strategy underlying this whole thing was that the military units in receipt of such favours, being under obligation to the government, would be willing to be employed against such other military units as were prone to turbulence. If such a policy was successful, the Raja would become strongly entrenched and then no problem, internal or external, would be too difficult for him to tackle. But the policy instead of helping him recoiled on him. It created a great storm. The units which did not receive the benefits felt sore and openly indulged in scathing criticism of the government and not unoften talked of overthrowing the Raja's ministry. On the contrary the units which had received the favours quietly looked on as spectators. Even at the capital all military units were not happy because they were not equally treated. But the units which were stationed away from the capital were far more angry and restless. They believed that since they happened to be away from Lahore, they were being deprived of the rewards and gratuities which the troops at Lahore were receiving. Thus a situation was created in which the troops at Lahore were adamant to stay on at Lahore while the troops away from there were insistent that they should be allowed to return to Lahore. It was with great difficulty that General Tej Singh was able to prevent the troops under him from marching back to Lahore. Still he failed to check the Ramgol Regiment[28] which returned to Lahore against his orders.

To fight against this policy of discrimination of Raja Hira Singh all military units—battalions, regiments and batteries, etc.—established special committees on democratic lines, called *panchayats*.[29] They were indeed a revival of the *panchayats* of the reign of Sher Singh. Once these *panchayats* were set up, they acquired great importance. They were the spokesmen of their units and as such formulated their demands, effected contacts with the corresponding organisations of other units, and negotiated for the redressal of their grievances. A central *panchayat* was sometimes created consisting of representatives of the primary *panchayats*. Such a *panchayat* was authorised to speak on behalf of the entire army and to conduct talks with the government on issues of importance to them.

The *panchayats* did not merely fight for improvement of emoluments or for removal of discrimination in the distribution of official favours. They also rendered great help in the maintenance of military discipline. The British Agent at Ludhiana, Col. Richmond was so much impressed by them that he wrote in October 1843:[30] "So favourable is my opinion of the efficiency of the system of the committees that I feel sure that a kind of Government will subsist for months to come and probably for a longer period". The system endured much longer than even the optimist Col., Richmond had expected. The *Calcutta Review*[31] had the following to observe regarding the *panchayats'* contribution to military discipline: "Europeans too often judge Asiatics by European rules and call false, unnatural or extraordinary what is merely new. It is not, however, a page of history to be lightly passed over by the Anglo-Indians, which exhibits the rude panchayats of the Sikh army setting at naught the legal authority of the Government and yet enforcing their own with iron and mysterious sway among their comrades. Woe betide to the ranks, mutilation of a hand, an ear or a nose, even death awaited them".

Officers of the army did not have any voice in the *panchayats'* debates. The *panchayats* only left military duties to them, all other matters such as questions of discipline, emoluments, movements, relations with other army units, government policy, etc., were reserved for their own deliberations. But military duties were an essential part of military discipline and could not be ignored. The *panchayats* in respect of such matters generally gave full cooperation to the commanders. The defaulters, if any were penalized.

Another dimension was soon added to the functioning of the *panchayats*. They claimed sovereign authority in the name of the Khalsa and asserted that the wielders of authority were accountable to them for the conduct of state affairs and showed no hesitation in inflicting punishment on those who were suspected of betraying the interests of the state. The concept of sovereignty of the Khalsa was an accepted Sikh political doctrine. It was the Khalsa which was the repository of sovereign power in the time of Ranjit Singh, or earlier in the eighteenth-century Sikh principalities of Banda Singh and the *misls*. The doctrine dated back from the time when Guru Gobind Singh in 1708 abolishing the personal *guruship* had conferred it upon the Khalsa. That is why the Khalsa has often been referred to as "the commonwealth of Gobind"[31a] by British writers. Just as this idea of Khalsa sovereignty was already present, so also the notion of identifying the Sikh army with the Khalsa of Guru Gobind Singh was already in existence.[32] The ministry of Raja Hira Singh provided the condusive circumstances in which it was not difficult for the army on the basis of the above two ideas to proclaim itself to be the very personification of *Panth Khalsaji* and as such asserted its supreme authority.[33]

Raja Hira Singh had barely been in power for two months and a quarter when the first crisis of his period arose. The cause was the dissatisfaction of the Queen Mother, Rani Jindan, with Hira Singh. She nurtured the grievance that she was not being given the respect due to her for her exalted status. At her instigation, or at least with her consent, her brother Jawahar Singh on 24 November 1843 escaped with the child Maharaja to the lines of the troops and appealed to them to save the Maharaja and his mother. The manoeuvre, however, failed because the army rejected his version and confined him, returning the Maharaja safely to the palace. Disappointed in this, the Rani began to work on the mind of Raja Sochet Singh, uncle of Raja Hira Singh. Raja Sochet Singh was already sore with his nephew because he had been ignored. At the critical time of winning over the army against the Sandhanwalias he had stood by Hira Singh like a rock, but for this he had been given nothing. Moreover, he felt that he had a better claim to *wuzarat* than Hira Singh. Rani Jindan's secret encouragement whetted his ambition still further and prompted him to work for his cherished goal with vigour and zeal. But his move also passed off peacefully, for the time being at least. Raja Gulab Singh came to Hira Singh's help and successfully persuaded Sochet Singh to shift his residence to his estates near Jammu. Raja Sochet Singh and his friend Rai Kesri Singh left the capital on 4 December 1843. About this time another explosive event occurred which unlike the above two occurrences brought the army into action. Princes Kashmira Singh and Peshaura Singh, sons of Maharaja Ranjit Singh by his wife Daya Kaur, were falsely accused of being privy to the Sandhanwalias' murderous plots against Maharaja Sher Singh and Raja Dhian Singh, and were attacked by the Dogra chief, Raja Gulab Singh. Their estates of Sialkot and Kurianwala were forcibly seized and a property worth 1½ lakh rupees was captured.[34] The Princes were taken captive and confined in Jammu. This act of high-handedness created a great stir in the army. The regimental *panchayats* expressed strong resentment against this. Their meetings were held almost daily where severe criticism was made of Raja Hira Singh and his administration. A significant new development of these critical days was the identification of the army with *Sarbat* or *Panth Khalsaji*. Even the army offices felt the impact of the stir in the soldiery. On 10 January 1844 a deputation of them met Raja Hira Singh and conveyed to him the strong feelings of the Khalsa. In the language of the news report they put it to the Raja:[35] "How had he dared to do it without consulting the Khalsa?" Next day, the officers again met Hira Singh and told him in so many words that Raja Gulab Singh had not done well in seizing the property of the Kanwars and that "the Khalsa was exceedingly displeased with the Raja on this account".[36] The report about the proceedings of the Darbar for 15 January 1844 mentions that the Dogra action against the princes created the feeling in the army that the Dogras were bent upon the destruction of the Khalsa".[37] The feelings of the men in the army ran so high that on 21 January 1844 Mian Labh Singh informed Raja Hira Singh that "the Sikhs were disposed to commit some outrage".[38] The following day General Kanh Singh Mann and Gen. Mehtab Singh Majithia presented a number of demands on behalf of the Khalsa. The more important of them were:[39]

1. Kanwars Kashmira Singh and Peshaura Singh should be released without delay and their lands restored to them.
2. Mian Waris Khan should be released without delay and reinstated in his post.
3. The Rajas should pay the revenues due on the districts under their management.
4. The Maharaja should be duly installed as sovereign. Rajas Gulab Singh and Sochet Singh should be present in Lahore on that occasion.
5. Sardar Jawahar Singh should be released on that day.
6. Raja Gulab Singh should give a satisfactory explanation about the assemblage of Hill men in Lahore.
7. The *jagirs* in possession of the Sardars should not be taken from them.

To these demands Raja Hira Singh replied that he would send a special agent to Raja Gulab Singh about these things. The officers said that the answer should come in ten days.

From the demands listed above it appears that the issue of the Kanwars had raised serious doubts in the minds of the Khalsa about the *bona fide* intentions of Raja Hira Singh and Raja Gulab Singh regarding the *raj*. The forcible eviction of the Kanwars from their estates and their imprisonment was regarded as only one of the measures intended to replace the Khalsa *raj* by a Dogra *raj*. The installation ceremony of Maharaja Dalip Singh had not yet been held and was being postponed on one pretext or another.[40] The non-Dogra chiefs were being gradually weakened by confiscation of their *jagirs* in full or in part, or by heavy fines.[41] On the other hand the Dogra chiefs were treated with great favour. They had not paid anything into the state treasury though the arrears due from them amounted to lacs of rupees. Rather, their *jagirs* were being increased. Then, hill men were being recruited in large numbers and assembled in Lahore. There were also rumours that property in the *toshakhana* was being sent in large quantities to Jammu.[42] All these things appeared to them to be part and parcel of a well-calculated Dogra policy to convert the Khalsa *raj* into a Dogra *raj*.[43]

Raja Hira Singh appreciated the seriousness of the situation[44] and immediately decided to release the Princes Kashmira Singh and Peshaura Singh. They were also allowed to reoccupy their *jagirs* of Sialkot and Kurianwala. Likewise, it was decided to hold the installation ceremony of Maharaja Dalip Singh on the scheduled date, 2nd February 1844. Regarding the other demands as well he made certain concessions though these concessions did not go very far. In this way the crisis for the time being was warded off.

But Raja Hira Singh was only trying to bide time. He made no qualitative change in his policy. Raja Gulab Singh, Raja Sochet Singh, Pandit Jalla and he himself still did not pay anything into the state treasury for the vast lands under their management or held by them in *jagir*.[45] On the contrary, Raja Gulab Singh was offered new territories in farm, namely, the districts of Chuch and Rawalpindi.[46] The non-

Dogra chiefs, on the other hand, continued to be treated shabbily. Jawahar Singh was still in prison and was being tortured.[47] Bhai Ram Singh was insulted[48] by Pandit Jalla on 29 February 1844. Khushal Singh was harassed.[49] Lehna Singh and Sham Singh were under suspicion. The worst of all, he had not forgiven the Princes Kashmira Singh and Peshaura Singh. The decision to harass them was resumed around the middle of February. A regiment of Raja Gulab Singh's hillmen marched[50] upon Sialkot soon after. Col. Dhonkal Singh was sent with his troops from Lahore to join in the attack of Sialkot. As was to be expected, there was once again a great stir in the army.[51] General Kanh Singh and other officers told Raja Hira Singh about this stir and advised him to dismiss Pandit Jalla and call Rai Kesree Singh to his assistance. The Raja gave evasive replies. The attitude of the Raja further embittered the Khalsa. The regiments of General Kanh Singh and Dooleh Singh deserted in the course of their march to Peshawar and joined[52] Prince Kashmira Singh. About this time the Khalsa was reported to be openly criticising the Raja's action against the Princes. The news report for 12 March 1844 says that they went as far as to state: "If the Rajas do not take care, the Khalsa will not leave one brick upon another in Jammu and Jasrota". It is also reported that Raja Sochet Singh wishing to fish in the troubled waters wrote encouragingly to the Princes and also sent them some money in support.[53] In view of the serious turn taken by the situation Raja Gulab Singh wrote to Hira Singh from Jammu to dismiss Pandit Jalla and to appoint Raja Sochet Singh and Rai Kesree Singh as his advisers.[54] Still Hira Singh went ahead with his policy of sending more troops against the Kanwars in Sialkot. On 21st March 1844 nearly all the General officers of the army plainly told Hira Singh that "if anything happened to the Kanwars the whole Khalsa would arise".[55] Next day the warning was repeated by the Khalsa themselves. They said that "the Khalsa was displeased and would go and release Sialkot and then march upon Jammu. They were tired of the Dograhs. If the Raja wished to remain master, he must consult the old Sirdars of the Khalsa. The Dograhs had been deceiving the Khalsa by saying that the English troops were collecting but they had all the time designs of their own".[56] The Raja felt alarmed and sent for some of the regimental *panchayats* but they refused to obey. Another shock for him was the release of Sardar Jawahar Singh from imprisonment by soldiers themselves on 24 March 1844. After that the soldiers of the regiment of Col. John Holmes sent a note to Hira Singh asking him to release Misr Beli Ram and his brothers. If they were alive, and if they were dead, to surrender Sheikh Emamuddin and to send away Misr Jalla. In case these demands were not conceded, they threatened to raze the houses of Raja Dhian Singh and Raja Hira Singh to the ground and march upon Jammu and Jasrota. Later on the same day 4 men of the *panchayats* of the same regiment came to the Darbar. They said that they had come on the part of the whole of the Khalsa and gave the Raja the orders of the Khalsa. They were emphatic that they were not petitioners but the bearers of the message of the Khalsa. The Khalsa wanted to know from him why he had maltreated Sardar Boor Singh, the widow of Maharaja Sher Singh, Jamadar Khushal Singh, Sardar Sham Singh Attariwala, and Kanwar Kashmira Singh and why he was showing favours to Sheikh Emamuddin, Pandit Jalla and Misr Lal Singh. Then they demanded the surrender of Sheikh Emamuddin, Pandit Jalla and Misr Lal Singh. If he hesitated or refused, he would himself be seized. The Raja said that he would obey the wishes of the Khalsa. In the afternoon the Raja sent for the officers of the army and for two men from each regimental *panchayat*. About 10,000 men came to the residence of the Raja. After some discussion a settlement was reached which said:[57]

1. Misr Jalla should be sent away to Jasrota.
2. Sheikh Emamuddin should be delivered up.
3. Sardar Jawahar Singh should be honoured.
4. Princes Kashmira Singh and Peshaura Singh should not be harassed and the operation against them should be called off.
5. The widows of Misr Beli Ram should be released.

On the following day Raja Hira Singh visited the regimental lines and assured every one that he was the well-wisher and the servant of the Khalsa. One special reason why he was at this time all politeness and obedience was that Raja Sochet Singh and Rai Kesree Singh were on the way to Lahore with the object of ousting him from power. When these two Dogra chiefs were defeated and slain on 26 March 1844, the attitude of Hira Singh underwent a change. He declined to dismiss Pandit Jalla, or surrender Sheikh Emamuddin, or Misr Lal Singh. He spared the lives of Kanwars Kashmira Singh and Peshaura Singh and allowed them to go wherever they wanted. But he did not restore their *jagirs*. Sardar Jawahar Singh was shown no special honour as had been promised. Rather, the Raja was on the look-out for an opportunity to reconfine him. His attitude towards non-Dogra chiefs also remained largely unchanged. They were still shabbily treated and their *jagirs* were confiscated whenever an opportunity arose. Thus the roots of the trouble remained precipitating critical situations from time to time. In such circumstances as these the army had to assert its supremacy as *Panth Khalsaji* on more than one occasion. Raja Hira Singh tried hard to manage the armed forces by means of donatives and special favours or to create rifts in their ranks so as to be able to play off one part against another, but all the measures he adopted failed to break the unity of the army or to crush its Khalsa spirit.

Frequently inducements were given by the authorities to allure the soldiery. When some units were chosen for the award of such favours, there were agitations by others until the benefits were also extended to those which had not got them before. Thus big gratuities or donatives were obtained by army men. Their monthly salaries were also raised.[58] But the Khalsa army was not a body of mercenaries that it should feel satisfied with such concessions alone. Just as it felt called upon, as we have seen above, to prevent Hira Singh and Jalla from undermining the basic character of the state, so also it felt concerned for its safety and integrity. It was a thoroughly patriotic army. Whatever be its grievances against Raja Hira Singh or his advisers, the army never tarried or hesitated to accord first priority to matters of defence of the state against enemies, external or internal. Among the internal revolts the most important ones were the risings of Fateh Khan Tiwana in Tank and Bannu, Painde Khan in Darband, and Zabardast Khan in Muzaffrabad. Some other chiefs of Hazara in revolt were the Sayyed of Kaghan, Sher Muhammad Khan of Gandgarh, Arsila Khan of Zaidah, Sultan Najaf Khan of Khatur, Ali Gauhar of Khanpur and Habibullah Khan of Pakhli. This shows that practically the entire region of Hazara was in a state of disturbance. Lower down, the region of Dera Ismail Khan, Bannu and Tank was similarly disturbed. All these revolts were put down and not an inch of the state's territory was lost. This was all due to the vigorous action taken by the Khalsa army.[59] As against the external danger, the response of the army *panchayats* was even stronger. When the British started constructing a fortified cantonment at Ferozepur, they felt greatly concerned. The regiments under General Gulab Singh Calcuttia were immediately moved to Kasur and there they began to temper with the loyalty of the Purbia sepoys of the British army. If ordered, they were even ready to cross over and destroy the new fortification under construction at Ferozepur or take Ferozepur and Ludhiana.[60] The most striking example of the army's concern for the country's defence is, however, provided by its consent to attack Bhai Bir Singh. The Bhai was a highly respected man. His anti-Dogra campaign was also very popular with the Khalsa regiments. Even when his private army was fast increasing and several important chiefs had joined him, the army was unwilling to accept the appeals of Raja Hira Singh for help against the Bhai. But when Attar Singh Sandhanwalia came over from across the Sutlej to join him, the situation suddenly took a new turn. Raja Hira Singh knowing the deep concern of the army for the defence of the country, appealed to its instinct of patriotism and secured its immediate consent to a march upon the Bhai's camp. The substance of his appeal on this occasion as reported in the *Punjab Intelligence Report* for 3rd May 1844, was:[61]

> "Raja Hira Singh drew up a paper to the following effect for submission to the officers of the army. 1st. The Sindhanwalas had left the Punjab at the time of the accession of Maharaja Sher Singh and after making their arrangements with the English they had tendered obedience to the Maharaja. Afterwards they had slain the Maharaja and his son and his Vizeer. Sirdar Uttur Singh again went away and confirmed his engagements with the English......4th. Now Sirdar Uttur Singh has agreed to give a six-anna share of the revenues of the Punjab to the English and having got permission from them had returned to the Punjab to establish the rule of the English. 5th. Bhai Bir Singh is a Fukeer or Devotee, he ought not to oppose himself to the Government. 6th. If the Khala is displeased with him, the Raja, they can assist Uttur Singh but they should remember that under the rule of the English the sacred cow will be slaughtered. 7th. A request should be addressed to Bhai Bir Singh to deliver up Sirdar Uttur Singh, otherwise he will be punished".

Some months later when the conflict between Raja Hira Singh and Raja Gulab Singh was at its peak, Raja Hira Singh used the same clever device to secure the consent of the army to march upon Jammu and with similar success. A proclamation to be issued to the troops was drafted by Pandit Jalla in collaboration with Diwan Amar Nath and Fakir Nuruddin. The draft mentioned, among other things, that Raja Gulab Singh "designed to oppose the Khalsa and really wished that the English should possess the Punjab". Diwan Amar Nath and Fakir Nuruddin did not like this reference to the English but Pandit Jalla insisted and in support of his contention argued as follows: "When the late Raja Sochet Singh and Rai Kesria Singh rose in arms against the Darbar and also when Uttur Singh Sindhanwalas crossed the Sutlaj—as soon as it was given out that they were supported by the British Government so soon did the Khalsa immediately march and destroy them..."[62] From this it appears that the army's patriotic sentiments were so intense that they could be, and were, exploited on occasions by the Dogra administrators.

There are two other aspects of the army's outlook which are relevant and need to be mentioned here. (1) The army was not interested in destablization as such. Most of the indiscipline found in its ranks was caused by the power-hungry chiefs. The same is true of the so-called greediness of its units. On the contrary the army had greatly succeed in saving itself and the state from immediate disintegration. Moreover, the army seldom attempted to disestablish an established government. For instance, it was not responsible for destroying the government of Maharaja Sher Singh and Raja Dhian Singh. On the other hand it promptly inflicted upon the culprits a punishment which they rightly deserved. As regards Raja Hira Singh's government, the army had several spells of confrontation with it but in spite of the strong language it often used, it never really attempted to destroy the government. When it finally decided to oust Hira Singh and Jalla from power, even then it was a defensive measure. Raja Hira Singh has planned[63] to replace Maharaja Dalip Singh by the infant son of the late Maharaja Sher Singh, to kill Jawahar Singh and to put under confinement Rani Jindan. It was only when this plot leaked out that the army decided to act against him. (2) The army was not prepared to tolerate any disrespect or humiliation of any member of Maharaja Ranjit Singh's family. Whether it was Dalip Singh, Kashmira Singh, Peshaura Singh, Rani Jindan or any other member of the reigning house, the army always showed the utmost deference for him or her unless a drunkard and debauchee like Jawahar Singh by his degraded and inhuman conduct had completely forfeited his entitlement to respect. On the question of harassment of Kanwars Kashmira Singh and Peshaura Singh the army went to the extent of *gheraoing*[64] the *Wazir* and did not let him go until he consented to treat the Princes well. On 9 May Mian Labh Singh imprisoned the mother of the Kanwars Kashmira Singh and Peshaura Singh and sent her towards Lahore. As soon as the troops learnt about that, they assembled and decided to release the lady. She was brought back from a distance of five *kos*. Col. Zorawar Singh who tried to restrain the men was shot dead.[65] Still another instance is that when Rani Jindan complained against Pandit Jalla for his rude and insulting behaviour towards her the army took a very serious notice of it.[66]

III

The fall of Raja Hira Singh strengthened the supreme position of the army still further. The new government headed by Rani Jindan completely depended upon its good will and support. When the Rani proposed the name of her brother for the post of *Wazir*, the army rejected it outright because it did not regard him as a fit person to hold that position.[67] Seeing the mood of the army the Rani set up a Council with herself as its president. The Council consisted of Sardar Jawahar Singh and Bhai Ram Singh[68] with Diwan Dina Nath, Fakir Nuruddin and Bakshi Bhagat Ram as secretaries. This arrangement continued for several months until in the month of May, taking advantage of the outbreak of a terrible pestilence of cholera in Lahore, the Rani quietly elevated her brother to the position of *Wazir*.[69]

The army being the predominant political force at this time, all military operations were undertaken by its sole direction. Raja Gulab Singh had accumulated large treasures during the ascendancy of Rajas Dhian Singh and Hira Singh. For the last many years he had not paid anything into the coffers of the state and it was estimated that the arrears due from him amounted nearly to a crore of rupees. It was also believed that Raja Hira Singh had removed lots of wealth from the Moti Mandir Lahore to Jasrota in the hills. Therefore, it was decided by the army *panchayats* as early as 23rd December 1844 when a grand *darbar* was held to celebrate emancipation from the Dogra rule, that the Dogra chiefs should be summoned to Lahore to clear their accounts and that in case they did not obey, expeditions should be sent against them. Shortly after, Sardar Sham Singh Attariwala was sent at the head of a considerable force to attack Jasrota and seize the deposits of wealth there. This happened in January 1845. The expedition was met with complete success. In the beginning of February 1845 a force consisting of about 9000 men was sent against Raja Gulab Singh. The Raja tried to be clever and employed much craft[70] to retrieve his position but ultimately he had to yield to the *panchayats* of the army. The *panchayats* gave him a guarantee of safe conduct and brought him to Lahore where he was received with great honour by the Rani, much to the dismay of Jawahar Singh and Lal Singh. He was even offered *wuzarat* which he politely declined. However, he had to give a written undertaking that he would pay a sum of 68 lacs by way of arrears, yield up nearly all the districts, which had been held by his family, excepting his own proper fiefs and to renew his lease of the salt mines on terms which virtually deprived him of a large profit, and of the political superiority in the hills of Rohtas.[71] This was undoubtedly a great success of the Khalsa army, though the government failed to realize all of this promised amount.

But the most striking example which shows the power of the army, its character as *Panch Khalsaji,* its concern for the family of Maharaja Ranjit Singh and its regard for military discipline is provided by the manner in which Wazir Jawahar Singh was penalized for his hand in the murder of Prince Peshaura Singh. The army regarded the crime of Jawahar Singh as intolerable and unpardonable and issued orders under the seal of *Panth Khalsaji* "to the Rani to repair to the camp with her son and to deliver up her brother and the murderers of Peshaura Singh, if he was really dead, intimating that disobedience would entail upon her their punishment".[72] The Rani tried to gain time by offering to parley with the *panchayats*, and Jawahar Singh made an attempt to save himself by flight, but all in vain. Ultimately the Rani, the Maharaja and Jawahar Singh had to obey the orders of the Khalsa and appear before the troops marshalled out in the *maidan* in perfect military discipline. Jawahar Singh was killed by the order of the Khalsa while the Rani and the Maharaja were safely taken to a side tent. Next day the dead body was handed over to the Rani for cremation.

As stated earlier, the army had never thought highly of Jawahar Singh's capabilities. Still when he had been charged with the duties of the *Wazir's* office they were prepared to give him a fair chance. Jawahar Singh, however, took his new position as a license to indulge in debauchery and drunkenness and thereby scandalised the whole Khalsa Darbar. Hardly three weeks had passed since his installation on 14 May 1845 that "the *panchayats*[73] proceeded in a body to the palace to remonstrate against Jawahar Singh's continuance in the government, reproaching that sirdar to his face with drunkenness and incapacity". They went to the Rani and requested her to replace him by Diwan Dina Nath, Bhagat Ram or Lal Singh, or the three conjointly. The Rani assured them that her brother would be asked to mend his ways. Since the *panchayats* did not want to disestablish the established government, they accepted the assurance and went away. Jawahar Singh thus had another chance to improve himself but he left the warning unheeded and soon involved himself in the plot to murder Prince Peshaura Singh. He not only got him assassinated but also celebrated the event by illumination. This was too serious an offence to be passed over lightly by the Khalsa army and hence the severe action taken against him.

The *panchayats* which served as the executive of *Panth Khalsaji* were able to maintain an iron discipline in the ranks of the army, a fact which has been conceded even by highly placed contemporary British officers. In the time of Jawahar Singh the system of *panchayats* was further tightened up by the institution of elected *chaudhuris* or magistrates. In this context the observation of Major Broadfoot in his letter to F. Currie, Secretary to Government of India, dated 26 January 1845, is not without significance. "The troops have now", he writes,[74] "in addition to their panchayats, magistrates elected by themselves, called chaudhuris of whom each company has two. The panchayats attend the Darbar but can do nothing till the approval of the chaudhuris has been obtained. These officers are usually private soldiers, independent of the government and unknown to it, nay to inquire about them is considered an intrusion". These *Chaudhuries* played a great role in punishing the excesses committed by the troops. One striking example of this is furnished by the manner in which six soldier offenders were dealt with. They had seized and violated the female child of a Khatri of Lahore. The Darbar dared not interfere but the *chaudhuris,* with the consent of the *panchayats,* set two of the men to the Darbar with the intimation that the army permitted them to be punished according to law. Each of the culprits had a hand and the nose cut off on the spot.[75]

IV

However, the democratic revolution which had happened in the state forces, though admirable in certain respects, ultimately gave rise to a most dangerous internal conflict. Conflicts had arisen earlier too but this conflict was of a different nature altogether. The former conflicts were between different groups of nobility or between different members of royalty. On the other hand the conflict that arose from the ascendancy of the army was between the army and the governing class. Despite all its shortcomings and limitations, the army stood for an ideology, a certain cause which it dearly cherished and in defence of which it considered no sacrifice too great. Col. Richmond who was the British Agent at Ludhiana for a period during 1844 thus writes about the spirit animating the Khalsa army:[76] "The cry of the Khalsa or commonwealth of the Sikhs, has as magical an influence on the followers of Nanak as the cry of Islam or of the cross had in by-gone days. The Sikhs, are still imbued with much of the activity of mind and resolution of purpose of a persecuted race become triumphant. They will still dare and endure much for the Khalsa". The Khalsa army considered the state as its own. In the building up of this state it had struggled hard and undergone untold hardships. Its defence, therefore, against all dangers, internal and external, was its sacred and bounden duty. It was a thoroughly national and patriotic army which viewed the steady increase in British forces south of the Sutlej with great alarm. It felt greatly dismayed when it found the governing class practically unconcerned about this growing external danger and awfully engaged in fratricidal intrigues. Col. Richmond depicts the character of the chiefs in the following words:[77] "Most of the present chiefs of the Sikhs must be regarded as mercenary. Their grandfathers were tillers of the ground, but the possession of authority and wealth acquired and preserved without labour has unnerved them and they are desirous of keeping their luxuries to themselves under any loss of independence. The Sikh chiefs perhaps now offer to hold their possessions of the British government".

The difference in the outlook of the two is quite obvious. Whereas the army represented the ideas of the commonwealth of Guru Gobind Singh and was prepared to do anything for the Khalsa, the chiefs only paid lip service to them. Wealth and power[78] had degraded them and rendered their outlook self-centred and selfish. Two things inevitably flowed from this. One, the chiefs felt that the rise in the power of the army was a great threat to their privileged positions. The Khalsa army had seldom advocated confiscations of their *jagirs* or other privileges. Rather, during the ministry of Raja Hira Singh it had often criticised the Raja's action of confiscating or reducing the *jagirs* and more than once pleaded with him to forego it. On the fall of Hira Singh many of the confiscated *jagira* were even restored with the approval of the army. Still the chiefs never trusted the army in full and were ever worried that it might change its attitude any time and dislodge them from their possessions.[79] This was particularly so because since the end of Hira Singh's rule most of the chiefs had assumed the authority and status of "petty sovereigns"[80] in their respective estates. Two, they failed to appreciate the seriousness of the danger from without. Though about this time the British were feverishly engaged on strengthening their military stations on the frontier, yet these chiefs advocated a soft and friendly line of policy and strongly argued against taking an alarmist view of the situation. Instead of getting prepared for the defence of the country, they counselled peace and patience.[81] What is still worse, many of the leading chiefs, as Raja Gulab Singh, Raja Lal Singh, and Gulam Mahiuddin were secretly carrying on intrigues with the British authorities. Blinded by selfish interests, they were even mentally prepared for a subordinate status of the state under British control. The role of the royalty had been and was no better. In the past Rani Chand Kaur, Maharaja Sher Singh,[82] Kanwar Kashmira Singh and Kanwar Peshaura Singh all at one time or another had offered to "become tributary and to lean for support upon foreigners".[83] At the present time Rani Jindan was also working in the same direction. The military might demonstrated at the time of the death of her brother had appalled and shaken her and she felt that so long as the power of the army remained unabated she could never have a true sense of security. Therefore, she favoured a British attack to get the ascendancy of the Khalsa army smashed. This attitude of the Rani was supported by her chief advisers, Raja Lal Singh and Misr Tej Singh in particular and other chiefs, including the principal commanders of the army in general. The army fell an easy prey to such machinations of their authorities because of the strong patriot urge the soldiers felt to defend the independence and integrity of the state in this hour of grave crisis. Thus it is obvious that on the eve of the First Anglo-Sikh War the Punjab was caught in the throes of a terrible internal conflict.

REFERENCES

1. Indeed, there was little money in the Moti Mandir to meet the demands of the troops for rewards and the promised raise in their emoluments. Raja Gulab Singh had taken away cart-loads of cash, gold and jewellery when he had marched out of the Fort along with his troops in January 1841. Rani Chand Kaur also had helped herself tc large quantities of treasure from the Moti Mandir. Further, all important chiefs as the Jamwal Rajas and Diwan Sawan Mal owed lakhs of rupees to the state, which they were not paying.
2. Khushwant Singh, *A History of the Sikhs,* Vol. II, p. 18.
3. H.T. Thornton, *History of the Punjab,* pp. 229-30 (First published in London, 1846-Reprinted in 1870).
4. S.R. Kohli, *Sunset of the Sikh Empire,* p. 40. Also see Munshi Sohan Lal, *Umdat-ut-Twarikh,* Daftar IV, Part II, pp. 18-19, 34.
5. H.T. Thornton, *op. cit.,* p. 236.
6. *Catalogue of Khalsa Durbar Records,* Vol. I, pp. 51, 56-77. *Punjab Intelligence Lahore* from 29th January to 9th February 1842 mentions that on Dhian Singh's recommendation it was decided to raise 10,000 troops from the hilly areas and orders to that effect were sent to officers at Nurpur, Pathankot, Kangra, the Doaba and other places. This may be in addition to the six thousand mentioned here, or it may be that out of the targetted 10,000 only 6000 were actually enlisted.
7. Edwards and Merivale, *Life of Sir Henry Lawrence,* Vol. I (London, 1872), p. 151.
8. *For. Dept. Sect. Cons.,* 17 January 1842, No. 66.
9. *For. Dept. Sect. Cons.,* 22 June 1842, No. 30—Clerk to Maddock, 16 May 1842.
10. *For. Dept. Sec. Cons.,* 25 January, 1843, No. 23. *Punjab Intelligence Lahore* for 27 November 1842.
11. *For. Dept. Sec. Cons.,* 11 January 1843, No. 88; *Punjab Intelligence Lahore* for 7 December 1842.
12. *Ibid.*
13. *For. Dept. Sec. Cons.,* 10 January 1843, No. 114; *Punjab Intelligence Lahore* for December 1841.
14. *For. Dept. Sec. Cons.,* 28 February 1842, No. 45; *Punjab Intelligence Lahore* for 29th January. Also H.T. Thornton, *op. cit.,* p. 242.

According to Debi Prasad (*Gulshan-i-Punjab*, p. 52) the Muslim troops had the secret instructions of Raja Gulab Singh to act in the manner they did.

15. *For. Dept. Sec. Cons.*, 22 June 1842, No. 30-Clerk to Maddock, 16 May 1842.

16. *For. Dept. Sec. Cons.*, 8 April 1842, No. 38-Clerk to Gen. Pollock, dated 2 March 1842. General Pollock calls it "a disorganised rabble". See *For. Dept., Sec. Cons.*, 21 March 1842, No. 26-Major Gen. Pollock to Lt. Col. Luard, dated 27 Feb., 1842.

17. *For. Dept. Sec. Cons.*, 22 June, 1842, No. 30-Clerk to Maddock, 16 May 1842. The rumours were so widespread that the Governor-General felt it necessary to assure the Maharaja on the question of Peshawar.

    The Sikh governor of Peshawar, Avitabile, was more loyal to The British than to the government which had appointed him. He is said to have made a proposal to farm Peshawar to the British government for a term of years.

    For. Dept. Sec. Cons., 8 June, 1842, No. 50-Clerk to Maddock, 15 May 1842. Also see H.T. Thornton, *op. cit.*, p. 244.

18. *For. Dept. Sec. Cons.*, 21 March 1842, No. 16-Pollock to Luard, 27 Feb., 1842.

19. *For. Dept. Sec. Cons.*, 8 June 1842, No. 54.

20. *For. Dept. Sec. Cons.*, 22 June 1842, No. 18. A little after in June 1842, a Sikh force of 5000 men advanced through the Jubhagi Pass and took up a position near Jallalabad.

21. *For. Dept. Sec. Cons.*, 31 January, 1842, No. 74-*Punjab Intelligence Lahore* for 1st to 11th January 1842.

22. *For. Dept. Sec. Cons.*, 28 February 1842, No. 45-*Punjab Intelligence Lahore*, 19th January-9th Feb., 1842.

23. *For. Dept. Sec. Cons.*, 30 March 1842, No. 97.

24. *For. Dept. Sec. Cons.*, 8 April 1842, No. 38.

25. Mr. Clerk had been empowered to do so by the Governor-General *vide* T.H. Maddock's letter to Clerk, dated 10 Feb., 1842. See *For. Dept. Sec., Cons.*, 14 Feb., 1842, No. 65. Sher Singh no doubt had sounded Clerk on this aspect but perhaps more with the object of testing the British designs regarding the Punjab than as a genuine request for help. The promptness with which the British got ready for intervention frightened the Maharaja. Had he been sincere about it, he would have welcomed it and not spurned it.

26. *For. Dept. Sec. Cons.*, 17 January 1842, No. 68.
27. *For. Dept. Sec. Cons.*, 29 July 1842, No. 134-Clerk to Maddock, 7 April 1842.
28. *Punjab Intelligence Lahore,* 1 January 1844.
29. Normally speaking there was one *panchayat* in each regiment and therefore sometimes the *panchayat* was also called regimental committee or committee of the regiment. The members of a *panchayat* were elected by the various companies constituting the regiment. Each company was allotted two seats. In artillery this function was performed by the various *deras.* All these *panchayats* functioned subject to the control of their electors. The *panchayats* held their meetings frequently.

    F.S. Bajwa, *Military System of the Sikhs* (Delhi, 1964), pp. 157-159.
30. *For. Dept. Sec. Cons.*, 23 March 1844, No. 505.
31. Vol. VI, 1846, p. 246.

31 a. Cunningham, *op. cit.*, p. 264.

32. Ranjit Singh often used to address the army as Khalsaji, particularly during the battles.
33. Sita Ram Kohli, *op. cit.*, pp. 41-42.

    This fact comes out very clearly from the abstracts of *Punjab Intelligence Lahore* pertaining to the period of Raja Hira Singh. For example see the report for 22nd January 1844—H.R. Gupta, *Punjab on the Eve of First Sikh War,* p. 179.
34. *Punjab Intelligence Lahore,* dated 9 January 1844; also Debi Prashad, *op. cit.*, p. 66.
35. *Ibid.*, dated 10 January 1844.
36. *Ibid.*, dated 11 January 1844.
37. *Ibid.*, dated 15 January 1844.
38. *Ibid.*, dated 21 January 1844.
39. *Ibid.*, dated 22 January 1844.
40. The ceremony was actually fixed on 2nd February 1844 but it was rumoured that as in the past it was again being postponed. Hence the suspicion.
41. A few instances showing how the non-Dogra chiefs were treated are given below:

    For constant harassment of Jamadar Khushal Singh—see *Punjab Intelligence Lahore* for 31 Dec., 1843; 5 January 1844. 2. Gen. Kanh

Singh Mann was fined Rs. 10,000 (6 January 1844) 3. Rattan Singh Gharjakhia was deprived of his *jagirs* (7 January 1844) 4. Kanwar Tara Singh deprived of some of his *jagirs* (20 January 1844). 5. Sardar Boor Singh actually beaten in the court (3 January 1844). Sardars Sham Singh Attariwala, Lehna Singh Majithia and many other leading chiefs were all under suspicion and were threatened with forfeiture of *jagirs*. When some senior army officers advised Raja Hira Singh against confiscating the *jagirs* of the *Sardars*, he said that increase to the army could not be given without resuming *jagirs*. To this the officers replied that he should first resume the *jagirs* of his own family (19-20 January 1844). Even Raja Gulab Singh sent Hira Singh a word of advice to continue the *jagirs* as they were at the death of Ranjit Singh (23 Jan. 1844).

42. *Punjab Intelligence Lahore* for 11 January 1844.

43. About this time Bhai Bir Singh also was very actively engaged in carrying on a regular propaganda campaign against the administration of Raja Hira Singh. His views had a great influence on the minds of the men in the army. Raja Hira Singh was greatly alarmed at this. He also suspected that all chiefs were inwardly the supporters of the Bhai (1st January 1844).

44. According to Debi Prashad the situation became so serious that Hira Singh was besieged in his house. *Gulshan-i-Punjab*, p. 68.

45. *Punjab Intelligence Lahore* for 27 January 1844.

46. *Ibid.*, dated 11 February 1844.

47. The food given to him was half salt and half flour. *Ibid.* dated 12 February 1844.

48. *Ibid.*, dated 29 February 1844.

49. *Ibid.*, dated 5, 6 February 1844.

50. *Ibid.*, dated 19 February 1844.

51. *Ibid.*, dated 26 February 1844.

52. *Ibid.*, 1 and 13 March 1844.

53. *Ibid.*, 14 and 15 March 1844.

54. *Ibid.*, 18 March 1844.

55. *Ibid.*, 21 March 1844.

56. *Ibid.*, 22 March 1844. It may be noted here that as a diversionary tactic the Raja was playing up the issue of a British cantonment at Ferozepur. He even sent one Sikh regiment to Kasur to keep a watch on the British at Ferozepur.

57. *Ibid.*, 24 March, 1844.
58. The raise was from Rs. 9 as under Sher Singh to Rs. 12½ in the time of Hira Singh. Under no other single administration was the increase so big as under Hira Singh.
59. J. D. Cunningham, *op. cit.*, p. 235.

    ......for the Panchayats, although bent on retaining their own power and on acquiring additional pay and privileges for their constituents, the soldiers, were equally resolved on maintaining the integrity of the empire, and they arranged among themselves about the relief of the troops in the provinces. On the frontiers, indeed, the Sikhs continued to exhibit their innate vigour, and towards the end of 1843 the secluded principality of Gilgit was overrun and annexed to Kashmir".
60. *Punjab Intelligence Lahore* for 30 March 1844.
61. H.R. Gupta, *op. cit.*, pp. 312-13.
62. *Punjab Intelligence Lahore* for 30 September 1844.

    The reference to the English was not included in the final draft. Still the statement of Pandit Jalla is very significant as it speaks eloquently of the Khalsa patriotism.
63. H.T. Thornton, *op. cit.*, p. 302.
64. Major G.C. Smyth, *op. cit.*, p. 107.

    "Raja Hira Singh was for 3 or 4 days surrounded by troops and virtually kept a prisoner in his house in the city. The Khalsa swore vengeance and extermination against the Raja, and all the Dogras in case any harm should happen to the princes". Also Debi Prashad, *op. cit.*, p. 68.
65. *Punjab Intelligence Lahore* for 19 May 1844.
66. S.R. Kohli, *op. cit.*, p. 88.
67. H.T. Thornton, *op. cit.*, pp. 307-19.

    Not only did the troops not agree to the Rani's proposal but also they caused letters to be sent to Lehna Singh Majithia and Kanwar Peshaura Singh inviting them to come to Lahore forthwith. Lehna Singh was offered the ministership and Peshaura Singh the supreme command of the army. Neither of these two proposals, however, fructified. Lehna Singh did not come. Peshaura Singh came but the Rani frustrated his chances.

    Jawahar Singh tried to soothe the troops and turn them in his favour. On one occasion he even took the young Maharaja to them to plead with them in the name of the Maharaja but they did not relax; rather they threatened to banish him from the city.

68. *Ibid.,* p. 311.

69. *Ibid.,* p. 316. It is sometimes said that the Rani purchased the army's consent for this. But the fact seems to be that at this critical juncture neither the troops nor the Sardars were in a position to question the decision of the Rani. It is also said that another factor that helped her was the concurrence of Raja Gulab Singh who happened to be in Lahore at that time.

70. He conducted negotiations simultaneously with the officers of the Lahore Darbar specially sent for the purpose and the army *panchayats* and tried to play off one party against another. Sardar Fateh Singh Mann and Wazir Bachna were paid a sum of 5 lacs as earnest money and when they set out with the money they were waylaid and killed, and all the money with them was seized and taken back to Jammu. For details see Cunningham, *op. cit.,* p. 242.

71. Cunningham, *op. cit.,* p. 242.

    However, before the payment could be made, the situation changed radically with the result that the promise was never fulfilled.

72. Thornton, *op. cit.,* p. 321; Debi Prashad, *op. cit.,* p. 88.

    Here we find an unambiguous assertion of the Khalsa's sovereignty which even the highest authority in the government could not set at naught.

73. *Ibid.,* p. 317.

74. *Foreign Secret Proceedings,* 4th April 1845, No. 111.

75. *Ibid.*

76. *Foreign Secret Progs.,* 23 March 1844, No. 487.

77. *Ibid.* Cunningham (*op. cit.* p. 256) expresses a similar opinion about the chiefs; "......the chiefs of the Punjab had clung to wealth and ease rather than to honour and independence".

78. Some idea of the wealth accumulated by big chiefs may be gathered from the following:

    a. Raja Gulab Singh possessed wealth running into quite a few crores of rupees. His arrears alone due to the Darbar were estimated at about one crore. He never paid these arrears.

    b. Raja Sochet Singh's wealth at his death was calculated to range between 30 and 40 lacs. He had sent 15 lacs to Ferozepur and nearly the same amount, may be even more, lay deposited in his fort on his estate (*Punjab Intelligence* for 11 April 1844).

c. When Jamadar Khushal Singh died in July 1844, his wealth was estimated to be from 30 to 40 lacs. Out of this about 30 lacs he had sent to his home in the vicinity of Meerut. (*Punjab Intelligence* for 2 July 1844).

d. When Diwan Sawan Mal died in 1844, it was stated that he had left 70 lacs in cash and 70 lacs worth of jewels and other property (*Punjab Intelligence* for 3 October 1844). According to Cunningham there was hardly any one among the important chiefs who possessed less than 15-20 lacs.

79 "As the authority of the army began to predominate, and to derive from its system of committees, a new danger threatened the territorial chiefs and the adventurers in the employ of the government. They might successively fall before the cupidity of the organised body which none could, control or an able leader might arise who would absorb the power of all others, and gratify his followers by the sacrifice of the rich, the selfish, and the feeble".

Cunningham, *op. cit.*, p. 256. The chiefs contemptuously called the sepoys *burshas,* meaning savages.

80. Thornton, *op. cit.*, p. 312.

81. Cunningham, *op. cit.*, p. 257.

82. *Ibid.*, p. 256.

83. *Ibid.*

4

British Hegemony

The war of 1845-46, of which a mention has been made in the preceding chapter, was concluded with a political settlement based on three treaties. Out of them two, signed respectively on 9th and 11th March 1846, related to the Lahore Darbar, while the third, signed at Amritsar a few days later on 16th March, concerned Raja (henceforward Maharaja) Gulab Singh Dogra. Of the treaties with the Lahore Darbar, the second was regarded as a supplement of the first and was accordingly given, by way of distinction, the somewhat less dignified name of 'Articles of Agreement'. In consequence of all these arrangements, the British government in India made immense gains in terms of territory as well as extension of political influence. The entire region of north-western India lying between the Sutlej and the Khyber Pass was thereby brought under their undoubted supremacy. No doubt, there were extensive areas still that were left unannexed and that stood outside their direct dominion, yet under the settlement they acquired in the whole of this region the role and position of a predominant power well-poised to bear down any resistance to its will. Unquestionably, the British were now provided with a foot-hold on this hitherto alien soil which, given the intention to do so, could be easily transformed into a springboard for acquiring still greater degrees of control.

For a proper appraisal of this settlement, it is necessary first to understand the views of its chief architect, Lord

Hardinge, on the subject. Fortunately, the personal papers of the Governor-General, written in his own hand, are now available in India, which furnish an authentic insight, unequalled by any other source, into the working of his mind several months before the hostilities started in December 1845. As it appears from these papers, he did recognise the desirability of the Punjab serving as a buffer against Afghanistan and other Muslim states of the north-west, and had no hesitation in saying that it was their "advanced post"[1] on the north-west frontier. In particular, he attached great weight to the long-standing rivalry between the Sikhs and the Pathans. "The Sikh power is naturally and necessarily", he emphasised, "opposed to the Muhammadan N.W. States of Asia".[2] However, he ruled out the practicability of this arrangement on the ground of the very serious ills with which the Sikh state was afflicted, such as insubordination of the army and unbridgable divisions in the ranks of the chiefs. He expressed his opinion saying that, "A weak Sikh State or Government of the same character, in that position, would be a source of continued embarrassment".[3] Such a state, he argued, could be of little service to the British Empire as a system of defence.

From this he proceeded to the consideration of the question of propping up the tottering (much too quickly in his opinion)[4] Sikh state. This course he also rejected on two grounds: (i) The system of protection was more harmful than useful because it tended to perpetuate misrule by depriving the people of their natural right of revolt and the ruler of all incentive for exertion in the cause of the welfare of his people. "Such a system is not politic", he pleaded,[5] "because the protected prince must become either a puppet indifferent to the good government of his country or must be discontented with his position and anxious to escape from his thralldom and thus likely to be ever foremost in intrigues against the power of his protector, and to the people it cannot but be unjust to establish a system under which a native government can exercise almost any degree of oppression towards its subjects, while they are checked by the power of the Paramount Authority from the exercise of their natural right of revolt against their oppressors. Moreover, he held it "neither politic nor just to try once again the experiment of maintaining a native dynasty under our military protection, which experiment has failed wherever it has already been tried".[6] (ii) The ills of the Sikh power were too serious to be remedied by such a system of protection.

Therefore, it appeared to him that annexation of the Punjab was unavoidable, if safety of the north-western frontier was to be preserved. His argument was that if the weakness of the Sikh government was irremediable (and he believed that it was so) they[7] "must adopt the other course of taking the Punjab under our dominion and advancing to the Indus". Working on this basis he then applied his mind seriously to the problems of organisation of administration and consolidation of power likely to ensue from the envisaged annexation. He visualised no difficulty to the maintenance of their power, once it had been introduced. His confidence was based on the composition of the population under the jurisdiction of the Khalsa Darbar. The total population was then, as reckoned by British expert opinion, about 3 millions, out of which the vast majority (ranging from 86 to 87.5%) was constituted by Muhammadans and Hindus. To these classes, he hoped, the British rule would not be unacceptable, the reason being, as he himself put it: "The Sikh ascendancy has not been attended with any advantages to these classes which they might not expect to enjoy in at least as great a degree under our Government".[8] He therefore expected no trouble in such parts of the kingdom as were predominantly inhabited by either Hindus or Muslims, be they the hilly territories or Multan or the Derajat or any other place like the Peshawar valley. About Multan and the Derajat in particular his feeling was that, "the sons of Sawan Mull, the late Governor of Multan, are not likely seriously to oppose or be dissatisfied with the introduction of British authority and the Muhammadan chiefs of the Derajat may yield as ready an obedience to our Government as to that of the Sikhs".[9] To facilitate the task, however, he thought it necessary and politic "to provide for former and present chieftains" and to make "by proper management their influence subservient to good government".

In the entire kingdom of Lahore he had fears only from the Sikh section of the population. He was convinced that "no degree of consideration shown to this class"[10] could induce them to change their attitude to the advent of British rule into their territory. But he had no worry about this because the Sikhs formed no more than one seventh or one eighth of the total population. Moreover, he believed that even in their case it was possible to devise measures to keep them in check. One of the measures on which he laid great stress was the necessity "to overawe them by the presence of a strong military and police force and to visit with prompt and exemplary punishment all their early attempts to disturb the peace of the country".[11] He was quite hopeful that in this task of keeping the Sikhs in order "more peaceable and contented of the Hindu and Muhammadan population may be useful auxiliarites".[12] Among other measures he stressed particularly the need of "guaranteeing to the powerful and most influential Sirdars a continuance of their possessions or of such positions of them as they have retained since the time of Ranjit Singh subject to such conditions as may appear applicable to each particular case",[13] as also of "a similar cause of conciliation, in some degree, with all the smaller Sikh landholders". In this connection he also pointed out that a strict enforcement of obligations attached to feudal tenures could go a long way in smoothing the way for the firm establishment of their authority in the Punjab.

The question of frontier defence against the possibility of Afghan danger was also given most careful consideration. He readily conceded that the best thing for them would be to have the Sikhs, as before, occupying a position of strength on the frontier, but he was extremely skeptical of a Sikh government strong enough to ensure what they wanted.

Therefore, he plainly expressed himself as: "If we must break up a respectable Sikh power, we must occupy this place of that Government and by a British force to undertake the defence of a new, long and diversified frontier and instead of a Sikh barrier have a British barrier against Afghans and other tribes of Asia beyond the Indus".[14] And on that basis he strongly urged that Peshawar should be occupied by "so large a force" that "the tranquillity of the valley of the Indus in that neighbourhood may be considered secure".[15] However, he added that this military measure needed to be supported by a political one: arriving at settlements with Yusafzai, Vuzeeree and other military tribes of that quarter along the lines of those effected with them by the Sikhs.

On the general administrative policy best suited to the British interest in the Punjab after its annexation, Hardinge made the following remarks:[16] "On the occupation of any newly conquered country in India, it must always be desirable so to frame the form of our Government that it may displace as little of the instruments and practice of the former regime as may be found practicable, consistently with the efficiency and security of a new and foreign administration". He frankly admitted his ignorance about the local institutions of the Punjab; even so he emphasised his point by saying that "there can be no danger in leaving all rights, tenures and customs at the first unaltered. This will inspire the people with confidence and make them contented. It is easy to reform hereafter and after sufficient experience whatever may be found injurious and objectionable".[17]

Nor did the question of administrative set-up to be introduced following the annexation escape the attention of the Governor-General. He wanted to place the entire machinery of the administration "under the control of an officer of the highest rank to be vested with all the powers of government and complete authority over all departments".[18] As for the functions of the subordinate officials, he preferred to continue, in the first instance, the old Sikh practice of combination of powers on the ground that it would be, as compared with the Regulation System of the older Presidencies, more economical and more intelligible to the new subjects. It is remarkable that Hardinge did not think it premature (even as early as May 1845, which is the date of the note under reference) to go so minutely into the qualifications of the kind of administrator he wanted to rule the Punjab.

It was with these ideas that the Governor-General Hardinge provoked hostilities with the Sikhs and then proceeded to engage in them with the determination to crush their power so as to clear the way for the fulfilment of his heart's wish. He did not anticipate much resistance from the Khalsa troops who had been represented to him to be no more than a vast rabble. There as about this time, says Lord Gough,[19] a mistaken estimate formed at British Headquarters of the real efficiency of the Sikh troops. The prevailing notion about them was that they were disorderly and of no great account from a military point of view, though it obviously lay in their power to produce anarchy in the administration of the Punjab, and it was supposed that they were not even fully competent to face Afghans or the Jammu hill-men. It does not seem to have been perceived that their conduct was not mutinous, as Hardinge and his advisers thought, but patriotic, inspired by the desire of saving their state from both internal and external enemies. A similar element of misreading was involved in their premises of the weakness of the Khalsa state on which they had built up their entire case for intervention. That this state was suffering from some serious internal troubles may not be contested, but that it was on the point of breaking up was an exaggeration. The state had hitherto survived all upheavals and not an inch of territory had been lost. The same army as appeared mutinous and turbulent to the British, was wonderfully maintaining the integrity and independence of their state and was determined as ever to continue to do so in future as well. The internal trouble, too, would never have been so serious, had not the British for their own reasons indulged in mischievous machinations.

That the Khalsa army was not wanting in capacity for united action or for the display of thorough discipline in the field was proved, to the great dismay and surprise of the Governor-General, in the battles of Mudki and Ferozshah. The British suffered heavy losses in these actions and before going in for the next action had to send for large reinforcements from Delhi. Both among officers and men at this time there was wave of demoralisation, which was not a happy augury for the next round of fighting with the enemy. Thinking prudence the better part of a valour, a secret link was established (at whose initiative is not clear but whosoever began it, must have received a prompt response from the other) between the Governor-General and Raja Gulab Singh, Minister to the Lahore Darbar at the time. In the secret negotiations that followed, the English, on the evidence of Cunningham[20] which was later confirmed by Boswell Smith, Murray and some other English writers, "intimated to Gulab Singh their readiness to acknowledge a Sikh sovereignty in Lahore after the army should have been disbanded". This being beyond the power of Gulab Singh, "the views of either party were in some sort met by an understanding that the Sikh army should be attacked by the English and that when beaten it should be openly abandoned by its own Government; and further that the passage of the Sutlej should be unopposed and the road to the capital laid open to the victors". This somewhat odd behaviour of the British was prompted by two considerations:[21] (i) It was felt that a quick victory over such a gallant and devoted enemy as the Sikhs was an impossibility; (ii) "The protracted hostilities would not only jeopardise the communications with the Jumna but might disturb the whole of the North-Western Province",[22] the vital point in their rear.

It was with the help of manoeuvres such as the above that the British were able to secure a decisive victory at Sabraon and effect an unopposed crossing of the Sutlej. When they arrived at Kasur, Raja Gulab Singh with a few other people of the Darbar waited upon the Governor-General.

During the talks that transpired there between the two sides, the Lahore deputation was shown the terms on which the British were determined to shape their future relations with the Darbar. The most conspicuous thing about these terms was absence of any mention of wholesale annexation of the vanquished state.

The decision against complete annexation was a serious departure from the original intention of Hardinge, as we have seen earlier, and he could not be really happy about it. Yet in his hour of victory he found himself confronted with circumstances in which it was impossible or extremely difficult to carry out the original plan and he had to submit to the inevitable. As such, his act of abstaining from wholesale annexation was an act of compulsion, and not an act of moderation or forbearance that it was represented to be for political reasons by the British Government of the day and most of the British writers of the nineteenth century. Hardinge neither had the freedom of choice, so essential to forbearance, nor does he seem to have had any faith in the underlying noble principle of forbearance with reference to the Punjab situation.

As for the necessities to which Hardinge had to submit, there were, first of all, the obligations of the afore-mentioned secret deal with Raja Gulab Singh. The part reserved for the Lahore Chiefs, Gulab Singh, Lal Singh and Tej Singh, had been so well performed that he had no justifiable excuse to go back upon his plighted word.

Secondly, and this was far more important, the victors were deterred from complete annexation by the formidable difficulties involved in the complete subjugation of the Punjab. One of the difficulties was that there was still a considerable part of the Khalsa army to reckon with: about 25000 men were assembled at Amritsar and Lahore and about 8000 on the north-west frontier, the latter being entirely fresh and full of enthusiasm. Besides, the country had several strong forts which could not be easily reduced. After what they had seen of the Khalsa in the late war, the British entertained the fear, and rightly too, that any attempt on their part at complete annexation would be met with the stiffest resistance. They even ventured to think that in the event of such a decision all ranks of the Khalsa would be immediately closed and they would rise, as one man, and fight shoulder to shoulder against their national enemy.[23]

As against this situation bristling with difficulties and risks, the inadequacy of the resources now at the disposal of the British put them veritably in a tight corner. Lord Gough's army at Lahore now numbered less than 20000 of all arms, of whom only 3500 were Europeans. For the sieges, which would have become inevitable in case of the entire country being annexed, "he would have required 70 or 80 siege guns with 1000 rounds for each; but he had only thirty guns with 300 rounds for each. Even with reinforcements from Scinde, where Sir Charles Napier had 16000 men and 60 guns, it is evident that the army at disposal would have been insufficient to undertake the real subjugation of the country".[24] The son and biographer of Lord Hardinge, who was acting as Private Secretary of the Governor-General during this period, makes the position absolutely clear when he says: "The extension of the British Empire to the Indus, however captivating to a certain school of politicians, was at that time impossible on military grounds. The absolute necessity of waiting for ammunition for 100 siege guns until the army could advance and the equally strong necessity of a siege train such as would deter the Sikh Darbar from making the war a war of sieges, were paramount considerations in which Sir Charles Napier (who had now joined the army) entirely concurred".[25] Continuing his arguments, he appeals to the critics of his father's decision against annexation to put to themselves this question:[26] "Could the Governor-General, with the military means at his disposal have achieved such a conquest after Sobraon? There was at that time a deficit in the Indian Treasury. The hot season was setting in, while four general actions had palpably weakened the strength of our European Regiments".

There was one more very important political consideration strongly weighing with the British government. Well aware of the foreign character of their rule, supported mainly by force, they could ill afford to have protracted operations anywhere in India, for the fear, quite genuine in such a government, more so in the situation of the two or three decades preceding the Rebellion of 1857, that such operations being interpreted as weakness might lead to disturbance of peace. Their best interests were always served, as they thought, by speedy results achieved through fast moving military operations. Therefore, the prospect of the war lengthening out compelled Lord Hardinge to decide for a lesser goal. He was confronted with a difficult choice: should he stick to his original object of complete annexation, unmindful of what it might bring in its wake, or should he accept something short of that and avoid the apprehended uncertainties. As a matter of expediency he chose the second alternative.

The alternative adopted by Hardinge, as the second best course open to him, was that of cutting down the strength of the Darbar government. His aims and objects and the measures necessary for their attainment figure prominently in the letter addressed by him to the Secret Committee from Kasur in February 1846. He wrote:[27] "A diminution of the strength of such a warlike nation on our weakest frontier seems to me to be imperatively required. I have therefore determined to take a strong and fertile district between the Sutlej and the Beas. This will cover Ludhiana and bring us within a few miles of Amritsar, with our back to the Hills. In a military sense it will be very important—it will weaken the Sikhs and punish them in the eyes of Asia. I shall demand one million and a half in money as compensation; and if I can arrange to make Gulab Singh and the Hill tribes independent including Cashmere, I shall have weakened this warlike republic. Its army must be disbanded and reorganised. The numbers of the artillery must be limited. The Maharaja must himself present the keys of Govindgarh and Lahore, where the terms must be dictated and signed".

And all these measures detailed by the Governor-General were immediately carried out; they formed the settlement of which the main object was to cripple the Khalsa state. All the cis-Sutlej territories belonging to it has been seized and annexed as a measure of security even before the war had actually begun. Now some other and much bigger portions were chopped off. The entire Bist Jullundur Doab was annexed to the British dominion. The hilly region called Kohistan was declared a British protectorate. In the same way the entire region comprising Jammu and Kashmir was detached from the kingdom of Lahore and made over to Raja Gulab Singh. These losses of territory, it was calculated, would weaken the Sikhs not only physically but also strategically. With Ferozepur and Jullundur in their possession and Jammu and Kashmir under their protection, the British were placed in a commanding position; except only on one side the territories of Lahore were encircled by a continuous ring of British or British-protected areas. This, it was thought, would ensure easy British victory, "should the Khalsa once more pit itself against the Company".[28]

What was left over after the surgical operations described above was handed over to Maharaja Dalip Singh to be administered by the Regent Rani Jindan and her minister Raja Lal Singh. This remnant of the Khalsa state was required to pay to the British, as war charges, a huge indemnity of one and a half crores of rupees. On finding that it could pay only 50 lacs, the whole of Kashmir was seized in lieu of the balance of one crore.[29] The maximum strength of its army was fixed at 32,000; 20,000 for regular infantry and 12,000 for irregular cavalry. All troops in excess of this number were to be disbanded after payment of arrears. The thirty-six guns which having been placed on the right bank of the Sutlej could not be captured by the British at the battle of Sobraon, were now seized by them. Further, the Darbar was made to surrender to the British entire control in respect of tolls and ferries of the rivers Sutlej and Beas up to Mithankot and of the River Indus from Mithankot to the borders of Bilochistan; the

Darbar's share being fixed at 50% of the net profits of ferry collections. The British also reserved to themselves the right of passage for their troops through the Punjab territories at any time they wanted and made it obligatory for the Darbar officials, at such times, to afford facilities in providing supplies and boats, though an assurance was at the same time given that all such services would be duly paid.

Only two things remained to complete the framework of a full-fledged subsidiary settlement, a British Resident and a British army. The former was introduced through the back-door, there being no direct provision for it in the Treaties, while the latter was rendered possible by a special request of the Darbar authorities who, through their disreputable role in the war just concluded, had lost all credit with the gallant soldiery of the state and were mortally afraid of them. Their request was also prompted by the fear that without outside help they would not be able to carry out their treaty obligations pertaining to the reorganisation of the Khalsa army.

Lord Hardinge, as explained earlier, was against the subsidiary system as such and was opposed to its extension to the Punjab, his reason being that it would come seriously in the way of re-establishment of a strong and independent Sikh government. Yet the temptation offered by the above request of the Darbar proved too much for him to resist.[30] No doubt, before giving his consent he made it clear that the stay of the British troops at Lahore would in no case be extended beyond December 31, 1846; still the result of his action was that the Punjab was now virtually under a subsidiary system, despite the contention made by him that the British force at Lahore was only for a limited period and for the specific purpose of helping the Darbar in the disbandment of their surplus troops.[31] He could not be unaware of the fact that such things once done could not be undone and that privileges once acquired could not be voluntarily abandoned. Thus was the idea of re-establishment of a strong and independent Sikh government killed even before its birth. If a subsidiary system, as he himself recognised, was a hurdle in the way of such an achievement, then surely he himself had blocked the path of progress, for with the presence of a British Resident and a strong British army in their midst, it was impossible for any Darbar government to have any sense of independence. Surely, there was a statutory guarantee of British non-interference in the internal affairs of the state but its fate could be no different from that of similar guarantees given elsewhere in India. And this is what actually happened. Within the first ten months, as we shall see later, all independence of theirs was at an end.

The new Punjab was no more than a dependant state; the sovereign rule of the people was gone; and the Maharaja was, in Hardinge's own words,[32] "in fetters, and under our protection, and must do our bidding", because by the terms of the treaty (clause I added) he could "neither make war nor peace nor exchange nor sell an acre of territory nor admit a European officer nor refuse us a thoroughfare through his territories or in fact perform any act without our permission". Indeed, as Hardinge himself put it:[33] "By the Treaty of Lahore, March 1846, the Punjab never was intended to be an independent state".

It will be seen from the foregoing account that Hardinge's main object, after annexation was ruled out, was to effect the maximum reduction in the strength of the Sikh power and to wait for another opportunity to finish it altogether. His was thus a "temporising"[34] approach, an approach of biding time, and the arrangement made was in all probability only calculated to serve a temporary purpose. In consequence, the attempt made by some writers to represent Hardinge's Lahore settlement as a device of creating a buffer against the Muhammadan power of Afghanistan seems no more than an exercise in futility. As previously mentioned, he had long ruled out its practicability. He had no hope that this object, even if desirable, was within the range of practical achievement. Nor is this view borne out by his thought and action immediately following the conclusion of the above settlement, to which we are shortly going to turn.

The task of reconstructing the Sikh government after the war devolved upon Raja Lal Singh. He was not fully competent for this and besides, had earned considerable notoriety for his bad faith and cowardice in the course of the war. His best merit was that he was considered a safe and convenient man by the British. Further, he was in the full confidence of the Queen Mother, Rani Jindan, and it was believed that nobody else would be acceptable to her. Raja Gulab Singh, equally unscrupulous but a far abler administrator, was willing, rather anxious, to undertake the duties of the Minister but this unfortunately suited neither the British nor the Rani, and so the matter was discreetly dropped.

The problem of the Raja was manifold: to disband the surplus army and to reorganise the remainder on sounder lines of economy and discipline, to improve the general administration to increase revenues and to win the goodwill of the chiefs. Each one of these tasks was of enormous proportions and presented formidable difficulties. Further complications were introduced by the almost empty state of the treasury and the presence of an officious and domineering British Resident who would not leave the native authorities free to work out their own solutions. The situation, as it was, called forth the skill, ability and diplomacy of a seasoned statesman, which qualities unfortunately were lacking in Raja Lal Singh. Nor did the Regent Rani Jindan offer any constructive and imaginative leadership, at this critical time, to make up for what the Raja lacked.

Still, it must be said that the Raja set about his task most assiduously and earnestly. When he started his work there was no money in the state treasury, because all the money there, 50 lacs, had been taken away by the British as war indemnity. In spite of this he was required by the British to start disbanding his surplus troops after due payment of their arrears. He had to carry out these orders, although simultaneously he had to find funds necessary for the running of the administration and payment of the state services, both civil and military. To tide over his difficulties he wished to make a proportionate deduction from the salaries of all his troops, but though there was nothing wrong about it, he was prevented by the Resident from doing so. He then decided to raise finance by reduction or confiscation of *jagirs*, which, though prejudical to the interests of the chiefs, was not wrong as a method of meeting a national emergency. He tackled Dewan Mul Raj of Multan with great courage and acquired[35] from him the outstanding succession fee of 18 lacs and all arrears of revenue, besides the entire Jhang division of his province, yielding a revenue of Rs. 1060200 and an agreement to pay for the rest of the territories Rs. 2154000, which amount his father used to pay for the whole province.

In this way the Raja managed to discharge successfully all his financial obligations. The troops under orders of disbandment were being gradually paid off and dismissed. The payment of the other troops was made regularly and no arrears were accumulated. Nor was any other part of the government disturbed on account of non-payment of money. But he was never free from financial worriers,[36] the state of the treasury being throughout very low. For this some drastic remedies were required, such as big cuts in the chiefs' *jagirs* and forcing the *kardars* and paymasters to disgorge all their ill-gotten money and to render accounts regularly in future. For this purpose he was gradually strengthening himself and might in due course have resorted to them, if he had not been dismissed for his involvement in the Kashmir affair.

In the political domain the worries of the Raja were much greater. The basis of his government being very narrow, his rule from the very first was an anathema to the big chief kept out of power, and they were feeling very sore. Here was a potential danger for his regime, and he was well aware of it. But he did not try to remove it by conciliating the chiefs and associating the more important of them with his administration; rather, instead of following this line of wisdom he tried to build up his strength with a view to their intimidation. For this purpose he conferred extensive territories[37] upon his own brothers, Ameer Chand and Bhagwan Singh and asked them to raise big levies of troops. He also raised a few thousands of Pathan and other non-Sikh soldiers.[38] These measures, however, produced results quite the opposite of what he had expected and wanted to achieve. The process of financial improvement was practically halted or dealt a severe blow,[39] and the disaffected Sardars' bitterness against the Raja's rule was all the greater because of the panic created by his new policy.

The critical situation thus created owed itself no less to the British than to Raja Lal Singh. Lord Hardinge had foreseen it as early as March 1846 and had even warned the Resident Henry Lawrence of the dangers inherent in the constitution of the new regime. But nothing tangible had been done to ward off the apprehended troubles. Rather by continued support to the notorious and unpopular rule of Raja Lal Singh, the British prevented the emergence of a stable and viable government.[40] Left to themselves the Sardars might have solved the problem between themselves.

In another way, too, the sharp turn the differences between the Raja and the other chiefs took around the month of August, was largely due to the ingenious role played by John Lawrence. The elder Lawrence, present at Lahore from March to August, had at least kept other chiefs at a distance, conducting all his business with the head of the government, Raja Lal Singh. John Lawrence, who came to Lahore in August to fill a leave vacancy caused by his brother's illness and was there till the following December, had no such scruples. He not only allowed the chiefs to meet him and discuss their grievances against the Raja but actually encouraged them to do so. As he himself admits in one of his letters written about this time, the Raja was "evidently a good deal alarmed"[41] at all this. The effect of this on the other chiefs was that they felt greatly encouraged and as a result the rift between the two was deepened.

In consequence, the position of Lal Singh's government was greatly weakened. Mortally afraid of his rivals, he became, henceforward, more and more urgent in his entreaties for the extended stay of the British Resident and troops at Lahore. It is significant that the first sounding in this regard began to be made soon after the arrival of John Lawrence and his assumption of charge of the Residency. On 7th September the matter was broached with the Acting Resident by Bhai Ram Singh and S. Ranjodh Singh. This was followed by Raja Lal Singh's personal visit to him on 10th September. The following day an interview was arranged between John Lawrence and the Maharani, at which the latter made a most earnest appeal for the continued stay of the British troops and the Resident.[42] Similar appeals came from the chiefs disaffected with the Raja.

Once things had come to such a pass, John Lawrence hastened to paint the gloomiest possible picture of the state of affairs at Lahore. He talked painfully of an impending financial crisis,[43] and made a sweeping and wholesale condemnation of the entire body of the Lahore chiefs, giving full vent to his preconceived prejudices against the Indian aristocratic classes. Not merely that, he even proceeded to suggest remedies. Writing to his brother at Simla on 27th August he said that the main demand of the chiefs was that they should be associated with the policy-making organ of the government.[44] As a way out of the difficulty, in the same letter he submitted a plan of a broadbased ministry but without much of his heart in it, for while he "expressed the hope that something of this kind would give tone and character to the Government", he did not at the same time hesitate to express the fear that "they will fail".[45] And then significantly he added that the continued presence of "a Sahib" was essential to the success of the scheme. A week or so after, taking advantage of the urgent appeals of the Darbar for the extended stay of the British troops, which he interpreted as their weakness, he turned his back upon his earlier plan and submitted another one. He wrote to his brother on September 8:[46] "I am convinced that matters cannot be carried on if we leave the country. The only plan which is both just and politic, so far I can see my way, is that we put the country in chancery—that is, manage it until the boy Maharaja arrives at years of discretion. This would be agreeable, I believe, to the chiefs". How could it be otherwise, for he himself had skilfully created a situation in which every one looked to the British?

On 11th September John Lawrence sent a long and elaborate despatch to the Governor-General, in which he recommended "the expediency of Government undertaking the management of the country in trust for the Maharaja until be arrives at manhood".[47] This recommendation was accompanied by a minute analysis of the possible reactions of different classes to the proposed step. He wrote: "It will not, I conceive, be eventually popular with the Sikhs who are strongly national, that we take the country ourselves. Those who would feel the advantages of our rule, who estimate the blessings of security to life and property, of perfect toleration to religion, of our encouragement of trade and agriculture, would no doubt rejoice, but there are many powerful classes who cannot fail to be inimical to our rule. Such are the chiefs and great holders of rent-free lands, the priests of both persuasions, Hindu and Mohammadan, and in particular, all people who live by service". In the interest of the success of the recommer.ded measure, he laid great stress on gradually reducing the power and consequence of the country's chiefs.

Two days after John's fertile imagination suggested to his brother a separate deal with Dewan Mul Raj "Should we find it necessary", he wrote, "to take the country, the plan will be to make a separate arrangement with Dewan Mul Raj and allow him to continue Dewan under us".[48] And the reason by which this proposal was backed was the desire to grab the sum of 21 lacs of rupees that the Diwan was bound to pay to the Darbar every year, and thereby also to weaken the Lahore state still further.

Let us now see Lord Hardinge's reactions in the matter. We have already noticed that to him the political settlement of March 1846 was at best a transitional arrangement and that he was on the look-out for a better opportunity to solve the problem finally and completely. A good peep into the working of his mind, showing at once his doubts and ambitions, may well be obtained from the following statement[49] which he made within three weeks of the signing of the Treaties of Lahore:

> "When I consider the character of the Ranee, her Minister Lal Singh and the absence of any man of master mind among the Sikhs to take the helm at this crisis, I confess I think the probability is adverse to the continuance of a Sikh government, which after all is a mere fragment of the population of the countries which they profess to rule, their numbers of men fit for the active duties of soldiers on the trans-Sutlej side not exceeding 100,000 fighting men".

It is not without significance that while his Agents at Lahore had right only to watch over the implementation of the treaties of March 1846, they were actually employed by the Governor-General as instruments for collecting and supplying detailed information about the military and revenue resources of the Sikh state, with the result that within a few months he had a complete picture before him. From the various returns[50] submitted to him from time to time, he was gratified to note that the country, if properly managed, could well afford the expenses of its administration.

The reports of deterioration in the mutual relations of Lal Singh and other chiefs, deliberately played up by John Lawrence, reactivised the Governor-General and he at once set to work out his next plan. He wasted no efforts on bringing about peace between the rival parties; nor did he pay any heed to the plan of a broad-based ministry contained in John's letter of 27th August. His mind, from the beginning of September particularly, was pre-occupied only with one idea—how to assume the entire management of the Punjab. As early as 10th September, much before his Agent at Lahore had made him aware of the Darbar's request and his own view of that, he had written to the Secret Committee:[51] "The other course which it may be open to the British Government to take and which has constantly occupied my attention since September 3, would be to carry on the Government of Lahore in the name of the Maharaja during his minority, a period of about 8 years, placing a British minister at the head of the Government assisted by a Native Council". Earlier in this letter he had made it amply clear that "the British garrison ought not to remain beyond the stipulated period if a native government continues to administer the affairs of the Punjab".[52] The reason given by him was that in such a case it would amount to countenancing misrule and oppression.

Elaborating his position further he said that Raja Lal Singh's government was oppressive and further that it was "impossible to place any confidence in the professions of the Maharani or the Vizier that the advice of a British Agent would be followed, if the garrison were to be permitted to remain".[53] Both these assumptions were exaggerated, if not totally wrong. The Raja's government was certainly not liked by the chiefs who were excluded from it, or by those who had lost their service as under the terms of the last treaty, but it was unfair to condemn it as being oppressive. Similarly, in the presence of their recorded preparedness to give written guarantees of good conduct and willing obedience,[54] it is difficult to agree with Hardinge that they were absolutely unreliable. But the Governor-General's objection was not to the Raja's government alone but, as the above statement of his shows, to any native government. This is most revealing and significant because this shows that the Governor-General was not prepared now to accept the Raja's government or any change in its place howsoever good that change might be, and further that he was now determined to have his pound of flesh for his agreement to continue his troops at Lahore beyond 31st December 1846. But this pound of flesh, it will be seen, was not on account of any existing oppression, but was actuated by his strong desire to capitalise on the weakness of the Darbar government betrayed by its repeated requests for the continued of the British garrison.

Another important point which comes out in the foregoing despatch of Lord Hardinge is that he was against withdrawing the garrison, and wished to avoid it if he could possibly help it. The plea advanced by him as the fear of anarchy into which he thought the state would be plunged after the withdrawal of the troops. In the face of such a fear he held that withdrawal of the garrison would be not only inconsistent "with the humanity or sincerity of our policy". But "equally opposed to our best interest".[55] But what he had in mind was no easy task to achieve. Being well aware that his plan would be resisted, he wanted to work quietly for the consent, forced or voluntary, of the Darbar government and the principal Sikh chiefs.

There was, however, one snag about his plan that it had a similarity to a subsidiary system to which he had on so many occasions publicly expressed his aversion. He was therefore at pains to explain that though subsidiary in form, his plan avoided the evils of that system. Pointing out the difference, he wrote:[56] "In the one case our troops are made the instrument for supporting misrule and giving countenance and strength to oppression; in the other, by British interposition, justice and moderation are secure by an administration conducted by native executive agency, in accordance with the customs, feelings and even prejudices of the people". Just how much justice was secured by Hardinge's system was amply laid bare by subsequent events. It brought about the subversion of the Sikh sovereignty quicker than the conventional subsidiary system would have done.

Nine days after his despatch of 10th September, Hardinge again wrote to the Secret Committee giving his detailed views on the vexed question of the Lahore garrison. In reply, he was given full freedom to deal with the question any way he liked.[57]

The following two or three months were taken up by the rebellion of the Kashmir Governor Sheikh Emamud-din. The rebellion was anti-Maharaja Gulab Singh and not anti-British, but as the British prestige too was involved in it, they felt greatly concerned, and Henry Lawrence personally led an army against the Sheikh. The Sheikh surrendered without fighting and then in his defence produced sealed documents proving the charge of instigation on the part of Raja Lal Singh. The Raja was tried in early December by a special court presided over by a special envoy of the Governor-General, Sir Frederick Currie. He was found guilty and immediately sent into exile.

The banishment of the Raja created an excellent opportunity for the reconstruction of the Sikh government on a broad basis, and were he earnest about the continuance of native rule in the Punjab, he would have found no difficulty in doing so. In this project the Rani too would have rendered great help to him. But this did not suit the policy of the Governor-General and he used the drastic punishment of the Raja for a different purpose: intimidation of other chiefs and bending them to his masterful will. At the same time he paraded it as another proof of the necessity of removing the native authority.

Negotiations about the all-important question of the British garrison at Lahore were taken up immediately under the very shadow of the Raja's exilement. As soon as Lord Hardinge's special envoy, Sir Fredrick Currie, who had been sent on the special mission for his consummate diplomatic skill, disclosed that assumption of absolute control by the British was the only basis on which the Governor-General could agree to allow his troops to stay on, the Regent and all her chiefs were stunned. The Rani forthwith withdrew her request for help and devoted all her energies to "an endeavour to win over the Sirdars of high and low degree, and unite them all together in a scheme of independent government of which she herself was to be the head".[58] The British were alarmed at these frantic efforts of her and resorted to many questionable devices to browbeat the reluctant chiefs. Hardinge, who had reached as close to Lahore as Bhyrowal to be able personally to guide the negotiations from close quarters, ordered sham troops movements[59] away from Lahore so as to exert a dramatic and decisive effect upon the negotiations in progress. To appeal to the self-interest of the chiefs, temptations and assurances about *jagirs* were given. In Harding's own language the guarantee to the chiefs of their *jagirs* "must...be a powerful stimulus to ensure their adhesion to the conditions imposed'.[60] Threats and warnings were also used.[61] Even then, for some time, all chiefs were not willing to accept the conditions which the British wanted to impose, and a compromise proposal was evolved to ask the Governor-General to permit the Agent with two battalions to continue for some months more. But this proposal, not unsound for a man sincerely desiring to help the native authority, was rejected outright by Hardinge saying that it is "so absurd that I consider it as equivalent to a desire to undertake the management of their own affairs, without our intervention..."[62] Ultimately, the British had their way, their persistent machiavellian pressure exerted on the chiefs proved successful and a treaty under the name of 'Articles of Agreement' was concluded on 16th December 1846, whereby the British Resident at Lahore became a virtual king of the Punjab. The treaty gave him "full authority to direct and control all matters in every Department of the state". For his assistance a Regency Council was created depriving the Rani of her regency powers. The members of the Council were entirely under his control and guidance; he could change them and appoint others as he pleased. In military affairs his power was as unlimited as in civil administration: he could withdraw Sikh garrisons replacing them by British troops in any and every part of the Punjab. The treaty was to have effect during the minority of Maharaja Dalip Singh and was to terminate on his attaining the age of 16 on September, 4, 1854.

The treaty of Bhyrowal, as it came to be called from the place of its ratification, was technically only a temporary suspension of Article 15 of the Treaty of Lahore of 9 March 1846 but in reality it effected a radical change in which all but form of power passed into the hands of the British, so that Hardinge was able to inform the Home authorities that, "our supremacy beyond the Sutlej is so real as if it were loaded with the real responsibilities of annexation".[63] Still because it was not a full-fledged annexation, he was a bit sore and confessed so in a private letter to his most trusted secretary and friend Sir Frederick Currie: "Personally[64] I may regret that it has not been my fate to plant the British standard on the banks of the Indus. I have taken the less ambitious course, and am consoled by the reflexion that I have acted right for the interests of England and of India". From the apologetic tone of the above statement it is not impossible to infer that Hardinge's decision of stopping short of complete annexation was, like his earlier one of March 1846, an act of submission to hard realities of the situation confronting him. In view of the certainty of stiff resistance from the whole Sikh nation in the event of a decision in favour of complete annexation and on account of the financial difficulties of the British government in India and the consequent dire necessity of civil and military retrenchment, he felt that the interests of his government would be better served by the adoption of a comparatively moderate course. It was for this reason rather than for any faith in the long ruled-out idea of the buffer state that he had to postpone the final decision on the fate of the Punjab.

Lord Hobhouse, President of the Board of Control and the Governor-General's immediate boss, did not at first appreciate the reasons that determined the attitude of the Government of India. He preferred complete annexation straight-way and declared the Sikh government "must he chose impossible".[65] However, eventually he came round and sent his approval of the treaty of Bhyrowal in these significant words:[66] "I have now only to congratulate you on all you have done and are doing. You will see by the newspapers that even the best guides of public opinion are now delighted with your arrangement and give you credit for biding your time and doing the right thing at the right moment". According to the son and biographer of Lord Hardinge, these words of Hobhouse offer the correct explanation of his father's policy in so far as "they embody the principles" by which "he was always guided in his dealings with the Punjab. "His policy", he writes, "varied from time to time, but only with the circumstances of the case".[67]

REFERENCES

1. *Hardinge Papers.* The date of this note is not given but it is definitely prior to May 1845.
2. *Ibid.*
3. *Ibid.*
4. "There is now every probability that the scepter of the Punjab will shortly fall from hands incapable of wielding it and the dynasty of Ranjit Singh will cease to exist". *Hardinge Papers.*
5. *Hardinge Papers,* a note dated May 1845.
6. *Ibid.*
7. *Ibid.*
8. *Ibid.*
9. *Ibid.*
10. *Ibid.*
11. *Ibid.*
12. *Ibid.*
13. *Ibid.*

14. *Ibid.*
15. *Ibid.*
16. *Ibid.*
17. *Ibid.*
18. *Ibid.*
19. Gough and Innes, *The Sikhs and the Sikh Wars*, p. 52.
20. *History of the Sikhs*, p. 279.
21. *Ibid.*, p. 279. This secret deal was, however, strongly denied by Hardinge and Henry but both of them being personally involved in the affair, this denial of theirs is not ununderstandable. See J. W. Kaye, *Lives of Indian Officers*, Vol. II, p. 292.
22. *Ibid.*, p. 278.
23. Henry Lawrence once openly confessed to Currie that any attempt by the British to subvert the Khalsa *raj* would not only meet with a determined opposition from the people but that the Sirdars too would join them and the Sikhs would not hesitate to sacrifice all for the sake of the Khalsa. Quoted in Khilnani, *op. cit.*, p. 63.
24. Gough and Innes, *The Sikhs and the Sikh Wars*, p. 143.
25. Charles Viscount Hardinge, p. 124.
26. *Ibid.*, p. 132.
27. *Ibid.*, p. 123.
28. Gibbon, *op. cit.*, p. 115.
29. This was a mere excuse. Had there been money enough to pay the entire amount, even then Kashmir would have been seized; then some other device would have been found for the occupation of this strategic area.
30. This was in spite of some misgivings of his that, as in Afghanistan some years earlier, their troops might be overtaken by disasters. Charles V. Hardinge, *op. cit.*, p. 127.
31. McLeod Innes, Sir H. Lawrence the Pacificator, p. 74.
32. Hardinge to Henry Lawrence, October 23, 1847—quoted in Edwardes and Merivale, *op. cit.*, p. 417.
33. *Ibid.*
34. Lawrence Archer, *op. cit.*, p. 2.
35. Khilnani, *op. cit.*, p. 31.
36. *Foreign Secret Proceedings*, 26 December 1846, Nos. 1079, 1101, 1119. Letters of John Lawrence to F. Currie, 1846.

37. *Foreign Secret Proceedings,* 26, December 1846, No. 1236—John Lawrence to Currie, 3 November 1846. Between themselves the two brothers had 45 lakhs of rupees worth of territory.
38. *Foreign Secret Proceedings,* 26 December 1846, No. 1249 and 1267 John Lawrence to Currie, 23 November 1846 and 17 December 1846. According to John Lawrence, not less than 10,000 troops extra to those of the Darbar were enlisted by Lal Singh and his brothers.
39. *Ibid.*
40. Boswell Smith *op. cit.,* p. 195. An extract from John Lawrence's letter of August 28, 1846.
41. *Ibid.,* p. 194—Letter dated 26 August 1846.
42. J. Lawrence to Currie, 11th September 1846.
43. *Foreign Secret Proceedings,* 26 December 1846, No. 1068—J. Lawrence to Currie, 4 October 1846.
44. Boswell Smith, *op. cit.,* p. 194.
45. *Ibid.*
46. *Ibid.,* p. 196.
47. Boswell Smith, *op. cit.,* p. 197.
48. *Ibid., op. cit.,* p. 196.
49. Edwardes and Merivale, *Life of Sir Henry Lawrence,* p. 385.
50. *Foreign Secret Proceedings,* 26 December 1846, Nos. 1325-1327. There are about 8 returns given here.
51. Charles Viscount Hardinge, *op. cit.,* p. 149; McLeod Innes, *Sir Henry Lawrence the Pacificator,* p. 77.
52. McLeod Innes, *op. cit.,* p. 74.
53. *Ibid.*
54. John Lawrence to Currie, 10th and 11th September 1846.
55. McLeod Innes, *op. cit.,* p. 76.
56. *Ibid.*
57. Charles V. Hardinge, *op. cit.,* p. 151.
58. Edwardes and Merivale, *Life of Sir Henry Lawrence,* p. 406. A revealing thing about Hardinge's mind is that the Rani, who had the biggest stake involved in the affairs, was excluded from the negotiations.
59. *Private Correspondence,* pp. 15, 16.

60. *Ibid.*, p. 16.
61. Currie to Maharaja Dalip Singh, December 9, 1846: "The Governor-General is determined to hold the Lahore Government responsible for the tranquillity of the frontier and will not permit the renewal of a state of anarchy, misrule, insubordination similar to the one which existed last year". See Khilnani *The Punjab Under the Lawrences*, p. 42.
62. *Ibid.*, p. 17.
63. Edwardes ad Merivale, *op. cit.*, p. 410.
64. *Private Correspondence, op. cit.*, p. 19.
65. *Ibid.*, p. 22.
66. Charles V. Hardinge, *op. cit.*, p. 152.
67. *Ibid.*, p. 157.

5
The Sword

I

When Jaswant Rao Holkar took leave of Ranjit Singh for good in 1806, the parting advice he gave the Maharaja was that he should build up a regular army, with artillery and infantry as its principal components. This was honest, advice based upon half-a-century of Indian experience. Balaji Bajirao, Madhoji Scindia, Hyder Ali, Tipu Sultan and Holkar himself had stood up to the British mainly on the strength of their regular battalions of artillery and infantry trained by European officers. Ranjit Singh at once saw the point of Holkar's advice. The feudal levies of horsemen which had composed the Dal Khalsa during the period of Ahmad Shah Abdali's invasions and their aftermath were now out of date. They could not be expected to hold their own against European armies equipped with new weapons and trained in new methods of war. Ranjit Singh inspected Holkar's western-model troops and was much impressed with their turnout and discipline. There was, however, one thing he could not puzzle out: why had they fled before Lord Lake's troops, which were similarly equipped and trained? It was to find the answer to this question that he paid the incognito visit to Lake's camp. The answer he found was that the British troops were even better trained than Holkar's. Ranjit Singh, therefore, resolved to change the entire organization of the Khalsa army, laying more stress on infantry and artillery than on cavalry, and, above all, to make proper arrangements for training.

The infantry proved difficult to organize to begin with. Indian army traditions accorded a very low rank and social status to foot soldiers. In Akbar's time they were bracketed with gate-keepers, palace guards, letter-carriers and palanquin-bearers. The Sikhs before Ranjit Singh promoted their status a little by using them for garrisoning forts; but they were still ranked far below horsemen. Sikhs were, therefore, not willing to enlist as foot soldiers. Ranjit Singh began by recruiting Hindustani deserters from the East India Company's troops, and he gave training jobs to the senior men among them. In order to make the infantry popular he used to attend its parades in person and to extend special favours to infantrymen. Once the branch became popular with the Sikhs, he began to be selective: he recruited the pick of the youth of the country, laying special emphasis upon good looks and physical fitness. Hindus and Muslims also came in and were selected on the same criteria. Two European officers, Allard and Ventura, joined the Maharaja's service later on, and helped in putting his infantry on a proper footing. In 1838 the infantry had a strength of 29,617 and drew a monthly salary of Rs. 2,27,660.

After organizing the infantry, the Maharaja turned his attention to the artillery. The Sikhs had no experience of heavy artillery and only knew how to use small swivel guns. In the beginning Ranjit Singh had to import both officers and gunners from outside the Punjab. Among the senior officers he recruited were two Europeans, Claude Auguste Court and Alexander Gardner. In order to cast guns, Ranjit Singh had a number of gun factories, of which local men, trained by the foreign officers, took charge in due course. In 1838-39, the artillery had a strength of 4,535, with 188 heavy guns and 280 swivels and its monthly salary was Rs. 32,906.

The cavalry continued to be a branch of the army and was divided into three groups, viz., the regular cavalry, the Ghorcharha Fauj and the Jagirdari Fauj. In 1838, the regular cavalry had a strength of 4,090 and drew a monthly salary of Rs. 90,375. The Ghorcharha Fauj was manned by representatives of the powerful families of the country whom Ranjit Singh thought it necessary to keep near his court for political reasons. It was his constant endeavour to win their loyalty and attachment. Therefore, he treated them generously. He bestowed distinctions and other marks of favour on them and even gave cash allowances to some of them. These sardars came along with their warriors, who were absorbed into the main army. For instance, the troops of the Nakkai and Kanhaya sardars were taken over bodily and formed part, respectively, of the corps commanded by Prince Kharak Singh and Prince Sher Singh. Almost all the military classes of the Punjab were represented in the Ghorcharha Fauj—Jat Sikhs, Hindu Rajputs, Muslim Rajputs, Pathans, Khatris, Brahmins and so on. The pay and emoluments were higher than in the regular army. The recruits were expected to bring their own horses and arms; but this was often relaxed. In 1838, the Ghorcharha Fauj numbered 10,795 and drew a yearly salary of Rs. 31,68,714.

The Jagirdari cavalry was raised on the basis of feudal levies. The chiefs and their men ordinarily lived on their own jagirs, presenting themselves for a review once a year at Dussehra time. The Maharaja used to take a strict muster of these troops personally to make sure that his fief-holders were carrying out their obligations; and failure to do so was punished severely. Even General Hari Singh Nalwa was on one occasion fined two lakhs of rupees for failing to produce the number of men he had undertaken to maintain.

The Ghorcharha Fauj was the aristocratic branch of the army by reason of its origin, and its officers vied with each other in maintaining its dignity. There was no prescribed uniform. This gave the officers full scope for trying to outshine their compeers in their dress, equipment and arms. Some wore velvet or silk coats, and over them a shirt of mail. Some had pink, others yellow, turbans, and all wore a belt round the waist, embroidered in gold, which supported a powder-horn and a Persian sword with the addition of a pistol in some cases. There were some who wore a steel helmet with a black heron's plume on it. Some also carried a bow and a quiver. All bore buffalo-hide shields on their backs.

Ranjit Singh's "feringhees", as the foreign officers were popularly called, were a colourful lot. Their number has been estimated variously: the highest estimate is 42 and the lowest 20. They were Italians, Frenchmen, Americans, Englishmen, Greeks, Russians, Germans, Scotchmen and Anglo-Indians.

He started recruiting them soon after the Treaty of Amritsar (1809), which he realized was a diplomatic defeat he had to swallow because of his being militarily weaker than the British. The first to join was an Englishman called Price, a deserter from Ochterlony's troops. Then came a number of Anglo-Indian soldiers of fortune, some of them sons of well-known British officers, including Robert Dick, son of Major-General Sir Robert Dick, and Jacob Thomas, son of the famous adventurer, George Thomas. But the first foreign officers who proved really valuable acquisitions were Jean Brancois Allard and Jean Baptiste Ventura, who joined Ranjit Singh's service in 1822. Allard was a Frenchman and Ventura an Italian. Both came of good families and both had served under Napoleon in the armies of Spain and Itlay. After the declaration of peace they had been demobilized and had unsuccessfully tried their fortune in Egypt and Persia. They had then come to Lahore, travelling through Herat, Kandahar, Kabul and Peshawar. Ranjit Singh took two months to examine their qualifications, verify their bonafides and put them to practical tests before he gave them employment. Allard was commissioned to raise to corps of dragoons, to be disciplined and armed exactly on the same lines as a cavalry corps in Europe. Ventura was put in command of the Fauj-i-Khas, which was a special brigade, the first in rank, discipline and equipment in the Khalsa army. Both were given liberal salaries of the order of Rs. 30,000 a year. Allard was alotted as his residence a commodious building, which stood where the house known as Kapurthala House in British times was subsequently constructed. The place is popularly known as *Kuri bagh* (Girl's Garden became it contains the tomb of Allard's daughter. Ventura was given Anarkali's tomb to live in: a marble tablet outside the Chief Secretary's room in the West Pakistan Secretariat, contiguous to Anarkali's tomb, commemorates this fact. Allard and Ventura were both promoted to the rank of General and were held in high regard by the Maharaja. Allard was decorated with the Order of the Star of the Prosperity of the Punjab and was entrusted with very important missions. He married a Kashmiri woman and had several children by her: the girl whose tomb has given the popular name of Kuri Bagh to his compound was one of them. He once went home on leave and, when he came back, he brought with him a personal letter addressed by the King of France, Louis Phillipe, to Ranjit Singh. He died at Peshawar in January, 1838, and his body was embalmed and brought to Lahore, where it lay in state before being buried in a cemetery outside the city walls.

Ventura made an excellent job of the Fauj-i-Khas. It consisted of four infantry battalions and two regiments of cavalry, and gave a good account of itself in many campaigns, especially in the hills and around Peshawar. Ventura married an Armenian woman from Ludhiana, but maintained a harem of Kashmiri and Punjabi women and lived in great style. The Maharaja thought so well of his administrative ability that he appointed him to officiate once or twice as Governor of Lahore.

Another prominent foreign officer was Colonel Henry Court, a Frenchman of noble birth educated at the Ecole Polytechnique of Paris. He commanded two battalions of Gurkhas to begin with and later on organized what was known as the French Legion. He was a man of culture and refinement and devoted himself to scholarly pursuits in addition to his profession.

The most dramatic of Ranjit Singh's foreign officers was Paole de Avitabite, an Italian by birth, who had risen from the ranks and had also seen service in Persia. He was a stout six-footer, gruff in his manners and ruthless in his methods of administration. He was, therefore, generally employed where a heavy hand was needed to put down turbulent elements. He was first posted as Governor of Wazirabad, but was later transferred to Peshawar as Military Commander. He also paid a visit to France, where he was received by King Louis Philippe, who awarded him the Cross of the Legion of Honour and honorary rank of General of the French Army.

Ranjit Singh used his foreign officers mostly for purposes of training. Although he gave them responsible positions, he never put them in supreme command of any major expedition. This did not proceed so much from lack of trust in their loyalty—although that was probably one factor—as from his anxiety to groom his own nationals for generalship. The administrative posts to which he assigned them occasionally were intended as a kind of compensation for their being kept out of supreme command, to which some of them naturally aspired by reason of their seniority. There was also a degree of political sagacity behind this. Difficult and unpopular administrative assignments could be handled more easily by foreigners than by local officers having family and personal attachments. It was Ranjit Singh's genuine desire to induce his foreign officers to settle down permanently in the Punjab; but with a very few exceptions, ties of home proved stronger in the long run than good jobs, high salaries, and the paraphernalia of luxurious living.

Azizuddin mentions an incident which caused the Maharaja much disappointment and disillusionment. While out on a walk during Mac Naughten's visit to Lahore, he met three Englishmen on the latter's staff and had a casual conversation with them about his European officers. He mentioned to the Englishmen that the European officers had all given him a solemn undertaking to fight for him against all his enemies. The Englishmen remarked that these undertakings could not be relied upon so far as fighting against the troops of the officers' own countries was concerned. On returning to the fort, Ranjit Singh related this conversation to Raja Dhian Singh and Fakir Azizuddin with much grief. He wondered what more he could do than he had done to make the foreign officers happy. He had given them princely salaries. (For example, Avitabile started on a salary of Rs. 5,000/-a month, equivalent to a lakh of rupees today. Allard and Ventura, as already mentioned, were given a starting salary of Rs. 2,500/- a month. These starting salaries were increased later on). He had conferred honours and jagirs on them. He had always treated them with consideration and confidence. Although he had recruited them only for training his men, he had kept them on after their training jobs were finished; in fact, he had sometimes had to find or create jobs for them.

Dhian Singh was anti-European. He, therefore angrily said that the European officers were all gold-diggers and opportunists. Azizuddin had the same liberal and cosmopolitan outlook as the Maharaja. So he remarked that, although it was a pity the European officers could not be made to regard the Punjab as their home, they had nevertheless made a valuable contribution to the regime. He though it had been worthwhile to engage them. The Maharaja remained in a pensive mood for a long time after this conversation.

II

The Ambitious Mother-in-Law

The marriage of Ranjit Singh, sixteen-year-old chief of the Sukerchakia misl, and Mehtab Kaur, fourteen-year-old granddaughter of Jai Singh, chief of the Kanhaya misl, in 1796, was hailed by the whole Sikh community as a great occasion. It was an alliance between the premier misl and one that was also prominent—an important enough event. But it was to acquire a greater importance than anybody could then foresee. It brought together two of the most dynamic Sikh personalities of the time, Ranjit Singh and his mother-in-law, Sada Kaur, who by both working together and working against each other determined the course of Sikh history for the next forty years.

Since her husband's death five years earlier in a skirmish with Ranjit Singh's father, Sada Kaur had been devoting all her time to bringing up Mehtab Kaur, her only child. There was, therefore, nothing to detain her in her husband's home after Mehtab Kaur's marriage, and so she accompanied the bride to her new home to live with her there. If her object in doing so was to bring the newly married couple close together, she was not successful in achieving it. The young people had their own reasons for not being fond of each other. In fact, it is likely that her meddling in their affairs drove them farther apart. However, this object was ancillary to a larger one, which was to groom her son-in-law for the leadership of the Sikh community. He had already shown promise of fitness for that role by the way he had ambushed and defeated the Bhangis at the tender age of twelve, when his father had suddenly died in the midst of an expedition against them. The role she envisaged for herself was that of the power behind the throne. It was not practical for a woman to think of ruling the whole Sikh community in her own name, and she had no man in her own family whom she could use as her ladder. She had thought out her plans immediately after her husband's death, which had left her faced with the gloomy prospect of being driven out of the Kanhaya misl by her husband's younger brothers as soon as her father-in-law died. These brothers-in-law of hers were imbeciles and she knew that, if she could get proper support from some quarter, she could throw them out of the misl before they threw her out. It was with the object of getting this support that she had conceived the idea of betrothing her daughter to Ranjit Singh and she had worked hard to bring the betrothal about, subduing her anger against the son of her husband's assassin. She had already enjoyed the first fruits of the prospective alliance: it had strengthened her hands so much that on her father-in-law's death in 1793 she had been able to make her mother-in-law and her two sons retire, leaving her to govern the misl. She had established her headquarters at Batala and raised a force strong enough to have defeated her family's old foe, Jassa Singh Ramgarhia.

Now that the long-projected marriage was an accomplished fact, the time had come for her to start preparing the ground for the ambitious plan which it was intended to serve.

The first thing for Sada Kaur to do was obviously to bring Ranjit Singh under her thumb. Unfortunately, he was tied to his mother's apron strings and seemed quite happy to let her manage the affairs of his state with the assistance of his father's dewan, Lakhpat Rai. Ranjit Singh had always looked up to Lakhpat Rai with the respect due to his father's principal officer and, therefore, had implicit faith in his ability and honesty. Sada Kaur began to poison Ranjit Singh's ears against Lakhpat Rai by suggesting that he was misappropriating funds. Ranjit Singh for some time turned a deaf ear to her allegations; but when they became persistent, he passed them on to his mother, who told him that he should not let evil thoughts about his father's trusted servant cross his mind. Once or twice he tried to get his mother or Lakhpat Rai to explain things to him and satisfy him; but matters of estate management and accounts were too complicated for his immature understanding. So he let them pass. Sada Kaur then tried to interfere directly and openly, which led to clashes between her and Ranjit Singh's mother. Matters reached such a state that there were constant charges and counter-charges, quarrels and fights, and even exchanges of abusive language. Ranjit Singh's home became intolerable for him. So he threw himself with abandon into his favourite pastimes of riding and hunting. He might have gone on with them indefinitely had not the Afghan invader, Shah Zaman, made his appearance in 1796 and again in 1797. On both occasions it was Sada Kaur who persuaded Ranjit Singh not to follow the example of the chiefs who had fled to the safety of the hills but to stay behind and fight. It was she who urged him to summon a meeting of the Sarbat Khalsa at Amritsar. It was the spirited appeal she made to the assembled chiefs and the threat that even if everybody else ran away she, woman, would fight the invader alone which banded the chiefs together under the leadership of her son-in-law.

But after the excitement of these emergencies was over, Ranjit Singh returned to the loneliness and misery of his home life. Torn between the intrigues of his mother and his mother-in-law—intrigues for power and influence and for the possession of his mind—he longed for somebody in whom his young heart could lodge its affections. His wife, Mehtab Kaur, was not willing to lend herself to such a role: she was even less of a companion than the two women fighting over him. So, four years after his first marriage, he took a second wife, Raj Kaur, daughter of the Nakkai chief. She brought sweetness and light into his life and provided for him a focus of interest in his home. Spending more time at home than he had ever done before, he began to look into the affairs of his estate and soon found that he could and must take their management into his own hands. The occasion for him to do so was providentially provided by the murder of Lakhpat Rai. This proved the signal for Sada Kaur's departure: taking Mehtab Kaur with her, she went away to Batala in a huff. She had gained a Pyrrhic victory. She had dislodged Ranjit Singh's mother and Lakhpat Rai, but she had not been successful in taking their place.

However, she did not have to return to Ranjit Singh's home to make him do big things. An opportunity of doing so otherwise came soon. The citizens of Lahore appealed to her as well as to Ranjit Singh to deliver them from the Sikh triumvirate misruling the city since Shah Zaman's withdrawal. Ranjit Singh mustered what troops he could and proceeded to Batala to consult his mother-in-law. She was waiting for him and, when he marched into the city, she marched by his side at the head of her own troops. She had helped in planning the surprise take-over which the whole affair was. Later on, again, it was she who advised Ranjit Singh to compel Chet Singh to surrender by the simple device of denying him provisions instead of storming Lahore fort. Yet again, when, after the capture of Lahore, the Bhangis, the Ramgarhias and Nizamuddin of Kasur joined forces and marched towards the city, it was Sada Kaur who fought Jassa

Singh Ramgarhia near Batala and defeated him—she had already learnt how to do so—, while Ranjit Singh himself tackled the rest of the combined forces at Bhasin.

Ranjit Singh repaid the debt a year later by winning back for her a part of her territory which Sansar Chand of Kangra had captured and by giving her in addition a part of Sansar Chand's territory. A year later still, it was she who provided the extra grain of moral courage he needed to tip the scales in favour of his deciding to assume the title of Maharaja. Hardly had another year passed when she joined him in the capture of Amritsar.

The turning point came with the birth of twin sons, Sher Singh and Tara Singh, to Mehtab Kaur in 1808. Until then Sada Kaur had been content to play second fiddle and had been happy to see her ambitions taking shape in the increasing power and prestige of her son-in-law. The birth of sons to her daughter gave her new ideas. Ranjit Singh had already been presented with a son, Kharak Singh, by his second wife, Raj Kaur, in 1802. The question that began to worry Sada Kaur's mind was whether Kharak Singh or the elder of her daughter's twins, Sher Singh, would be chosen to succeed Ranjit Singh. The relations between Ranjit Singh and Mehtab Kaur being what they were and Kharak Singh being the eldest born, he was the obvious choice. Could she change that? In any case, it would be wise to strengthen her own position and that of her daughter and grandsons independently of the fortunes of the Sukerchakia family. She began by raiding the territory of her ancient enemies, the Ramgarhias, who sought Ranjit Singh's protection as his vassals. Ranjit Singh had to interfere and bring about an amicable settlement: and he had to do so more than once.

The rift widened when tribute was levied on Adinanagar, one of the estates of the Kanhayas. It was the general practice of the Durbar to make the various chiefdoms pay for their protection. How else was a central army to be maintained? Even the estates of the Maharaja's own mother and Prince Kharak Singh were not exempt from this, but Sada Kaur thought that her estates should enjoy complete exemption. The gift of Whadni near Ferozepur, instead of satisfying her as ample compensation, made her think that she was beyond the Durbar's jurisdiction when the English began to challenge Ranjit Singh's right to levy tribute or annex territories beyond the Sutlej. A month before Metcalfe came to negotiate a treaty with Ranjit Singh on this subject, Sada Kaur supported the Malwa sardars against the Maharaja. At a later stage, when the British began to make preparations for compelling Ranjit Singh to sign the treaty by a show of force, she was among the first to send word to them that they could count on her support. Later still, when Ochterlony actually advanced at the head of the British task force into the Malwa states, she was present with the Malwa sardars to greet him. Ranjit Singh forgave her all these things out of gratitude for what she had done for him in the beginning of his career. True she had embittered his domestic life with her intrigues; but she had meant well and she had so often been a source of courage and strength to him.

The breaking point was reached when Sada Kaur refused to attend the wedding of Kharak Singh in 1812 and even forbade Sher Singh and Tara Singh to attend it. Mehtab Kaur was by then dead and the boys were living with her; but instead of giving them enough to live upon decently, she would send them every now and again to their father with petitions for jagirs. When Ranjit Singh gave some small jagirs to Kharak Singh, Sada Kaur began to rail against him for partiality and to complain that he was letting Sher Singh and Tara Singh live in penury. Ranjit Singh countered this by proposing that she should give half her estate to the princes, who were after all her only heirs. The wrangle continued until Ranjit Singh made up his mind to settle the problem once for all and proposed, in 1820, that she should make over the administration of her estates to Sher Singh, as she was then in her seventies and deserved some rest. This was the last thing she could agree to. So she decided to cross the Sutlej and go to the British to seek their protection. The excuse she put forward for the journey was that she was going to inspect her Whadni property. Hearing of this, Ranjit Singh invited her to come to Lahore and discuss with him the whole question of jagirs for her grandsons. She met Ranjit Singh in his camp at Shahdara and he was able to talk her into signing a document assigning the management of her estates to Sher Singh; but she had signed the document with a mental reservation and tried to escape to Batala to seek British help for stopping its execution. She was intercepted by Kharak Singh and brought back to Lahore, where she had to be put under house arrest. Sher Singh was put in charge of her estates; but she did not reconcile herself to this logical and inevitable dispensation to her dying day, to such an extent had the high ambition of her youth degenerated into senile avarice. From her confinement she sent a message to Ranjit Singh that she wished to be put to death rather than be deprived of her property. Ranjit Singh wept before the maidservant who had brought the message and said that Sada Kaur had been more than a mother to him. He appealed to the maidservant to make her mistress understand that what had been done was what she herself would have done if she had taken a reasonable view of things. The property would sooner or later have gone to her grandsons and it was necessary that they should learn to look after it before it actually became theirs.

Sada Kaur is remembered as one of the most high-spirited and capable women in Sikh history. Her contribution to the building of the Sikh nation would, however, have been much greater than it was if she had subordinated the interests of the Kanhaya misl or, to be more accurate, her own interests, to the larger interests of the Khalsa Durbar. Her mistake lay in failing to see that Ranjit Singh was not just a rival misldar but the symbol of the unity of the Sikh nation as a whole. If the Sikhs were to be unified, they had to have one leader and it was Ranjit Singh, and not she, who could fulfil that role. It was a sad failure of vision on her part to try to destroy the image she had done so much to build.

III

Of all the men with whom Ranjit Singh exchanged turbans as a pledge of eternal brotherhood. Fateh Singh Ahluwalia was the closest to him. Heir to the prestige of the saintly Jassa Singh Ahluwalia, who was the nearest thing to a king the Sikhs had ever had and who had led their combined forces against Ahmad Shah Abdali, he was among the first chiefs whose hand of friendship was grasped by the young Sukerchakia misldar. It was in no small measure to his influence that Ranjit Singh owed his selection to march at the head of the combined Sikh troops against Shah Zaman in 1796 and again in 1797. Soon after he had captured Lahore, in 1799, Ranjit Singh sent for Fateh Singh and enlisted him among his chief political and military advisers. The exchange of turbans took place a year later at Taran Taaran in the course of an impressive ceremony watched by thousands of people assembled from all parts of the Punjab to bathe in the sacred tank.

After the ceremony the two allies together captured Pindi Bhattian and Dhanni-Potohar, both of which were granted to Fateh Singh. They next proceeded jointly against Nizamuddin of Kasur. In 1802, Ranjit Singh, Fateh Singh and Sada Kaur marched side by side as victors into Amritsar.

The friendly relations between Ranjit Singh and Fateh Singh were put on an even firmer footing when they together signed the Treaty of Lahore with the British in 1806, undertaking to see to the expulsion of Jaswant Rao Holkar's armies *60 miles* beyond Amritsar. In the same year Fateh Singh accompanied Ranjit Singh on his expedition to the south of the Sutlej and a year later to Jhang. These expeditions were followed by a joint campaign against Sialkot, Akhnur and Sheikhupura. Then came the visit of Metcalfe in 1808. Fateh Singh Ahluwalia and Dewan Mohkam Chand were sent to Kasur at the head of 2,000 horsemen to receive the English envoy at Kasur. Fateh Singh was present when the Treaty of Amritsar was signed in 1809. He also accompanied the Maharaja to Kangra in the same year, and was left in charge of the defences of Lahore and Amritsar when the Maharaja marched to Multan in 1810. In the following year he accompanied Ranjit Singh on his visit to Shah Mahmud at Rawalpindi and later helped in the reduction of Sardar Budh Singh of Julundur. In 1813 he fought alongside the Maharaja against Wazir Fateh Khan and took part in the Bahawalpur, Rajauri and Bhimbar campaigns. He was also present at the siege of Multan in 1818. During the Maharaja's Kashmir campaign in 1819, he once again remained in charge of Lahore. Two years later, he assisted the Maharaja in reducing the fort of Mankhera.

Suddenly in 1825 came the news like a bolt from the blue that Fateh Singh Ahluwalia had left Kapurthala and fled to Jagraon, across the Sutlej, with his whole family. What had happened to spoil a beautiful friendship—a friendship which had stood foursquare even to the winds of intrigue and hostility which had blown in the Treaty of Amritsar? As subsequent investigations showed, the source of the mischief was Fateh Singh's agent in Lahore, Chaudhri Kadir Bakhsh, who had been sending alarming reports to his master about the Durbar's designs on his estates. The reports falsely suggested that the estates would shortly be attached, as had happened to most other misls. Fortunately for the friendship, the British were at that time anxious to remain on the right side of Ranjit Singh. In any case, they could not with any justification interfere in view of the Treaty of Amritsar. As far as Jagraon was concerned, it had been granted to Fateh Singh, on payment of a nazrana, by the Maharaja, who was, therefore, its overlord for the purposes of the British. As regards Fateh Singh's estates north of the Sutlej, British interference in them was precluded by the Treaty of Amritsar.

The British, therefore, advised Fateh Singh to rely on his friendship with the Maharaja and go back to his home north of the Sutlej. Ranjit Singh also sent his envoys to allay Fateh Singh's fears. At last Fateh Singh came back. He was received with full honours by Prince Nau Nihal Singh and Raja Dhian Singh. The two friends met once again. Fateh Singh unsheathed his sword, laid it at Ranjit Singh's feet and asked him to sever his head with his own hand for the act of infidelity of which he had been guilty. Ranjit Singh stood up from his seat, embraced his friend and returned his sword. There were tears in the eyes of both of them. Fateh Singh was given a robe of honour, an elephant with a silver howdah and a necklace of pearls.

His estates north of the Sutlej had been seized under the Maharaja's orders by Fakir Azizuddin—not too happily, because the Fakir had a great liking for this amiable man. Fakir Nuruddin was sent to deliver them back to Fateh Singh's officials, and there was no happier man in the whole of the Punjab at that moment than the Fakir.

IV

An Embarrassing Admirer

Among those who helped Ranjit Singh in the capture of Amritsar in 1802 was a band of Akalis under the leadership of Phula Singh. While chiefdoms were being won and lost around them, these dedicated soldiers of the Khalsa—"immortals", as they genuinely believed themselves to be—devoted themselves to the care of Sikh shrines with occasional sorties to the surrounding country to win their bread at the point of the sword. Their most dearly cherished dream was to see a Khalsa kingdom established; but they were not organized and equipped well enough to realize this dream themselves. They were, therefore, eagerly waiting for a man who could do so: they would place all their fanatical zeal and all their self-disciplined bravery at his service. They saw the lineaments of such a man for the first time in the youthful Ranjit Singh. When, therefore, after driving the Afghan invading armies away and making himself master of Lahore, he appeared before Amritsar, they were only too ready to strike a blow for him.

Phula Singh and his Akalis were difficult men to get on with. Their whole way of life was a paradox. On the one hand, they were humble and pious people, continually praying and doing menial jobs for the love of the Guru in the holy places and gurdwaras, on the other hand, they believed that they were entitled to exact from the community whatever they needed for their upkeep. Their needs were not many and they seldom appropriated to themselves more than they needed; but what they needed they took by any means open to them. To serve a temporal master was against their creed. In fact, it was an article of faith with them to defy and prey upon the powerful and the rich, while serving and helping the poor and the weak. In the matter of religious doctrine and practice, they were uncompromisingly orthodox. While they were dreaded by the rich and the privileged, they enjoyed a good deal of popularity among the Sikh masses.

Phula Singh himself was a combination of the best and the worst features of the Akali character. His best quality was his dashing gallantry and his worst was his blind fanaticism. Ranjit Singh made use of both these qualities at the same time by throwing him and his Akalis into battle at critical moments in engagements against similar muslim fanatics, as for example, at Kasur and at Nowshera. It, however, took Ranjit Singh some time to bring under control the other qualities of this strange man. One of these arose, paradoxically enough, from his very admiration for Ranjit Singh as the Sikh king of his dreams, and it was his impatience with any concessions made by Ranjit Sigh to the exigencies of statecraft. It was Phula Singh who was the chief author of the fracas between Metcalfe's Muslim bodyguard and the Akalis at Amritsar, and his intention in provoking it was that the negotiations for the Treaty of Amritsar should break down, because he thought that Ranjit Sigh would compromise his position as an independent ruler, if he signed the treaty. Little did he know that he was, in fact, hastening the treaty by his rash act. Worse than this was his habit of going on plundering sprees every now and again. This, again, arose from his misconception about the right of Akalis to defy lawful authority and make direct exactions from the community. Ranjit Singh had to reprimand him repeatedly and make him return his acquisitions—that is, those of them which he had not already disturbed among his followers or the poor. It was not until Ranjit Singh took him and his band of Akalis into his service and thus brought him under his direct control that his free-booting activities stopped.

Ranjit Singh treated Phula Singh both as an individual and as the leader of a movement, and he made good use of the difficult material that he was in both these capacities. As an individual he was a brave and brilliant soldier. As the leader of the Akali movement, he represented a force which, if not harnessed to the purposes of the state, could undermine its very foundations. It was a good piece of human relations work to make a proudly independent Akali leader accept royal service, and it was an equally clever achievement of statecraft to make the Akali movement serve the interests of the state. However, it cost Ranjit Singh a good deal of patience and tolerance to achieve these results. Akali Phula Singh was a particularly violent specimen of those Akalis who considered it their life's vocation to go about insulting people, and there were not a few occasions when he practised this upon Ranjit Singh until he had been tamed. He did not stop short of even at having an attempt made on Ranjit Singh's life, or at least making a show of one. Immediately after the Rupar meeting between Ranjit Singh and the British Governor-General, at which Ranjit Singh had been asked to desist from annexing any territories in Sindh, an Akali rushed towards Ranjit Singh with drawn sword. There was no need of questioning the man, after he had been overpowered, to find out whose was the master-mind behind him. Ranjit Singh at once understood that this was another demonstration of the fire-eating Akali leader's impatience with his compromises and of his overzealous vindication of the Khalsa Durbar's prestige. Akali Phula Singh continued in the Maharaja's service until he met his death at Nowshera in the manner in which he had so often gone out to meet it.

Akali Phula Singh seems to have had some kind of a strange respect for the Fakir brothers. Not only did he spare them the indignities to which he used to subject big people simply for the fun of doing so, he even listened to mild rebukes from them, and this cannot have been from fear; for the man knew no fear and, in any case, he had nothing to fear from them. In fact, the Akalis as a class treated the Fakir brothers with respect after their own fashion and used to address them as "Babaji" or "Saeenji"—words which are used in addressing holy men. During the period before they were brought under control and when they used to indulge in occasional acts of extortion and freebooting, Fakir Nuruddin was stopped one day by a band of Akalis near the Shahidganj mosque in Landa Bazar and asked to pay them what they used to call a "gappha", a gift of money. Fakir Nuruddin mentions that they did so in a very respectful manner as if they were begging. He did not have much money on him and, therefore, asked them to call at his house. When they did so, he gave them two thousand rupees. The Maharaja got to know of the incident and had the men arrested and produced before him. He seemed to be so angry that the Fakir apprehended he would award them very severe punishments. To avoid creating bad blood, he submitted to the Maharaja that this was not a case of robbery or extortion, since he had given the money voluntarily. The Maharaja was visibly displeased at being frustrated in meting out the punishment which he thought the men deserved, but had to let them go. However, Nuruddin was amply repaid for his clemency—or sagacity: the Akalis never bothered him again.

Raj Kaur, Ranjit Singh's second wife, triumphed over his first wife, Mehtab Kaur, by presenting him, in 1802, with his first son, who was named Kharak Singh on the advice on the astrologers. So great was the happiness of the Maharaja and his people at the birth of the heir-apparent that Lahore was *en fete* for several weeks. Robes of honour were bestowed on the Sardars of the Durbar and every soldier in the capital was given a necklace of gold. Large sums of money were distributed among the poor from the royal treasury.

The infant grew up into a good-natured and well-behaved boy. He learned the arts of war and was sent out on military expeditions—in the beginning for training, later on in nominal command and later still in actual command. He gave a creditable account of himself on all occasions, and it could be hoped that in the fulness of time he would grow into a reasonably good military leader. But he was simple-minded, gullible and mentally indolent. He left the management of his estates entirely in the hands of his tutor, Bhaia Ram Singh, a Brahmin convert from Meerut who, having originally joined the Maharaja's bodyguard, had rapidly risen to prominence with the help of his brother, Jamadar Khushal Singh, the Maharaja's *deorhidar* (Lord Chamberlain). Reports of mismanagement and irregularities on the part of Ram Singh soon began to be brought to the Maharaja. He dropped gentle hints to the Prince and asked him to take a little more interest in his private affairs. The Prince was, however, so much in the hands of Ram Singh that all these admonitions were wasted upon him. At last, in 1816, the Maharaja lost his patience and ordered the arrest of Ram Singh on a charge of embezzlement. Ram Singh went on protesting his innocence and his inability to pay the amount he had been held accountable for. The Maharaja sent for Kharak Singh and informed him in open court that he was going to appoint another man, Dewan Radha Ram, in Ram Singh's place. Kharak Singh pleaded for the release and reinstatement of Ram Singh, claiming that he was speaking for his mother. The Maharaja told the Prince to explain the position to his mother and obtain her consent.

On the following day, Maharani Raj Kaur appeared in court and was questioned on the subject. She left the matter to the Maharaja's discretion. Bhaia Ram Singh, however, subsequently made good the missing money and was allowed to resume the management of Kharak Singh's estates on his providing a cash security for the regular payment of the *nazrana* due to the Durbar. The *nazrana* nevertheless fell into arrears more than once and had to be realized by coercive measures. The manner in which it was realized on a particular occasion in respect of Kharak Singh's Sheikhupura jagir illustrates how little ties of blood or other personal factors influenced Ranjit Singh in the matter of realizing Durbar revenues. The occasion was the death of Maharani Raj Kaur. Hardly was her cremation over when Durbar troops went to Sheikhupura and invested Kharak Singh's fort there. Kharak Singh had it conveyed to the Maharaja through his servant, Ilahia, that this action had aggrieved him very much, as he was in mourning for his mother. The Maharaja sent the reply that the action had been taken exactly because the Prince was in mourning and might not, therefore, be able to look after his estate. He, however, added that, if the Prince could furnish a written undertaking to pay 5 lakhs of rupees—presumably the amount due from him—, the Durbar troops would be recalled.

Prince Kharak Singh was utterly lacking in ambition and worldly sense. His real interest lay in praying, reading the Granth and sitting with legs folded and head bowed in the company of holy men. Perhaps he was a throw back to one of his ancestors in the time of the earlier Gurus—that is, before they became soldiers of fortune and adventures. There was a religious strain in Ranjit Singh's character too; but it was kept in check by the more dominant practical strain. In the case of Kharak Singh the practical strain had no stimulus to keep it active and in time became defunct. His lack of spirit and his simple-mindedness were a source of great anxiety to Ranjit Singh, became he knew that his successor would need qualities of another order to cope with the forces that his death would release.

Kharak Singh's simple-mindedness seems to have bordered on imbecility, as would appear from some incidents narrated in the author's family papers in which he figures. Two of these are reproduced below:

One day Ranjit Singh was admonishing Kharak Singh to learn to look after his private affairs so that he could fit himself to succeed him on the throne. To demonstrate how fast that event was approaching, he pointed to his beard and said, "Look at my grey beard, my son". The heir-apparent stepped forward, took the Maharaja's beard in his hand, closely examined it, and exclaimed, "By God, it has gone all grey". This was in private audience; but there were courtiers present. One of them was Fakir Azizuddin, who mentions how horrified he was. As regards the Maharaja himself, Azizuddin says that there came a profoundly sad look into his face. What room was there for royal or paternal anger in dealing with an infantile intelligence of this order?

On another occasion, while Prince Kharak Singh was inspecting the royal stables in the company of Fakir Nuruddin under royal command, a horse passed by. Turning to the keeper of the stable, the Prince asked, "Isn't this the horse that was killed in the battle of Nowshera?" "Yes, Your Highness, it is", promptly replied the quick-witted stable-keeper.

Kharak Singh's succession to the throne remained problematic for a long time, especially because of the Maharaja's dissatisfaction with his management of his estates; but the Bhaia Ram Singh affair proved a blessing in disguise for him. On one of the occasions when the Maharaja questioned the Prince on the subject, he lost his temper with him and told him to get out of his sight. The Prince took this to heart and avoided appearing in court for a long time. The Maharaja's ministers, especially Azizuddin, interceded on the Prince's behalf and advised the Maharaja to do something to make amends for the Prince's loss of face. The Maharaja decided to swallow the bitter pill, do what appeared to be the right thing and leave the consequences to fate. Accordingly, on September 27, 1816, a grand Durbar was held, at which the Maharaja put the saffron mark of succession on Kharak Singh's forehead. Even this did not matter entirely. Speculation remained rife until Ranjit Singh's last moments as to whether Kharak Singh or Sher Singh would succeed him. The stakes were even between the rivals. Kharak Singh was the eldest son, connected through his mother with the Nakkais and through his wife with the Kanhayas of Fatehgarh, and backed by the majority of the sardars and the army as the rightful heir. If he was not admired for his intelligence or ability or even his appearance, he was liked for his simplicity and piety. Sher Singh had a finer appearance, a quicker intelligence and a more impressive bearing. The Dogra group, led by Raja Dhian Singh, the Prime Minister, was supposed to be backing him. His chief disadvantage was that there were doubts about his parentage. Mehtab Kaur, rumour had it, had not given birth either to him or to his alleged twin brother, Tara Singh, but had bought both of them and foisted them upon the Maharaja. Ranjit Singh had acknowledged both the boys; but the general impression was that he had done so only to save appearances. In any case, Sher Singh's connection with the Kanhayas through his real or supposed mother, Mehtab Kaur, was not much of an asset for him owing to the strained relations between Ranjit Singh and Mehtab Kaur's mother, Sada Kaur.

Ranjit Singh's deathbed decision—taken on the advice of Fakir Azizuddin—that Kharak Singh should succeed him with Dhian Singh as his Prime Minister was the best compromise practicable. Kharak Singh was the rightful heir, and he needed Dhian Sigh's guidance and support. In the event, this strange association did not work. The simple-minded Kharak Singh succumbed to court intrigues, allowed himself to be deposed and imprisoned within four months of his accession and was slowly poisoned to death in another year's time. Fakir Azizuddin speaks of these events with profound sorrow and says that, if he could have foreseen them, he would not have given the advice he gave to Ranjit Singh about the succession. But one wonders that other advice he could have honestly given in the circumstances.

6

Administrative Machinery

I

The Legendary Laili

One of Ranjit Singh's ruling passions was his love for horses. He had more than twelve hundred of them in his stables, of which as many as a thousand were reserved for him personally. He took great care of them and used to inspect them almost daily. Riding was his favourite exercise, and he would make time for it even on the busiest day. Two horses were, therefore, always kept close to wherever he might be, saddled, bridled and all ready to be mounted. Not seldom, when anything annoyed or worried him, he would abruptly adjourn court, call for a horse and go for a long ride. This used to be an indication that something big or unusual was in the offing. He sometimes used to say that where he felt surest of himself was in the saddle, and so he often took important decisions on horseback. He did not give up riding till his last illness. After successive paralytic strokes had made it impossible for him to mount a horse unaided, he would have himself lifted into the saddle. Once there, he could look after himself, because he was a born rider.

The vanity he lacked in regard to his own appearance he made up for in regard to the appearance of his horses. They were decked out in the most expensive and gorgeous trappings—bridles and saddles overlaid with gold and studded with precious stones, strings of jewels round the neck, including the Koh-i-Noor itself on special state occasions, and gold bangles round the ankles. The jewels and ornaments of his horses were worth as much as fifty lakhs of rupees. There was hardly a horse among those reserved for him which had been purchased for less than twenty thousand rupees. Most of the horses were of local breeds, but quite a few of them were Persian, for example, Gauharbar, Sufaid Pari and Laili. There was a small number of thoroughbred Arabs too.

The Maharaja was always on the look-out for new additions to his stables and he was always ready to compound cash tribute for horses. In fact, whenever he took any new territory, his first demand was horses, especially if the territory had a well-known breed or if the chief was reputed to have a good stable. It was a standing joke among the courtiers that, if there were enough good horses to compound the total tribute due to the Durbar, the Maharaja would accept the whole lot of them and then tap other sources to raise money or have to sell horses to keep his government going. Nobody could, however, reason with him on this subject; even Azizuddin and Nuruddin do not seem to have dared to do so. He was like a wayward child where horses were concerned.

The things he did to acquire the Persian horse Laili are strange enough to read like a fairy tale. Not content with this, some unsympathetic historians have twisted them and woven them into a weird tale of cruelty and extortion. According to the author's family papers the true facts are as narrated below:—

Sometime in 1822 the Maharaja heard that one of the Barakzai brothers—either Dost Muhammad or Yar Muhammad—had a beautiful Persian horse, named Laili. It was, however, not known whether the horse was at Kabul or at Peshawar. When, in 1823, Fakir Azizuddin visited Peshawar to collect tribute from Yar Muhammad, the presents given to him for the Maharaja included a number of horses; but Laili was not one of them. Azizuddin had been instructed by Ranjit Singh to inquire about Laili and, if possible, to acquire it; but Yar Muhammad pretended that Laili was not in his possession and Azizuddin took him at his word. A year or two later information was received that the horse was actually in Yar Muhammad's possession. The Maharaja offered to buy it, but was told that it was dead. The Maharaja had reliable information that the horse was alive and in Yar Muhammad's possession. Further negotiations were, therefore, discreetly conducted, but with the same result. Ultimately, in 1828, the Maharaja's patience was exhausted and he sent a force under Budh Singh Sandhawalia with the dual object of nipping in the bud new trouble threatened by the tribesmen and acquiring Laili from Yar Muhammad. Budh Singh was killed; but the battle was won by the Durbar troops. However, when Generals Allard and Ventura, who were with Budh Singh, dealt with Yar Muhammad for having secretly helped the tribesmen, Laili was not among the horses that he presented to them for the Maharaja. The Generals demanded Laili, but were told that it was dead. They, therefore, took Yar Muhammad's brother as a hostage. The Maharaja was not satisfied with this and sent a further force to Peshawar under Kharak Singh's command to acquire Laili by whatever means possible—by purchase, by threat, by force or even by the deposition of Yar Muhammad. Before, however, Kharak Singh could reach Peshawar, Yar Muhammad had been defeated and slain in an uprising of the tribesmen and his brother, Sultan Muhammad, had fled.

In 1830, when Sultan Muhammad was installed as Governor by Prince Sher Singh and General Ventura, Laili was again asked for. Sultan Muhammad hemmed and hawed as Yar Muhammad had done, and it was not until Ventura had arrested him in his own palace that he delivered the horse. It was carried off to Lahore as a valuable trophy of war and received there with great joy.

The traveller Baron Charles Hugel quotes Ranjit Singh as having told him that Laili had cost him sixty lakhs of rupees and 12,000 of his soldiers; but a child's evaluation of its doll or a collector's evaluation of a rare object of art he had acquired should never be taken seriously. Besides, all the military operations during which Laili's acquisition was attempted were not intended solely for him. Some historians even doubt if Ranjit Singh actually acquired the Laili he had been after, because Laili is a feminine name in common use, whereas the animal that went under that name in Ranjit Singh's stables was a male. Azizuddin and Nuruddin do not explain this apparent discrepancy, but seem to have no doubt that the horse which Ranjit Singh acquired as the famous Laili of the Barakzai stables, whose name was a legend in the whole of Persia and Afghanistan. Whatever may have been the truth, Ranjit Singh was happy with his acquisition and used to take a special pride in exhibiting it to his foreign visitors. Azizuddin and Nuruddin also speak of it in glowing terms. They describe its colour as dark grey, which also does not agree with the meaning of the word *"Laili"*, that is to say, black. But, here again, they offer no explanation. The identity, the sex and the colour of Laili must, therefore, remain a mystery. As against this triple mystery, the more famous Laili—the legendary beloved of Majnun, the archetypal made lover of Arabic, Persian and Urdu poetry—can claim only a single mystery, namely, the question of her complexion. The general belief is that she was as black as night, as her name suggests. To Majnun, however, she appeared as fair as dawn. Hence the famous Persian proverb, *"Laili should be seen with Majnun's eyes"*. We, for our part, cannot do better than try to visualize Ranjit Singh's Laili as he saw him or her.

II

The Bungalow on Wheels

One of the marvels of Ranjit Singh's palace was a bungalow on wheels with silver walls and a shawl canopy for a roof and furnished with carpets, cushions, curtains and multi-coloured chandeliers. It was pulled by eight elephants and stood so much higher than the ground that one had to use a ladder to ascend it or descend from it. The royal children and their playmates used to go for joyrides in it on festive occasions, and what made this a special treat for them was the fact that, having no springs, it jolted them enough to give them the feeling of riding eight elephant chariots at a time, one for each elephant that pulled it. The Maharaja was often personally present to organize and inaugurate the joyrides, and it was always an amusing spectacle to see the Lion of the Punjab employing all his skills of statesmanship, diplomacy and generalship to deal with this most difficult sample of his subjects, this human material in the making. The children of the Fakir family used to be among the holiday-makers, and the author's family papers contain some first-hand accounts of these royally supervised joyrides and reminiscences of direct encounters with the Maharaja.

Ranjit Singh was very fond of children, especially good-looking and intelligent ones, and delighted in being surrounded by them, playing with them and exchanging little jokes with them, whenever he could find time for this. The royal children even enjoyed the freedom of the private durbar, and it was not an unusual thing for the smaller ones among them to toddle or crawl about or even climb over the Maharaja. Most foreign visitors to his court have mentioned this, either with approval as a mark of his humanity or with disapproval as a sign of lack of order. But since even in his most relaxed moments Ranjit Singh's mind was always, consciously or subconsciously, planning the future of his kingdom, he utilized his contacts with the children of his courtiers and sardars for picking out promising boys from among them. These boys were brought up under his personal supervision, taught to read and write, instructed in riding and in the use of arms and, as they grew up, assigned increasingly important duties. In this way he recruited many young men to serve him, and some of them rose to high positions in the army or in the civil administration. Among these were some children of the Fakir family. The most prominent of them all, however, was Hira Singh, the son of Raja Dhian Singh.

Hira Singh was born in 1818, when his father replaced Jamadar Khushal Singh as Deorhidar, establishing himself in a short time as Prime Minister and, with Fakir Azizuddin, the most important figure in the Durbar. Hira Singh was thus brought up right under the Maharaja's eye. Not only because he was the Prime Minister's son, but also because he was an exceptionally good-looking, bright and winsome child, he engaged the Maharaja's special attention all along. Being an apt pupil, he soon began to excel all other boys in riding, swordsmanship and musketry. Added to this was a certain pertness and quick-wittedness about the boy which particularly pleased the Maharaja. He thus became the Maharaja's special favourite. When he was about 8 or 9 years old, his father began to bring him occasionally to the court. There also he conducted himself in an excellent manner, quietly watching the proceedings but coming out with apt remarks, whenever invited or permitted by the Maharaja to speak. He offered a pleasing contrast to the Maharaja's own sons, Kharak Singh and Sher Singh. Kharak Singh was not only plain-looking and dull-witted, but was also farouche and felt ill at case in the court. He was, therefore, never there except under compulsion. Besides, he was most of the time out in the field or on his own estates. Sher Singh was good looking and manly, but did not distinguish himself by his wit or wisdom. Again, he also was most of the time away from Lahore—either with his grandmother, Sada Kaur, or on some campaign or outer. The Maharaja, therefore, began to like the presence of Hira Singh in his court.

There came a time when Hira Singh began to be given a seat in the Durbar by the Maharaja's side along with the two Princes, Kharak Singh and Sher Singh. Since the Princes were mostly absent, this evolved in practice into his being the sole occupant of a chair by the Maharaja's side. In full Durbar, where the Ministers, Councillors and Sardars used to take their seat in order of rank, Hira Singh's special seat acquired a princely importance. In private audience this led to a situation which has caused so much comment on the part of foreign visitors. Hira Singh used to be seated by the Maharaja's side, while his father, the Prime Minister, stood behind the Maharaja with folded hands. There was nothing in this which need have shocked or surprised anybody. Hira Singh was for Ranjit Singh a trinket, a pet, a flower, an emblem of his childish delight in bright, colourful and lively things. He was also Ranjit Singh's compensation for his disappointment in his own sons. He saw in him what he would have liked Kharak Singh and Sher Singh to be. Perhaps he also saw in him what he would have himself liked to have been when he was his age.

Hira Singh grew up preciously into a strikingly handsome younger with bright eyes, a ready wit and a fine bearing, an excellent horseman, a dashing soldier and a polished courtier—a combination of qualities inherited by him from his father and those imparted to him by the training he had received at Ranjit Singh's hands. In 1828, when he was hardly ten, he was given the title of Raja, with a jagir to live up to it, and the command of several regiments. Ranjit Singh now began to think of finding a bride for him. Anirodh Chand, son of Ranjit Singh's old ally and adversary, Sansar Chand, chief of Kangra, who was now dead, happened to visit Lahore with two of his beautiful sisters. Ranjit Singh sought the hand of one of the girls for Hira Singh. Anirodh Chand, scion of a very old and proud family, looked down upon Hira Singh as an upstart and, therefore, did not welcome this proposal. Giving a noncommittal reply, he left to attend the wedding of the son of Fateh Singh Ahluwalia; but negotiations were re-opened through two Hindu Sardars, and Anirodh sent a written agreement to give the hand of one of the girls. He had, however, not consulted his mother. When she came to know of the proposal, she flew into a rage and, taking her daughters with her, went over to British territory. Anirodh Chand soon joined her there and gave away both his sisters in marriage to the Raja of Tehri-Garhwal. Ranjit then found a bride for Hira Singh in another family of a less proud descent and the marriage was celebrated in 1829 with great pomp befitting the marriage of the Maharaja's adopted son; for that was what Hira Singh had, in fact, become.

In the game of musical chairs that was played for ten years after Ranjit Singh's death, Hira Singh installed himself in the Prime Minister's chair in 1843, only to lose it after a year along with his clever but pampered head, which was cut off by the Khalsa army and hung up over one of the main gates of Lahore. The Fakir children, Hira Singh's playmates in the festal chariot, enjoyed careers of a different order. They kept their heads and carried them on their shoulders into the British period along with their jobs—jobs no less useful, if less imposing, than Hira Singh's. They had sounder hearts to guide their heads. They also had Azizuddin and Nuruddin to prevent them from getting involved in the dangerous game of court intrigues.

III

Pigeons, Blind Women and Tigers

While Ranjit Singh loved pageantry, jewellery, sumptuous clothes (even if on other people's persons), spirited horses and magnificently caparisoned elephants, there was another side to his nature which cared for humbler and gentler things. Children were on the borderline; for, though he was fond of all children, he was partial to good-looking and intelligent ones. In the matter of pets, however, he made no such distinction. His pets were little homely creatures like tame pigeons and domestic fowls. It used to give a mild shock of surprise to his foreign visitors, and perhaps a less mild one to the lordlier people among his Sardars, to be ushered into his presence while he was feeding the palace pigeons and fowls with his own hand. The spectacle of a man covered with a flock of pigeons, flying over his head, perching on his shoulders and pecking at his hand, or a brood of chickens running around him, scurrying about and fighting with each other over the crumbs thrown to them—this spectacle was different from the picture they had in their minds' eye of the great Maharaja. Bahadur Shah, last of the Mughal Emperors, once sent him some fan tail pigeons and performing monkeys. They were received with no less joy than costly presents of jewellery, robes of honour and horses—even horses—used to be received. Some additions were made to their repertoire of skills under the personal supervision of the Maharaja, and performances by them used to be among the entertainments to which special visitors were treated.

It is significant that Ranjit Singh kept no eagles or hawks, which it was fashionable for big men in those days to display on their hands or wrists as a symbol of manliness and power. Even in hunting hares Ranjit Singh's main objective used to be to give an opportunity to his greyhounds to exercise their limbs. The horsemen accompanying the greyhounds had strict orders never to chase and run down a hare. If Azizuddin prayed silently for the safe escape of the hares while they were being chased by the greyhounds, Ranjit Singh did not yield the palm to this gentle mystic in soft-heartedness. Should he happen to hear to fowl scream or a goat bleat piteously when caught for being slaughtered, the Maharaja would at once order its release. The royal cooks, therefore, had to take good care to avoid this.

This responsiveness to cries of distress often led to curious incidents during the royal progress through the streets of the city. It was all right for people to stop the Maharaja by shouting, "Dohai Sarkar", in order to lay genuine complaints before him: this was a routine affair. But sometimes people used to stop him with this cry for all sorts of fanciful things. One of these was to touch his body. Some of the people who wanted to touch him literally believed that his touch had the power of turning base mental to gold. One such person was a blind old woman, who, after she had stopped the Maharaja with the usual cry of distress and been led up to him, lifted a brass cooking pot she was carrying, and before anybody could intervene, rubbed it all over his clothes, besmearing them with soot and grease. She had probably been in her kitchen when the royal procession had approached and had run out with the cooking pot without cleaning it. The royal attendants rushed up to her, pulled her away and tried to snatch the pot from her hand. The Maharaja stopped them and, bending down to the blind woman, said. "Old mother, why did you do this? Do you know you have spoilt my clothes?" "Maharaja," cried the woman, "have my head cut off for spoiling your clothes, but please don't let them take away my cooking pot. It must have turned to gold". "Yes, old mother", said the Maharaja, "it has turned to gold and nobody will take it away from you". Then he had the pot filled with gold coins and ordered that two court messengers should carry it to the old woman's house. It transpired on inquiry that the old woman was a poor widow, who had lost her only son, and who, therefore, deserved at least some of the gold she had been given.

Ranjit Singh's clemency sometimes took strange forms. In the course of hare hunts it happened now and again that a tiger hiding in the jungle was surprised. The Maharaja's orders were that, except in rare circumstances—when, for example, a single man found himself unexpectedly confronted with a tiger—firearms should not be used. Tigers were to be killed only by being surrounded by a number of men armed with spears and lances and swords. The Maharaja used to say that it was cowardly and unfair to shoot a tiger because he had no weapons with which to retaliate from a distance. Those who distinguished themselves in this dangerous sport were recruited by the Maharaja to good posts in the army. One night, the hunters came upon a tiger cub, captured it and put it in a cage, which was placed near the Maharaja's tent. Later in the night the Maharaja heard a continual rustle in the reeds near his tent as if some creature were moving about in them, and this was accompanied by an intermittent sound resembling the moaning of a cat. The Maharaja sent for one of the shikaris and asked him to listen to the sounds. The shikari listened and opined that this was the cub's mother who probably wanted to get to him. The Maharaja ordered the release of the cub. "Even a tigress is a mother," he remarked. The shikari remonstrated and proposed that the tigress should be permitted to come to the cub and should then be captured or killed; but Ranjit Singh silenced him with a look.

IV

Unequal Sweethearts, Equal Wives

If there was one thing in which Ranjit Singh failed to excel or even equal the average monarch of Oriental history, it was the size of his harem. It comprised forty-six women belonging to four categories. In the first category were nine whom he married in the orthodox Sikh manner. The second category also consisted of nine, all of them widows, whom he adopted as his wives by casting his mantle over them, as sanctioned by custom. To the third category belonged seven courtesans. All these categories enjoyed the status of queens. Not so the fourth category, which consisted of concubines.

While it was only human for Ranjit Singh to like some of these women more than the others, he was equally kind and considerate to all of them. Even the haughty Mehtab Kaur, his first wife, who had rejected his approaches as a youthful bridegroom and had gone away to her paternal home, continued to receive from him until her death such affection as she was willing to accept during the occasional visits they paid each other. He could not otherwise have acknowledged Sher Singh and Tara Singh as his sons, irrespective of whether they were actually such or not.

While there must have been mutual jealousies and intrigues among the ladies of the harem—in what house-hold, whether royal or common, do they not exist?—there is no evidence in the author's family papers of any conflict or quarrel which became a public scandal or which openly involved the Maharaja or any of his courtiers and sardars. This was due to the unfailing tact and impartiality of Ranjit Singh. He had his occasional love affairs; but even in the thick of them he never neglected any of his wives. If there was any person who was in a position to know all about what happened in the royal harem, that person was Fakir Nuruddin, who was in charge of all affairs relating to the Maharaja's palces. Due allowance being made for his reticence, it is remarkable that there exists in his papers hardly any account or mention of anything scandalous that happened in the harem. In fact, the author's family papers do not contain much of interest about Ranjit Singh's wives and sweethearts. Whatever little they do is reproduced below.

One day, a personal servant of Prince Sher Singh presented himself to the Maharaja's second wife, Raj Kaur, mother of Prince Kharak Singh, with the message that his master sought permission to pay his filial respects to her, or "to touch her feet" as the custom was. "God preserve my own son, Kharak Singh, and his son, Nau Nihal Singh," said Raj Kaur angrily, "why should I let that son of a washerman touch my feet? Go and tell him that he cannot get himself accepted as the Maharaja's son by tricks of this kind". Fakir Nuruddin was present. On hearing this, he said to Raj Kaur, "Maharani, you should not utter proud words like these. They do not please God". Raj Kaur laughed the matter away. Soon after that she suddenly died, followed shortly by Ranjit Singh himself. Within less than two years, Kharak Singh and Nau Nihal Singh died on the same day.

Kharak Singh was stricken with grief at his mother's death. The Maharaja sent him a number of doshalas and lengths of gold and silver brocade, which were carried by a deputation of the principal sardars and courtiers. The funeral of the Maharani was performed with great ceremony and her body was cremated in her own garden outside Bhati Gate in Lahore. The Maharaja was so shocked by the news of the Maharani's sudden death that he said angrily in court, "So death has struck a blow at the royal family, too". This was the first time that Fakir Nuruddin had heard him utter a blasphemy, and he shuddered to hear it.

Nuruddin speaks with particular regard, approaching admiration, of two daughters of Raja Sansar Chand of Kangra whom Ranjit Singh married after an expedition conducted especially for their sake. The elder one of these was called Mehtab Devi but was better known as Guddan, while the younger one was called Raj Banso. The latter committed suicide by taking opium, and the former burnt herself as a *sati* on Ranjit Singh's funeral pyre. Raj Banso's suicide took place in circumstances which caused Ranjit Singh more than ordinary grief. The Maharaja occasionally used to hold a Durbar of his maharanis. At one of these Durbars, he asked a dancing girl, named Allah Jowai, which of his maharanis she thought to be the most beautiful. Allah Jowai hesitated to reply, because by doing so she would offend all the maharanis but one. The Maharaja, however, insisted on her replying and put her under an oath. Thus cornered, she pointed to Raj Banso and said, "This, Maharani is the moon and the others the stars of your harem". "Perhaps you are right," remarked Ranjit Singh, "but don't you think that Moran Sarkar is just as beautiful as Maharani Raj Banso?" Being bracketed by her husband with an excourtesan so deeply wounded the pride of the blue-blooded Rajput princess that, as soon as she returned to her bedchamber, she took a large dose of opium, lay down in her bed and never woke up again. The Maharaja was stricken with great grief and remorse and performed her cremation with his own hands on a costly pyre of sandalwood. He very rarely held durbars of his maharanis after that.

The next maharani about whom Nuruddin has something interesting to say is Gul Bahar Begum, a courtesan of Lahore. She combined beauty with wit and wisdom, and the Maharaja often profited by her advice on complicated questions. She was fond of exhibiting herself in public and often went out riding on the same elephant with the Maharaja. Having no issue of her own, she adopted a Muslim boy, whose progeny is still living in Lahore. She also built a mosque, which is still extant. After the annexation of the Punjab, the British Government paid her a pension of twelve thousand rupees a year until her death in 1863.

Ranjit Singh's favourite queen, however, was Moran, a dancing girl of Amritsar, with whom he fall violently in love at first sight when he was twenty-two. Before he could win her father's consent to her marrying him, he had to agree to a rather awkward condition. It was customary among the families of courtesans in Amritsar for the bridegroom to build, light and blow ablaze with his own breath a fire in his father-in-law's house. Moran's father, boggling at the idea of marrying his daughter outside his clas, made the observance of this custom a condition, hoping that it would frighten the royal suitor away. Ranjit Singh unhesitatingly accepted the condition. It was, however, actually fulfilled in the house of Moran's godfather, Mian Samdu, a wealthy citizen of Amritsar, instead of in her father's house. The wedding was celebrated with great eclat. The bridegroom's party, which formed a procession of elephants, horses, palkis and people on foot stretching from Lahore Fort to the Shalamar Garden, a distance of several miles, went all the way to Amritsar. The bride was given away by Mian Samdu with a dowry of several lakhs of rupees worth of jewellery, clothes and household effects, as if she had been a princess.

Moran was not only the most beautiful—with Raj Banso and perhaps also Guddan—but also the stateliest of Ranjit Singh's queens. She was the only one in whose name Ranjit Singh struck a coin. The coin bore the figure of a peacock in keeping with the queen's name, which is the plural of the Punjabi word for that bird and which she acquired because of her style of dancing. There is a mosque named after her near the Mati Chowk in Lahore. There is also a village in the district of Amritsar which bears her name. She did not subscribe to the custom of the veil and used to appear unveiled in public along with the Maharaja like Maharani Gul Bahar Begum and unlike the other maharanis, who observed strict purdah.

With a poet's interest in affairs of the heart, Fakir Azizuddin recalls several occasions when Ranjit Singh confessed to him or to other members or his immediate circle how dearly he loved Moran. One such confession, evoked by the sight of Lord William Bentinck helping Lady Bentinck off the boat when they arrived for the Rupar meeting in 1831, is recorded even by Sohan Lal in his Umdat-ut-Tawarikh. "The Maharaja said that at that moment he was reminded of Bibi Moran, for he had exactly the same kind of love and unity with her and could not bear separation from her even for a moment". And yet Moran is not known to have played any prominent part in the politics of the court of Ranjit Singh. Nor is any other woman. It was only after Ranjit Singh's death that the Court of Lahore became a hotbed of feminine intrigue. It is, therefore, difficult to see the justice of opinions like the one expressed in the passage quoted below from Sir Lepel Griffin's "Ranjit Singh":—

> "Like most men who have been distinguished in history for administrative vigour and military genius, Ranjit Singh was very susceptible to feminine influence". Yes, he was susceptible to feminine influence, but as a man and not as a ruler this was one sphere in which he managed to keep these two capacities apart.

7
On the Borderline

On the borderline between Ranjit Singh's harem and his court, between his private and his public life, there was a no man's land, a land of wine and song and dance. It was here that he used to spend his hours of relaxation—an evening once or twice a week with late-night variations when there was a festival or a special state occasion. Some hostile critics have described this as debauchery; but the fact is that there was little of debauchery in the way he used to spend his time in the company of his singing and dancing girls. He loved singing and dancing for their own sake and took a connoisseur's interest in them. The performances, therefore used to be displays of art and not the orgies of dissipation which some people have imagined them to be. The Maharaja would sit apart, sometimes alone and sometimes accompanied by guests—he had no particular boon companions. He would drink his special wine, an extract of raisins with ground pearls mixed in it, watching the performance and occasionally applauding or asking some performer to come up and receive a gift of money at his hands. Being fond of repartee and *badinage,* he would now and again engage in a wordy duel with some particularly vivacious girl; and usually such a one served as cup-bearer. There was, however, never any coarseness or vulgarity in the process. The singing and dancing soirees thus used to be quite sober and dignified affairs. Quite often the Maharaja even conducted state business during the soirees. In fact, people with whom he had something to discuss in private were sometimes invited to them so that he could talk to them quietly.

Some writers have tried to magnify the battles of his Amazons, which used to be waged on special occasions, into bacchanalian revelry; but they were nothing of the kind. For all their excitement, they were mere innocent frolic without any abandon or impropriety. Ranjit Singh seldom let himself go. Even when he did so, he never became a barbarian or a profligate. Illiterate as he was, he had acquired a degree of refinement from his association with persons of culture and learning, such as the Fakir brothers, and was always on his guard against lapses from the royal standards he had been told of. As regards the singing and dancing girls, they mostly came from professional families with generations of training behind them to perform in royal courts and aristocratic assemblies and a rigorous code of etiquette of their own to observe. Those of them who came from other sources were given the necessary training. Western visitors, unfamiliar with the oriental institution of professional singing and dancing girls, seem to have allowed their imagination to be led astray by occasional departures from traditional observances witnessed or heard of by them. In particular, they seem to have lost sight of the occasion: for example, Holi is a festival which is celebrated by all and sundry by a free-for-all of colour splashing, and the use of bows and arrows with heads of balls of coloured powder was merely a refinement.

The royal troupe consisted of a hundred and twenty-five girls chosen for their good looks from all over the Maharaja's domains. They remained members of the troupe generally upto the age of twenty-five, after which they were given to the Maharaja's offices as a favour or a reward for good work. At one time the *prima donna* was a girl known as Bashiran, whom the Maharaja, because of her brown eyes resembling those of a cat, used to call "*Billo,*" the nearest English equivalent of which is "Tabby". She was the

Maharaja's special favourite and had a jagir of eight thousand rupees a year given to her, double the jagirs given to the other girls. She had musical talent of a high order and her *forte* was singing *ghazals* from the Diwan of Hafiz. One day, the Maharaja, in a playful mood, offered to give her jewellery worth fifteen thousand rupees and a further jagir of four thousand rupees a year if she could win the affections of Fakir Nuruddin. "No, thank you, Maharaj," said Billo in a scandalised tone. "Do you want me to be stricken blind for looking with sinful eyes at that holy man?"

Fakir Azizuddin, however, did not prove impervious to Billo's charms. It happened like this. One evening he went to see the Maharaja about an urgent piece of business, while the latter was sitting on a platform overlooking a tank in front of the Samman Burj, listening to Billo's singing. As the Maharaja looked absorbed, the Fakir took a chair by his side and waited for the song to end. Billo was singing one of her best *ghazals* from Hafiz, and she was doing so in her best style. The combination of the spiritual and the aesthetic proved too strong for the supersensitive mystic; who suddenly went into an ecstatic fit and, shouting "Allah-o-Akbar", jumped into the tank. The royal attendants jumped in after him and pulled him out. He, however did not regain consciousness for a long time and did so only after several of the royal physicians had attended to him. Fakir Nuruddin does not seem to have been one of them. From that time on, whenever Fakir Azizuddin was announced while the Maharaja was attending a singing and dancing performance, the Maharaja would clap his hands as a signal for the performers to stop. In particular, he would order the Mirasis (accompanists) out, saying, "Run away, you cuckolds, our Fakir Sahib is coming". The Punjabi word for cuckold, "bharua", is a term of affectionate and familiar abuse employed in speaking to inferiors and does not necessarily have any derogatory moral connotation. Why the poor Mirasis were ordered out has not been explained. Perhaps Fakir Azizuddin, with his highly developed aesthetic sense, did not like the way they have of prompting the singing girls by leading them or joining in their singing in their high-pitched voices. Besides, they are very seldom favoured with pleasing looks. There was, however, one number which Fakir Azizuddin does not seem to have grudged the Mirasis. It was the opening song in Persian, which, freely translated, runs thus:—

"God grant that thy star be always in the ascendant. May fortune always favour thee May the flower of thy prosperity always blossom and may it rankle like a thorn in thine enemies' eyes".

Billo was not only the *prima donna* but also commanded the company of Amazons, which consisted of thirty or forty of the singing and dancing girls, handpicked for beauty of face and figure, playfulness and agility. Their uniform was as follows: a lemon-yellow banarsi turban with a bejewelled crest; a dark green jumper over a blue satin gown, fastened with a gold belt; deep crimson skin-tight pyjamas of *gulbadan* silk; and a pair of pointed golden shoes. As for jewellery, they wore a pair of gold earrings set with stones, a diamond nosestud, a pair of gold bracelets and a ruby ring on the middle finger. Their accoutrement was completed by bows and arrows; but their arrows were less deadly than the glances of their eyes.

Honourable Subjects

There is a curious inner contradiction in the criticisms levelled at Ranjit Singh by hostile critics for his territorial acquisitions. Ranjit Singh had as good a right to found a kingdom for himself by the strength of his arms as any other man before or after him. Now sure of their ground in questioning this right in theory, such critics have, by a devious logic, maligned him for exercising it in practice. They have characterised his levying of tribute on the chiefs and sardars falling within the ambit of his projected kingdom and his annexing of their estates for their failure to pay it as inherently wrong acts—acts which in themselves constituted high-handedness, treachery, avarice and what not. They, however, do not say how else a kingdom can be, or has ever been, founded and maintained. Impartial critics, on the other hand, have acknowledged the fact that in achieving his ambitions Ranjit Singh used the barest minimum of force or craft necessary. Baron Charles Hugel, for example, says: "Never perhaps was so large an empire founded by one man with so little criminality; when we consider the country and the uncivilized people with whom he had to deal, his mild government must be regarded with feelings of astonishment". Similarly Captain Murray says: "It is difficult to suppress admiration in contemplating the career of such a man, who, with so many disadvantages, succeeded, with so few crimes, in elevating himself from a simple sardar to be the sovereign of a large kingdom, including Hindus and Mohammadans, as well as Sikhs, the only state in India not substantially under British dominion".

Even Sir Lepel Griffin, who has compiled a catalogue of what he considers as the Maharaja's wrongful confiscations of the estates of his friends, allies and servants, makes the following concessions to him:—

"With all his rapacity Ranjit Singh was not cruel or blood-thirsty. After the victory or the capture of a fortress he treated the vanquished with leniency and kindness, however stout their resistance might have been, and there were at his Court many chiefs despoiled of their estates but to whom he had given suitable employ, and who accepted their position with the resignation born of Eastern fatalism, which takes the sharpest sting out of defeat. The sardars who had been the leaders of the several confederacies which he overthrew were all in this fashion reduced from equality and rivalship to honourable subjection; and, in addition, there was a large group of Muhammadan Khans and nobles who would have received short shrift from Govind Singh, but whom Ranjit Singh attached to his fortunes, thereby materially strengthening his position in the western districts. The heads of the Mussulman tribes of Sial, Ghebas, Tiwanas and

Kharrals, and the family of Nawab Muzaffar Khan of Multan were included in this group".

Sir Lepel Griffin could have added several other names, as for example, those of Nawab Kutbuddin of Kasur, the Nawab of Bahawalpur, Sardar Sultan Muhammad Khan, several other Barakzais and a number of Saddozai princes.

Sir Henry Lawrence sums up the Maharaja's considerateness in this respect in the following words:—"Members of deposed ruling families may be seen in Delhi and Kabul in a state of penury, but in the Punjab there is not to be seen a single ruling family whose territories may have been conquered by Ranjit Singh, and which may have been left unprovided by him. Not only the Sikh ruling houses, but those of other faiths, too, we provided for by him with equal munificence".

Azizuddin and Muruddin cite many instances of the assessment and realization of tribute, nazrana and other charges in which the Maharaja evinced an anxiety to avoid causing any undue hardship. Except in cases of open defiance or intransigence, it was customary for lengthy negotiations to be conducted with the vakils of the sardars and chiefs until a sum considered fair and reasonable by both the sides was agreed upon. Even after this, time was often allowed for making the payment. Not seldom assessments made and accepted were subsequently reduced. One particular practice in which the Maharaja always considered the needs of the people affected was the realization of the nazrana on the death of sardars and chiefs. It was part of his plan to abolish excessive private wealth so as to augment the resources of the state, on the one hand, and to reduce wasteful private expenditure on the other. Nevertheless, he always saw to it that the widows and children of deceased chiefs and sardars were left with ample resources to live decently. When any estate was taken over for default in the payment of nazrana or even for disobedience, the proprietors and their families were given adequate alternative jagirs. The estates of widows were taken over only in cases where there were no male heirs capable of managing the estates and protecting them against others, and in many such cases the Maharaja cast his mantle over the widows and brought them under his personal protection.

Fakir Azizuddin mentions an interesting case in this connection. Bhai Gurbakhsh Singh was an old and trusted servant of the Maharaja. During his last illness he sent a request to the Maharaja to pay him a visit. When the Maharaja arrived, he found five heaps of money on the floor, consisting of a lakh of rupees each. The Bhai had three sons and a daughter. "Maharaja," said he, "I have made the distribution of my wealth as I am sure you yourself would have made it. Please grant these four heaps to my children with your own blessed hands. The fifth heap belongs to the Khalsa Durbar. Be gracious enough to accept it from my hands". What the Maharaja would have done, left to himself, is not known. However, he accepted the dispensation proposed by the clever Bhai.

Despite his studied effort to be coldly impersonal in the matter of collecting funds for the Durbar, Ranjit Singh sometimes could not help being affected by human considerations. It as to this that the Fakir brothers owed their narrow escape on one occasion from having to pay a hundred and fifty thousand rupees to the Maharaja. It was September, 1814. The Maharaja had just returned from his disastrous expedition to Kashmir, and the finances of the Durbar were in a low state. He asked Fakir Azizuddin if he and his brothers could together provide him with a hundred and fifty thousands rupees. Azizuddin replied with folded hands that, although his whole property and even his life were at the disposal of the Maharaja, all he possessed at the time was sixty thousand rupees. The Maharaja did not pursue the subject any further. Azizuddin mentions that he felt very unhappy at his inability to carry out the Maharaja's behest fully and unhappier still that the Maharaja had not accepted his humble offer of sixty thousand rupees. Although he does not say so—keeping up appearances in such matters was one of the aristocratic virtues of the day—it is open to conjecture that he could not at that time very well afford to part even with the amount he had offered. Ranjit Singh must have inferred this from his tone and manner and dropped the matter out of consideration for a loyal servant.

Showers of Gold

March, 1837, was a gold month for the Punjab: it saw the wedding of the Maharaja's grandson, Prince Nau Nihal Singh, at Amritsar. The Maharaja had told his ministers and sardars that he wanted the wedding to be remembered by all who saw it and talked about by their children and their children's children. Preparations began early in 1837. Invitations were sent to the highest British officers, the Governor-General, the Commander-in-Chief and the Governor of Agra, and to all the principal chiefs and sardars between the Indus and the Sutlej. The Governor-General and the Governor of Agra sent their regrets; but the Commander-in-Chief accepted the invitation. So did most of the chiefs and sardars.

"On Magh 21, 1893 Sambat," reads an account of the wedding (in Persian) in the author's family papers, "Misr Beli Ram, the Bhai Sahibs and Sardar Attar Singh were commanded to go first to Prince Nau Nihal Singh and then to Prince Kharak Singh to take auguries about the date of the marriage. They were also told that they should take whatever they needed for distribution at the augural rites from the storehouse of Misr Lal Singh. Accordingly, Prince Kharak Singh took the augury and, having obtained a quantity of rupees, sovereigns and woollen wrappers from the storehouse, distributed them among the augurs. The Maharaja was informed of this, whereupon he commanded the presence of Prince Nau Nihal Singh. On Magh 29, 1893 Sambat, Captain Wade informed the Maharaja that Sir Henry Fane, the Commander-in-Chief, would come to attend the wedding. Prince Nau Nihal and the Bhai Sahibs paid their respects to the Maharaja in the afternoon and threw five hundred rupees over his head as alms to the poor. The Maharaja then commanded that Bibi Nakkain and Rani Chand Kaur should proceed to Amritsar. A sum of two hundred and fifty rupees was given to the royal ladies and orders were issued to the officials concerned to make arrangements for the entertainment of the Commander-in-Chief at Atari. On Phagan 1, 1893 Sambat, after the usual charities, Prince Kharak Singh was given a horse with a gold saddle, robes of honour, jewellery and cash and commanded to proceed to Amritsar to make arrangements for the wedding. Orders were issued to Laddha Singh and Fakir Imamuddin to arrange for the entertainment of the Prince and for a royal salute of guns. On Phagan 30, 1893 Sambat, the Prince was granted four thousand gold ducats for presentation during the *pashkara* ceremony, and orders were sent out to Sardar Hari Singh Nalwa, Raja Gulab Singh, General Avitabile and Misr Rup Lal to attend the wedding. Accompanying a letter of Dewan Sawan Mal from Multan came a hundred rolls of gold-embroidered bedspreads, a hundred pairs of gold bangles and other articles; also three lakh and eight thousand rupees. The Jamadars of the four clothes stores were awarded one thousand and one hundred rupees each for making liveries. On Phagan 5, 1893 Sambat, Prince Nau Nihal presented himself to the Maharaja. The Maharaja told him that he ought not to believe mischief-mongers and assured him that he would attend his wedding.

On Phagan 6, Fakir Azizuddin presented Captain Wade to the Maharaja. On the following day orders were issued for the posting of foot, horse and artillery to receive the Commander-in-Chief at the bridge. On the same date gold and silver articles were entrusted to Prince Nau Nihal Singh along with sweetmeats. Orders were issued for the daily entertainment of the Commander-in-Chief's camp in accordance with the advice of Bhai Ram Singh and Sham Singh Atariwala. The rations were 300 maunds of fine flour, 205 maunds of gram, 1000 maunds of firewood, 15 seers of butter, 50 seers of ghee, 15 seers of sugar candy, 1515 eggs, 1000 he-goats, an unspecified quantity of curd, and 40 maunds of sweetmeats. Bhai Ram Singh was ordered to proceed to Atari, to take stock of the stores and to purchase 101 head (each of camels, cows, buffaloes and horses. In addition, 150 do-shalas, 25 banarsi dopattas, 50 lachas, 56 large-sized uniforms, 2 gold-threaded doshalas, 2 gold saddles, 2 elephants with gold-encrusted howdahs and numerous gold ornaments were ordered to be kept ready. It was also ordered that 2 gold-enamelled utensils, 2 gold tumblers, 4 gold bowls, 8 gold flasks, 8 sets of silver utensils and an equal number of sets of brass utensils should be procured. In the way of provisions it was ordered that 2 store-rooms should be filled to capacity with flour, 2 with fowls, 2 with molasses and one with firewood and that 1000 cartloads each of fodder and grass, 100 cartloads of charpais and 500 clay vessels should also be provided.

"On Phagan 10, Captain Wade requested that Commandant Chet Singh be ordered to keep boats ready at the Hari Ghat for the crossing of the Commander-in-Chief. The Vakils of Nabha and Patiala were asked whether their chiefs would attend the marriage, and they replied in the affirmative. On Phagan 15, Captain Wade informed the Maharaja in the garden of Chhota Ram of the arrival of the Commander-in-Chief. In answer to a query by the Maharaja, the Captain expressed the opinion that it would be best for the Commander-in-Chief's camp to be near the garden of Jawala Singh on the bank of the Ravi. He also proposed that the military parade should be held in the ground below the fort. On Phagan 19, the Maharaja left Lahore to attend the wedding, entered Amritsar by the Lahore gate and, showering gold and silver coins, proceeded to the Bhangi fort. All sardars presents made their obeisances to him and the wedding rites began.

"Maharani Nakkain flung gold and silver coins over the heads of the Maharaja and Prince Kharak Singh. The Maharaja threw five hundred rupees and a handful of sovereigns into the ceremonial oil. Then he prepared with his own hands the ceremonial mixture of perfumes, oil, flour and ground pears for the bridegroom. The oil and the mixture were applied to the bridegroom, by one of the Bhai ladies. The Maharaja awarded her five hundred rupees for this and, at her request, also granted her a jagir. Sovereigns and rupees were also received from Atari as a good omen, and these were made over to the bridegroom. After watching a dancing performance for some time, the bridegroom left for his residence.

"On the 22nd, Prince Nau Nihal Singh proceeded through the bazar, showering gold and silver coins, and arrived at the Bhangi fort for the marriage ceremony. In the afternoon of the 23rd, the Maharaja, showering gold and silver coins on the way, proceeded to the Bhangi fort. There Raja Ladwa and Raja Suchet Singh presented elephants, horses, clothes and cash to the bride as her dowry and trousseau and also showered money over the heads of Prince Kharak Singh and Prince Nau Nihal Singh. The Maharaja awarded him 1,100 rupees as entertainment money.

"On the 24th a report was received from Kishan Chand to the effect that the Commander-in-Chief had arrived near Amritsar. At that juncture Raja Gulab Singh arrived with five hundred of his best horsemen. Fakir Azizuddin was commanded to arrange for a salute of guns from Gobindgarh fort. Soon thereafter Raja Jaswant Singh Makarwala presented himself with horses and sumptuous dresses and he showered one thousand rupees over the Maharaja's head. After an exchange of courtesies he was dismissed with a present of two thousand and one hundred rupees.

"In the afternoon the Maharaja proceeded to the Shish Mahal, showering money on the way. Pleased with the wedding arrangements in Bhangi fort, he offered thanks to God and then entered the Shish Mahal. On the 25th, the Maharaja sent Prince Kharak Singh to receive Sir Henry Fane, the Commander-in-Chief. On the same day, some trans Sutlej rajas paid their respects to the Maharaja and then took their leave. As there was unexpected delay in the arrival of the Commander-in-Chief, the Maharaja advanced to welcome him personally, accompanied by the whole court. He met the Commander-in-Chief and his party coming on elephants. The English officers stood up on their elephants and saluted the Maharaja, and the Commander-in-Chief transferred himself on to the Maharaja's elephant to travel together with him the rest of the way. The party entered the Shish Mahal with proper pomp and ceremony. A salute of guns was fired. Host and guest showered five thousand rupees over each other's head. The Maharaja pointed to a medal around the Commander-in-Chief's neck and inquired about it. The Commander-in-Chief explained that the medal and his knighthood were both awards from the British Government in appreciation of his services. Then the Maharaja presented nine thousand rupees and a hundred gold ducats to the Commander-in-Chief and ten thousand and five hundred rupees to the English members of his party by way of ziafat (feast money). To these were added two horses, two elephants, viands, sweetmeats, forty ornamental bedsteads, silver utensils and two tents with silver poles, all of which were despatched to the Commander-in-Chief's camp. In the afternoon, Fakir Azizuddin was deputed to escort the Commander-in-Chief to the Bhangi fort for participation in the wedding ceremony. On arrival the Commander-in-Chief showered money over the Maharaja's head. For some time, host and guest were engaged in conversation. Then those present gave the Commander-in-Chief a thunderous ovation for his attendance at the wedding and the *tambol* ceremony began. The Sardars, Ministers, members and relations of the royal family and well-wishers made the following cash presents:-

(There follows a long list of cash payments, ranging from Rs. 40 to Rs. 77,519.)

"After the tambol ceremony, four robes of honour, four horses, two elephants, several jewels and many lengths of expensive cloth were presented by Prince Kharak Singh to the Commander-in-Chief, Captain Wade and Lieutenant Fane. Similarly, Prince Nau Nihal Singh presented twentyone robes of honour to the principal dignitaries.

"In the evening, the Maharaja took his British guests to the Shish Mahal, wherefrom, after a short stay, the Commander-in-Chief returned to his camp, while the Maharaja proceeded to the Durbar Saheb for thanksgiving. In the afternoon the Maharaja went with prince Nau Nihal Singh and troops to Boopa Rai. A severe storm of rain and hail was raging. In the Morning of the 27th, after an inspection of the troops, the Maharaja accompanied the Commander-in-Chief to Atari. At the time of his departure, two thousand and five hundred gold ducats were showered over the elephant of Prince Nau Nihal Singh. A salute of guns was fired when the royal party reached Atari. Sardar Sham Singh Atariwala came on foot to receive the Maharaja. The Maharaja accompanied him to his haveli (mansion), where the Sardar presented fifteen horses and a hundred gold ducats to his royal guest and twenty-five gold ducats each to the Commander-in-Chief and Princes Kharak Singh, Nau Nihal Singh and Sher Singh. From there the Maharaja proceeded to the baradari and the Commander-in-Chief to his camp. In the evening Fakir Azizuddin escorted the Commander-in-Chief to the Shalamar Garden, Where there was a display of fireworks.

"On the 28th, the Maharaja rode around his pavilion and inspected the thousands of people who had assembled there. He ordered a cordon of foot and horse troops to be thrown round the crowd, prohibiting entry or exit without the permission of the troop commander. Then he sent the principal sardars into the crowd with bags of money and with orders to give a rupee to each person. The distribution took 8 hours.

"Thereafter the Maharaja despatched Prince Nau Nihal Singh to Amritsar along with the bride's palanquin. The troops were ordered to march to Mianmir and halt there. The Maharaja then took his guest of honour to the Shalamar

Garden for festivity and entertainment. The Commander-in-Chief was fascinated by the setting and the arrangements. The Maharaja inquired if he had seen another garden like the Shalamar. The Commander-in-Chief replied that he had seen one in Paris on which many lakhs of rupees had been expended. Then the Maharaja asked the Commander-in-Chief if he had witnessed another wedding like that of Prince Nau Nihal Singh. The Commander-in-Chief replied that he had not and added that when the Governor-General received an account of the wedding he would feel sorry that he had not attended it.

"At Kasur, after a feast on Chet 5, the Commander-in-Chief witnessed a parade on the Durbar artillery. On the 6th, the Commander-in-Chief, seated with the Maharaja in a silver bungalow constructed under the personal supervision of Fakir Nuruddin, witnessed a grand review of the army. On the 7th, Prince Nau Nihal Singh arrived at Lahore from Amritsar and was given a salute of guns. In the evening Fakir Azizuddin escorted the Commander-in-Chief to the fort, where there were illuminations, singing and dancing.

"On the 9th, in the afternoon, the British officers and their ladies paid a visit to the Maharaja. The Maharaja took to ladies to see Rani Nakkain, the mother of Prince Kharak Singh, who presented jewellery and cash to them. The Maharaja directed Fakir Nuruddin to have it announced by beat of drum that no suspicious characters should be allowed to enter the city, nor should any person interfere with the personnel of the Commander-in-Chief, on pain of severe punishment. The Commander-in-Chief and Captain Wade called on the Maharaja again on the 10th. On the 12th, the Commander-in-Chief joined the Holi celebrations and said that he had enjoyed them very much. On the same date the Maharaja delivered to Captain Wade a letter addressed by him to the Governor-General, expressing his gratification at the participation of the Commander-in-Chief in the wedding celebrations. On the 15th, under orders from the Maharaja, Prince Nau Nihal Singh presented a guard of honour to the

Commander-in-Chief, who complemented the Maharaja on the discipline and turn-out of the guard and the commanding ability of the Prince. On the 18th, Fakir Azizuddin escorted the British guests into the presence of the Maharaja, who thanked them for their participation in the wedding. The Commander-in-Chief in his reply expressed his gratitude for the excellent hospitality accorded to him. On the advice of Fakir Azizuddin the Maharaja gave his British guests further robes of honour as parting gifts. Prince Sher Singh was deputed to conduct them on their return journey. The Commander-in-Chief left for Ferozepur on the 19th. The Maharaja sent Guru Sadhu Singh to Kartarpur with robes of honour and with instructions that the guests should be entertained on their return journey at every stage and presented with robes of honour.

"On Aswaj 19, 1894 Sambat, the following presents were received from the Governor-General through Munshi Shahamat Ali in connection with Prince Nau Nihal Singh's marriage and produced on the same day before the Maharaja by Fakir Azizuddin:-

(1) a necklace of diamonds and pearls,

(2) a pair of armlets,

(3) a turban ornament,

(4) a pair of bracelets,

(5) a pair of diamond-studded bangles,

(6) 11 other pieces of jewellery,

(7) 105 western-style dresses,

(8) a gold bird-cage,

(9) a horse,

(10) a crystal service set.

"The Maharaja granted 500 rupees to Munshi Shahamat Ali and a similar amount to the present-bearers along with trays of sweetmeats".

This is a bare report of events drawn up by officials too busy running the show to enjoy it, not to speak of describing it. Some of the British guests both enjoyed and described it, and we cannot do better than draw upon their accounts to add a little colour and detail to the official outline. The party that received the British Commander-in-Chief five miles outside Amritsar consisted of 3,000 horsemen, all splendidly attired. The most striking figure in the party was the Prime Minister, Raja Dhian Singh, who was covered with jewels hanging row upon row, about his neck, in his turban, on the belt of his sword and dagger, and over the whole of his dress. Even the saddle and bridle of the Persian horse he rode were embroidered with gold, the saddle cloth being of silver tissue. Prince Sher Singh were a tiara of diamonds, emeralds and rubies. The officers of his suite blazed with jewels and cloth of gold and silver. The heir-apparent, Prince Kharak Singh, who led the advance party, does not seem to have attracted much notice. The Maharaja himself, when he met the Commander-in-Chief half way, was dressed plainly in yellow with a single row of pearls down the breast. His Sardars of State were clad in cloth of gold. While the Commander-in-Chief was travelling together with him on the royal elephant, the Maharaja plied him with innumerable questions about the composition of the British regiments, from the Colonel down to the privates, the English mode of casting artillery and manufacturing other weapons of war, the battles in which Sir Henry had fought and the strength of the East India Company's army. At the tambol ceremony the Maharaja and the bridegroom, whose face was covered with a golden veil, sat under a kind of Christmas tree laden with artificial oranges. The tambol paid in cash amounted to upwards of fifty lakhs of rupees.

The wreath used for the investiture of the bridegroom was of diamonds and pearls strung together with gold thread. The religious part of the ceremony was followed by an all-night performance by the royal troupe of dancing girls, about

80 strong. At that time the Maharaja was in state dress, his breast shone with rows of great pearls and on his arm scintillated the famous Koh-i-Noor.

The money distributed among the sight-seers by putting a cordon of horsemen round them exceeded a million of rupees. The bride's dowry consisted of 101 horses, richly caparisoned with gold and silver trappings, 101 cows, 101 she-buffaloes, 10 camels, 11 elephants, gold and silver ornaments valued at several lakhs of rupees, gold and silver utensils, precious stones, rich silk fabrics and 500 pairs of cashmere shawls. The clothes forming part of the bride's trousseau alone covered an acre. The Shalamar Garden, on the night when it was the scene of festivities, looked like an Arabian Nights fairyland. There were rows of oil lamps on every possible spot where they could be put or hung. Even the branches of the trees had lamps growing on them. A highlight of the Holi festival was a battle fought by the Maharaja's guard of Amazons, between thirty and forty in number and armed with bows and arrows. The ammunition they used consisted of balls filled with powder of various colours, one of which exploded in the nicely combed beard of the Afghan Ambassador, giving his grave diplomatic face a momentary expression of horror at this indignity. He had to pay for this involuntary reaction by having his face, and especially his eyes, bombarded with colour balls. The British Commander-in-Chief had only one eye bombarded. Nobody says what happened to the Maharaja's single eye.

We can best conclude this account by adding to the list of wedding presents one from the chief British guest, Sir Henry Fane, which for obvious reasons escaped inclusion in the official list: it is a passage in Sir Henry's *Five Years in India*". Here it is:-

> 'Ranjit among his subjects has the character generally of a kind and generous master and one of the best princes that have ever reigned in India. As evidence of his being really a good and amiable man may be cited his kindness

to children (two or three of whom he had crawling about the Durbar), and the fact of his never having, since he conquered the country, put a man to death for even the most heinous crime. His exceeding kindness and good nature throughout our entire visit, to all in any way attached to us, makes us believe that such is his real character. At all events it is certain that without the punishment of death this chief yet manages to keep his wild people in perfect subjection".

8
Death of A Lion

W. G. Osborne, Military Secretary to the Earl of Lake, Governor-General of British India. Began his account of the funeral obsequies of Ranjit Singh in a letter to his superior with the following words.

"Ranjit Singh is dead, poor fellow! and died as like the old Lion as he had lived. He preserved his senses to the last, and was (which is unusual with native princes) obeyed to the last by all his chiefs...".

It took a lot to kill the old lion—three strokes of paralysis in four years, several bouts of fever and dysentery, experiments by a whole host of allopathic, homoeopathic, ayurvedic and unani doctors and quacks and, last but not least, his absolute refusal to allow himself any rest.

The realization that his days were numbered came to Ranjit Singh on June 20, 1839, with a fresh attack of fever, after an uneasy respite, and a discharge of blood from the nose. For the first time he voiced the anxiety that had been preying upon his mind for years about the future of his kingdom after his death. It was to Fakir Azizuddin that he did so. Azizuddin, with his usual tact, avoided betraying the thought that the end was not far off. As if implying that the Maharaja needed rest to help his recovery, he suggested the delegation of powers to Kharak Singh, who had already been designated as the successor as early as 1816. He also suggested the formal appointment of Dhian Singh as Prime Minister. The Maharaja was not one to delude himself. He asked Azizuddin point-blank whether it would not be a good idea to make a formal proclamation of succession. Azizuddin agreed that it would be a good idea and proceeded to draft the proclamation. It was read out on the following day at a durbar held after a review of the troops by Kharak Singh and Dhian Singh.

On June 22, the Maharaja became unconscious. The physicians in attendance, including Azizuddin, gave up all hope. Accordingly, in Sohan Lal's words (all the quotations that follow are from his *Umdat-ut-Tawarikh*): "It was decided, as a point of policy, to get ready a bier worth Rs. 10,00,000 for the last day of the Sarkar". It was also decided that "a *sankalp* (ceremonial offering) of 100 horses with gold and silver harnesses and brocade, velvet and embroidered trappings and saddle-cloth and 500 cows be performed". The gatekeepers of the eastern, western and southern gates of the fort and the gate of Hazoori Bagh were ordered to guard the gates carefully and to allow nobody to come in. "As soon as this terrible news became known in the town of Lahore, noise and hue and cry arose from streets and bazars".

But the maharaja, when he regained consciousness, thought all this to be premature. He, therefore, "issued an order for the performing of his *sucheta* and from all sides cries of congratulations arose high. After the performance of the *sucheta* the Sarkar ordered the presentation of the musicians, the bards and the singers and after that inspected the *Chaukis*. After that the Sarkar issued an order to John Holmes, askir him to march .... at midnight and go to Amritsar along with his platoons, 250 horsemen and some cannon and to establish himself firmly at the gates of the fort of Gobindgarh and not to show any kind of confidence in any one of his own (the Maharaja's) relatives and the like. An order was issued to the camp of Raja Hira Singh to establish themselves near the tomb of Anarkali .... the Raja Kalan (Dhian Singh) .... proposed in agreement with the

Sarkar that .... the Sarkar should perform *sankalp* with his own blessed hand of so much property as (it) is reported to be the practice of the kings (to distribute at such a time), adding that all kinds of things and horses were present in the treasury of the Sarkar". Besides Rs. 22,000 in cash, the articles proposed for distribution were: "*lakhna* ornaments and jewellery, including the pearl necklace of Misr Dewan Chand, 11,000 armlets with green stones, ornamental bracelets, 8 gold rings, gold vessels, dishes, cups, jugs, 4 in number, 1 silver pitcher, 1 silver wash-basin, 1 ganga sagar, a silver short-stool, special suits of clothes, 11 *pashmina* badris having only one seam, 51 gold chairs, 1 silver chair, bejewelled and gold swords, one very well-inlaid shield, 1 bejewelled dagger, another of gold, 1 gun with a gold cover, 2 elephants with gold *howdahs*, 2 elephants with silver *howdahs*, 19 horses with silver, gold, plain, bejewelled and gold-threaded saddles, 101 pairs of bejewelled garlands without any string, 11 velvet, banat, plain and other canopies with poles of gold and silver". .... "At night the Raja Kalan (Dhian Singh), Sardar Ajit Singh, Raja Hira Singh, the Bhai Sahibs, Fakirji (Azizuddin) and Misr Ram Kishan remained present...".

On June 23, the Maharaja got up early in the morning and, calling for his special conveyance, went out for a drive. On his return, "he performed a *sankalp* of horses, elephants, 5 gold vessels, cups, jugs, etc., 51,000 rupees and a pair of bangles". Later in the day the royal physicians held a discussion. "Fakir Azizuddin said that everything was in the hands of God .... In the meantime the Sarkar once again became senseless .... At the time of noon, when four hours of the day had passed, the Sarkar woke up and became alert as usual .... After that he took invigorating medicines, like gems, and, placing his head upon the pillow, lay down to take rest ...".

On June 24, "the Sarkar took medicines of gems and in his special conveyance went out to Baradariwala garden and returned. After that he went out to enjoy the sacred sight of a sadhu...". On his return he performed one more *sankalp*.

On June 25, the Maharaja was too weak to go out and became unconscious more than once. Raja Dhian Singh proposed that, as it was too hot in the Shish Mahal, the Maharaja should go down to the ground floor. The idea was that he should be made to lie down on the floor so that he should die in the lap of mother Earth in the traditional Hindu manner. The Maharaja, however, showed displeasure at the suggestion: he was not yet ready to die. The Ministers, therefore, "proposed that from under the compound pieces of wood should be heaped upto the roof so that he might be made to go down at the time of loosening them". By the afternoon, "bodily and mental movements of the Sarkar became suspended" and the pulse became weak and intermittent.

Early in the morning of June 26, "the Sarkar had the honour and pride of enjoying the sacred sight of the Adi Granth and Baba Granth and made a prostration before them". He was administered a new medicine, which revived him a little. Taking advantage of this, he made a further *sankalp* of eight lakhs of rupees, his special conveyance, elephants with gold and silver howdahs and horses with gold and silver trappings. Thereafter, "the Sarkar undid the weapons from his waist and handed them over to the servants with the words that..... the last moment had drawn near". The servants broke down. There were tears in the Maharaja's eyes, too. A little later, "51 cows, 11,000 gold ducats, many swift-footed horses and many suits of clothes were given away in *sankalp*".

Bhai Govind Ram brought up the subject of the Koh-i-Noor. The Maharaja, he recalled, had often remarked that none of the kings who had possessed the diamond before him had taken it away from this world along with himself. He had, therefore, had a mind to entrust the affairs of his kingdom to Kanwar Kharak Singh, make a pilgrimage to the various sacred places and present the Koh-i-Noor personally to the temple of Jagannath. Now that the moment of his departure from the world had come all of a sudden, asked the Bhai, what was his pleasure? the Maharaja made a sign to say that the diamond should be sent over to the temple of Jagannath. Then Bhai Govind Ram mentioned that the Maharaja had already ordered Raja Dhian Singh to do so: the latter had, however, replied that it was for Kanwar Kharak Singh and not for him to carry out the order. The order, Bhai Govind Ram continued, had accordingly been communicated to Kanwar Kharak Singh. The latter, however, had stated that the diamond was with Misr Beli Ram. On hearing this, Jamadar Khushal Singh asked Misr Beli Ram to produce the diamond; but the latter began to put forward excuses and replied that it was in Amritsar.... "The Sarkar produced wrinkles upon his forehead on hearing this discussion. After that, according to a request by Bhai Govind Ram, two armlets with diamonds worth Rs. 2 lakhs, several bejewelled ornaments, 8 top hats of the Persian style, 2 elephants with gold seats and Rs. 5 lakhs in cash were given away in *sankalp*. After that the Sarkar put on all his ornaments and then removed them from every limb of his body and, making a prostration by resting his head upon the earth, gave them away in *sankalp*".

"On the 15th of Har (27th June, 1839 A.D.), a Thursday, within three hours the Sarkar had nine successive motions and the movement of his lips stopped and.... his pulse left altogether its normal course....Fakir Raza (Azizuddin) said, with his eyes full of tears and his heart full of anxiety, that he was a Mussulman and knew that it was the last hour .... With these words he came out and all began to weep and cry .... After that the Sarkar got up again at about noon and felt severe pain developing into his final restlessness and uneasiness ...". A little later, Raja Suchet Singh came to present himself. "The Sarkar opened his eyes once and cast an unconcerned look and closed his eyes again, and the pulse left beating altogether. After that the Sarkar was made to lie straight .... upon the bed, which had been set right with all the requisites of the last day, like *doshalas, tulsi* leaves, gold ducats, linseed and so on and, lighting up a gold lamp, gave it away by way of *sankalp* along with other things. After that they made him sit upon a wooden stool and, washing his blessed hair with Ganges water and curd, dressed him in new clothes .... Bhai Gobind Ram said into the ear of the Sarkar, at the moment he was expiring, the words, 'Ram, Ram,' three times. The Sarkar repeated them twice but at the third time his lips did not open and his life went out of him by way of his eyes .... Emphatic orders were issued for closing up the doors of the fort and Rajaji (Dhian Singh) ordered that a gold and silver bier must be got ready along with other things very soon. This dreadful news became known to the ladies and they began to cry and weep .... and got ready to burn themselves alive. The Raja Kalan went to them to set their grieved hearts at rest and said that the Kanwar (Kharak Singh) would be looking to their needs, considering them as his real mothers as before ...., remarking further that everything other than the Sarkar himself would be available .... to them".

Raja Dhian Singh next went into the octagonal tower to set at rest the minds of Rani Kattochan (Guddan) and the other ranis. Rani Kattochan, daughter of Sansar Chand, used to observe strict purdah. On this occasion she came out of the seraglio "without any hesitation, with her open face, with her bright looks and with her glowing forehead" into the presence of Dhian Singh and said that "assurances were necessary for those who had to live after the death of the sarkar and added that she was going to accompany the stirrup of the Sarkar" into the other world. The other ranis gave him a similar reply.

The Maharaja's body lay in state on the floor during the night. "All those who were present remained weeping and crying all night, while the Brahmins kept on reading the Gita and the Bishan Shahasaranam and the Bhais remained busy in reciting the Granth Sahib".

On June 28, "Kanwarji (Kharak Singh) took his bath and put on clothes like *dhoti, uparna* and so on and making the

Sarkar sit on a wooden stool, bathed him in the water of the Ganges and made him put on a turban and a suit of clothes perfumed with saffron, and decorated the body of the Sarkar with ornaments, such as a bejewelled plume, a bejewelled turban gem, a bejewelled hand-chain, a pearl necklace, a bejewelled armlet and a diamond ring. After that he made the Sarkar lie down on the bier with one pillow under his head and another under his cheek and, sending for a doshala from the clothes store, spread it over him. After that all the chieftains and near attendants presented doshalas".

At this stage "the news came that the ladies had made a *sankalp* of all their estates, ornaments and other belongings and, handing over the receipts of the revenue tax of the spring crop to the *kardars*, had presented themselves near the gate, fully decorated and adorned. Kanwarji (Kharak Singh) ran to the door .... to receive them and threw himself at their feet. The ladies uttered prayers for him and put their hands upon his back and patted him". Then the ladies left their special conveyance and entered "with glowing foreheads, bright looks, resplendent cheeks, laughing and dancing ...., looking like figures of the spiritual world, and approached the Sarkar".

When Raja Dhian Singh had gone into the octagonal tower on the previous evening to give assurances to the ranis, one of them, namely, Hardevi, had tauntingly reminded him of a previous statement of his that "he would always remain with the stirrup of the Sarkar". Dhian Singh had kept quiet; but he now appeared in fine clothes and covered with ornaments and "declared that he had a mind to join the stirrup of the Sarkar". Kharak Singh and others threw down their turbans at his feet, saying that the kingdom could not go on without him. A heated debate followed as to whether the scriptures required or permitted ministers to burn themselves with their kings. The question was at last resolved by the intervention of Rani Kattochan, who in a tone of authority commanded Dhian Singh to agree that he would remain in the service of the new king for a year, after which he would be free to retire and go away to the sacred places. This was agreed upon by all concerned and reduced to writing. The funeral procession then left the fort. "The Sarkar was lifted up on a glorious bier and weeping and crying .... arose from all sides.... All the surviving ladies, including Gul Begum, wept very bitterly and fell senseless on the ground". The four ranis who had resolved upon burning themselves on the Maharaja's pyre, followed his bier on foot, dressed in their bridal costumes and jewellery. The streets of the city were lined with people, row upon row. As the cortege passed, people cried and prayed aloud, Muslims, Hindus, Sikhs, all in their own way. The ranis kept taking off their jewels and throwing them to the poor.

The bier was taken to the garden near the gate at the foot of the Badshahi mosque and the Maharaja's body, after being given a bath, was laid on a pile of sandalwood. Prayers were offered for about an hour by members of all communities in their respective ways. Then the four queens, led by Rani Kattochan, walked up to the pyre. Rani Kattochan seated herself in the middle of the pyre with the Maharaja's head in her lap. The other three ranis seated themselves round her, with seven maidservants forming an outer circle. Before the pyre was lit, Rani Kattochan asked Kharak Singh and Dhian Singh to go up to her and, placing Dhian Singh's hand on the Maharaja's chest, made him swear aloud that he would befriend and support Kharak Singh. Thereafter she made Kharak Singh swear in a similar way that he would never go against Dhian Singh. Kharak Singh then set the pyre alight. There was a gentle shower after some time. A pair of pigeons came out of the sky and fell into the flames.

EPILOGUE

A Wreath of Choice Tributes

Sir Alexander Burnes

"I never quitted the presence of a native of India with such impressions as I left this man. Without education and without a guide he conducts all the affairs of his kingdom with surprising energy and vigour, and yet wields his power with a consideration quite unprecedented in an Indian prince".— Travels into Bukhara, etc., 1834.

Captain J. D. Cunningham

"Ranjit Singh found the Punjab a waning confederacy, a prey to the factions of its chiefs, pressed by the Afghans and the Mahrattas and ready to submit to English supremacy. He consolidated the numerous petty states into a kingdom, he wrested from Kabul the fairest of its provinces, and he gave the potent English no cause for interference".— History of the Sikhs, 1849.

Alex Gardner

"The Maharaja was indeed one of those master-minds which only require opportunity to change the face of the globe".— Memoirs of Alex Gardner, 1898.

General John Gordon

"He managed better than others more learned to transact the current duties of his State by means of his retentive memory, quickness of mind, and keen observation... . His court was brilliant with oriental pageantry, but personally he was free from pomp and show, and so scrupulously simple in his dress among his gorgeously clad Sardars as to be distinguished among the distinguished".— The Sikhs, 1904.

Victor Jacquemont

"His conversation is like a nightmare. He is almost the first inquisitive Indian I have seen......The most skilful of our diplomats is a complete simpleton (in comparison with him)". Letters from India, 1834.

Sayed Muhammad Latif

"He entertained great respect for learning and learned men. His Secretaries were in perpetual attendance on him and he had the papers read out to him in Persian, Punjabi or Hindi, and he saw that his orders were drawn up in due form and that the drafts met his views... . His appearance was prepossessing, his manner and address were delightful, and his features were full of animation and expression. His remaining eye was large, quick and searching, and its fire and brilliancy displayed at once the great acuteness and energy of mind of its owner".— History of the Punjab, 1891.

John C. Marshman

"He possessed the same grand creative genius as Sevajee and Hyder Ali".— History of India, 1874.

W. L. M'Gregor

"...... it is evident that he is no common character, but possessed of powers of mind rarely met with, either in the eastern or western world".— The History of the Sikhs, 1846.

Captain Murray

"Ranjit Singh has been likened to Mehemet Ali and to Napoleon...... There are some points in which he resembles both; but estimating his character with reference to his circumstances and position, he is perhaps a more remarkable man than either....... There was no ferocity in his disposition and he never punished a criminal with death even under circumstances of aggravated offence. Humanity indeed, or rather a tenderness for life, was a trait in the character of Ranjit Singh. There is no instance of his having wantonly imbued his hands in blood".— History of the Punjab, 1846.

Captain Leopold Von Orlich

"In battle, he was always seen at the head of his troops and foremost in combat.......... In energy of will and endurance he was unequalled by any of his people. The want of education was covered by the splendid mental powers with which nature had endowed him, and prudence are knowledge of mankind enabled him to maintain himself in his high position. By means of excessive liberality he attached faithful servants and brave warriors to himself".— Travels in India, 1845.

W. G. Osborne

"He was one of that order of minds which seem destined by nature to win their way to distinction and achieve greatness.......... He rules with a rod of iron, it is trúe, but in justice to him it must be stated that, except in actual open warfare, he has never been known to take life, and his reign will be found freer from any striking acts of cruelty and oppression than those of many more civilized monarchs".— The Court and Camp of Ranjit Singh, 1840.

Lt. Col. Steinbach

"The treasures (of Ranjit Singh) may be estimated to have amounted at his decease to about eight crores of rupees in cash, or the same number of millions of pounds sterling with jewels, shawls, horses, elephants, etc., and several millions more............ it is doubtful if any court in Europe possesses such valuable jewels as the court of Lahore".— The Punjab, 1846.

9
The Annexation: End of an Era

The idea of annexing the Punjab was none of Lord Dalhousie's invention; it had been in existence long before he became the Governor-General of India. As a matter of fact, every Englishman of political leanings in India as well as in England since the late disastrous British adventure in Afghanistan, if not since England became alive to the Russian danger looming large to the north-west of India consequent upon the Russo-persian Treaty of Tarkomanchai (1828), had overtly or covertly cherished this idea, to wit: Sir Henry Fane's (Commander-in-Chief of the East India Company's army secret appraisal of the military resources of the Kingdom of Lahore in 1837, Lord Auckland's suggestion in 1841 of making Raja Dhian Singh "independent cf his master",[1] Clerk's (British Agent at Ludhiana) intrigues and formulation of a plan intervention at a time when the Punjab was rocked by a large scale mutiny in the army, Lord Ellenborough's massive military demonstration at Ferozepur to keep the Sikhs in awe and his subsequent war-like preparations against them, Major Broadfoot's (British Agent at Ludhiana) deliberate provocations and machinations and Lord Hardinge's war with the Punjab state in 1845. All these were secretly inspired by the keen desire to have this border state included within the confines of the British Empire in India. Sir F. Currie's significant remark[2] that "if it (Punjab) cannot be Sikh, it must, I suppose, be British" represented no idiosyncracy of an individual but a belief commonly held among the British statesmen of the time. The independence of the Punjab was considered by them as a big stumbling block in the way of their advance to the natural frontiers of India on the north-west—a feeling which had been enhanced in intensity by the annexation of Sind in 1843 having pushed the Sind frontier far ahead of the Punjab frontier in the north. To keep an effective watch over the strategic land of Afghanistan, proximity to that country was a great desideratum. That explains the very keen anxiety of Lords Ellenborough and Hardinge and others placed below or above them to push into the Punjab as early as possible. No means, fair or foul, if otherwise feasible, were spared to bring about conditions of chaos and lawlessness there which would give them the necessary opportunity for interference. If after the First Anglo-Sikh War (1845-46), the extreme step of annexation was not taken, it was for no lack of desire to do so, but was due to certain practical difficulties such as the indecisive character of the Sikh defeat, the strength of the unvanquished Khalsa army, the large number of forts that must be reduced if the state was to be annexed, the heavy losses suffered by the British in the war and the resultant exhaustion of their resources. It was not the will that was lacking; only the will gave way to expediency dictated by the realities of the situation. That this was so, will be clear from the following extract which occurs in a private letter of Lord Hardinge to Sir F. Currie, dated 16 December, 1846.[3]

"Personally, I may regret that it has not been my fate to plant the British standard on the banks of the Indus. I have taken the less ambitious course, and I am consoled by the reflection that I have acted right for the interests of England and of India".

These words were written on the occasion of the signing of the Treaty of Bhairowal. They were much more valid a year earlier, when the Treaty of Lahore was signed in March, 1846. The Treaty of Bhairowal gave to the Government of India as represented at Lahore by its Resident, "full power to direct and control all matters in every department of the state" during the period of Maharaja Dalip Singh's minority, and yet the Governor-General was sorry that he had not been able to fulfil his desire of annexation. The same may be said of the Home Authorities. The Treaty of Bhairowal like its predecessors was unanimously approved by the Court of Directors, the Board of Control and the Cabinet, and yet it is a fact that Sir John Hobhouse, the President of the Board of Control, was, in the words of Lord Hardinge,[4] "for annexation direct and immediate".

Therefore, when Lord Dalhousie arrived in India in January 1848, the issue of annexation of the Punjab had under discussion for several years. He was not responsible for the origin in the same way as he was not accountable for the general line of the official policy of "abandoning no just and honourable accession of territory or revenue", first enunciated in 1841[5], though he has often been charged with that. The fact is that a tremendous change had occurred in the thinking of the East India Company on the subject of relations with the Indian States since its political ascendency was firmly established in 1818. Since 1835, it had begun to claim, as the paramount power succeeding the Mughals, all the prerogatives which the Mughal Emperors used to exercise in regard to their vassal states. Besides, the deteriorating state of administration in the subsidiary states, despite repeated warnings from the Company's Government, had caused the principle of annexation to be accepted as the legitimate solution of these areas of misrule as well as an essential part of the policy of consolidation which was the avowed object of the Company during this period.[6] The spirit of the times will be found reflected in Sir Charles Napier's boast, "Were I emperor of India for twelve years.........no Indian prince should exist. The Nizam should be no more heard of. Nepal would be ours".[7] Col. Sleeman rightly lamented: "Few old officers of experience, with my feelings and opinions on the subject, now remain in India and the influence of a school characterised by impatience at the existence of any native state, and its strong and often insane advocacy of their absorption—by honest means, if possible—but still their absorption, is too great over the rising generation.....".[8] It was in these circumstances that Dalhousie arrived in India.

When a member of the Imperial Government in England, Dalhousie had "approved of the policy"[9] observed by his predecessor Lord Hardinge in abstaining from a more effective occupation of the Punjab. But his views underwent a radical change, when two Englishmen, Agnew and Anderson, were murdered at Multan followed by the desertion of their entire Sikh escort to the side of Dewan Mool Raj, the ex-Governor of Multan and when the Lahore Darbar frankly confessed that they were unable to trust any part of their own army to crush the revolt and hand over the criminals to the British. He was essentially a man of imperious disposition who could tolerate no opposition or resistance either to his own will or the writ of the mighty power he proudly represented. His reaction, therefore, to the happenings in the Punjab was quick and sharp. "When the period shall have passed during which military operations are impracticable", wrote he to Sir F. Currie on 15th May, 1848, "I shall consider it my duty to put forth, if necessary, the whole power that the Government of India can command for the purpose of inflicting signal and severe punishment on those guilty of this outrage and of exacting from the state of Lahore that national reparation which it is my firm determination to obtain for the national injury done to the Government of the Hon'ble Company".[10] Thirteen days later, he expressed himself even more forcefully: "Here has been a deed committed in Multan with which all India and all England will ring, the rebel Governor applauding and rewarding the deed, thereafter actively engaging in open and formidable revolt and the state of Lahore confessing itself incapable to give us justice on the murders, still less to put down the rebellion or afford reparation for public injury".[11]

It will be observed from above that Dalhousie, from the very start, held the Lahore Darbar for a heavy reparation for its failure to act against the rebels on its own, characterising it as "a grave question to be settled between the British Government and the State of Lahore.[12] It seems to be an extraordinary inference in view of the fact that the Regency Council which represented the Lahore Darbar had hardly any power to act independently of the British Resident. The Resident had been at the head of the Government of Lahore ever since the Treaty of Bhairowal, signed on 16th Dec., 1846; the Councillors of Regency were merely "executive officers".[13] to do as they were bid," under his control and guidance". The Resident's "power" was unlimited in military affairs". He could "withdraw Sikh garrisons, replacing them by British Troops, in any and every part of the Punjab".[14] And when the military emergency arose, he pursued his own course, ordering the troops backwards and forwards, occasionally consulting the Darbar or informing them of his determinations, but never allowing them to adopt their own plans for restoring the peace of the country. The Resident was, in fact as well as in law, the Government of Lahore. When the news arrived of the outbreak at Multan, he transferred none of his authority to the Councillors; he gave all the orders himself. Hence Lord Dalhousie's attempt to separate the Resident from the Government of Lahore and to decide to penalise the latter for an outrage which was committed by a rebel Governor, was unwarrantable and pregnant with sinister possibilities which gradually unfolded themselves in the months to come.

In making the distinction between the Lahore Darbar and the Resident, Lord Dalhousie seems to be motivated by the anxiety to lift the issue above the level of a mere problem of internal law and order, and to give it the appearance of an inter-state question to be decided in accordance with international law, as applicable to independent states, forgetting or deliberately ignoring the fact that one of the states concerned here was subordinate in every sense of the term, internally as well as externally. It is "in pursuance of the commonest right of nations that he demands "delivery and punishment of the criminals",[15] from the Lahore Darbar, and when the latter regret their inability, not from any motives of hostility to the British, but from the peculiarity of the circumstances, the Governor-General makes it a charge against them and demands reparation.

Consistently with the approach of treating the issue on the plane of international law, the Governor-General declared as early as July, 1848 that "We shall have a perfect right to do so (annex the Punjab), if the British army shall be called upon to take the field against Mooltan". "The result, therefore, of my consideration of this portion of the subject is", he informed F. Currie, "that if the British should be required to take the field against Dewan Mool Raj, our right to do what we please with the Punjab will be beyond cavil or dispute".[16] In his above reference to the British army, he also included the nine thousand strong British contingent kept at Lahore at the expense of the Lahore Darbar, which, in the words of the Treaty of December 1846, was specifically intended "for the protection of the maharaja and the preservation of the peace of the county" and when later on Major General Whish, an officer from this contingent, proceeded against Multan and started shelling it, Dalhousie declared the fact to be "conclusive". "The Treaty, my dear Sir, is in fragments, a *casus belli* has arisen, if ever one arose between two nations before.....", Wrote he to Currie on September 4, 1848.[17]

With the kind of approach indicated above, Lord Dalhousie found it impossible to agree to the idea of making the Punjab a strong buffer state. As early as June, 1848, and that is long before the revolt of Dewan Mool Raj had developed into a widespread general rising, he communicated to Sir F. Currie that "Whatever the issue of this immediate outbreak may be, it must, I fear, be regarded as going far to prove the impracticability of our being able to ensure the construction of a firm and self-sustaining government to rule the Punjab".[18] He went on the examine the reasons of his holding this opinion, "The account you give of the materials out of which it is to be formed, as they have been exhibited by the test these events have applied to them, is very discouraging and Mr. John Lawrence's estimate of the chiefs and leaders is not a whit more favourable than yours". And then: "The debt due by the state of Lahore is very large, notwithstanding the windfall found in the Tosha Khana. There seems a very faint probability of the 22 lacs being annually made good". He ends the argument on an emphatic note of injured innocence. "Are we to go on being generous and magnanimous, maintaining for other six years a government which can neither punish its criminals, control its army, pay its army, pay its annual contribution or discharge the principal of its debt? Especially are we to maintain it for six years at this sacrifice, when we can hardly doubt that at the end of these six years, the chiefs will be as impotent under a boy sovereign of 15 as they are now, the army as insubordinate, and consequently the frontiers of our territory as unsafe and the neighbourhood as turbulent as they were likely to be in December, 1846". Writing privately to the Resident at Lahore on 13th July 1848, he finally rejected the idea of the buffer state.[19] "I thought and I think still that the firm establishment of a Hindu Government between the British frontier on the Sutlej and the Khyber is the most advantageous circumstance that could be desired for British India. I am desirous of fully and fairly carrying Lord Hardinge's policy into effect, honestly and candidly, if it can be done". But he says in the same breath that it is an impossibility and in support of this he repeats all the old arguments of the poor material of the chiefs of the Darbar, the hostility of the army, and the financial insolvency of the Lahore state, concluding therefrom that... "the experiment which has endured for now two years, has proved a failure...".[20] The reference here is to the experiment of the British-Protected government at work since March 1846, more particularly since December 16,1846, when the Treaty of Bhairowal inaugurated the constitutional arrangement that was in existence at the time of the Multan revolt. But one may reasonably ask: Who was responsible for the failure of this experiment ? The Sikhs or the British ? And further, was the experiment really meant to be successful ? One only wishes that the Governor-General should have taken the trouble of honestly going into the causes of this failure, before pronouncing his final verdict on the matter, for to an impartial investigator the boot may appear to be more on the British leg than on the Sikh.

When Sir Henry Lawrence returned from furlough and resumed the duties of the Resident at Lahore from Sir F. Currie on February 1, 1849, he made a last-minute though a half-hearted effort to change the determination of Lord Dalhousie in favour of establishing a buffer state in the Punjab. Sir Henry was unhappy with the way the Government of India had handled the Punjab affairs since 1847, that is, during his period of leave.[21] But the Governor-General had by now finally made up his mind for annexation, as he informed F. Currie to this effect on December 19, 1848: "My resolution has been formed after long, anxious and conscientious consideration; and neither Sir H.L. nor any body else can shake it".[22] The formation of the Sikh-Afghan alliance against the British about this time had introduced a convenient new factor into the situation, which had further weighted the scales against Henry's views. Lord Dalhousie's argument now ran: "The materials for it do not exist; and even if they were to be found, it has now become evident that the object for which the establishment of a strong Sikh Government was desired by us would not thereby be accomplished".[23] He saw no utility of the Punjab state, "if the Sikhs made up their differences with the Afghans and would collaborate rather than fight with them". Therefore, even before the last cannon was fired at Gujarat, he informed Sir Henry that he intended "the utter destruction of the Sikh power, the subversion of its dynasty and the subjection of its people".[24] Sir Henry on the other hand did not regard the annexation of the Punjab as inevitable. He was inclined to the view that the policy of protecting and preserving the Sikh kingdom till the majority of Maharaja Dalip Singh, to which the British Government was pledged by the Treaty of December, 1946, had not been honestly pursued.[25] He held that nothing occurred in 1848 that was not contemplated and expressly provided for in the Treaty of Bhairowal. The insubordination of the Khalsa army was known to the British. It was precisely to curb it that the Sikh Government had invited the British power to manage their affairs till their Maharaja came of age. The British as the guardians of the Maharaja and enjoying unlimited powers under the treaty were legally bound to suppress all internal tumults and maintain peace and tranquillity in the realm. In broad terms, Sir Henry believed (may be intellectually only) with his colleagues Col. Sleeman and Major Outram that any policy of indiscriminate annexation of Indian states was wrong in principle as well as in expediency in so far as it tended to destroy break-waters against the forces of anarchy and portended ill for the security of the British Empire—a view that was not adequately appreciated until its vindication by the rising of 1857. Hence conscientiously, Sir Henry did not hesitate to tell the Governor-General in unequivocal terms: "My own opinion, as more than once expressed in writing to your Lordship, is against annexation. I did think it unjust; I now think it impolitic. It is quite possible I may be prejudiced and blinded, but I have thought over the subject long and carefully".[26] But regarding it as a lost cause or lest his own career should be marred, he not only tamely yielded to the masterful will of his master but also offered him "the assurance that "so long as I am your agent, you will find me act with faithfulness and without reserve".[27]

Sir F. Currie who was the Resident at Lahore from March 1848 to January, 1849, was more pliable than Henry Lawrence, so that Lord Dalhousie expressed a sense of personal obligation to him for the "readiness" with which he had entered into his views.[28] But even he, till the close of June at least, was not positively thinking on the lines of annexation, though the idea was not wholly unfamiliar to him. For reasons of expediency he recommended the assumption by the British of direct administration of affairs, leaving titular sovereignty to the Maharaja Dalip Singh on the analogy of William Bentinck's action in Mysore in 1831. The idea was immediately rejected by the Governor-General who replied to him in these words: "For my part, I do not see how it is practicable for us to assume more directly the administration of affairs than we do, except in one way—by subverting the state and declaring the Punjab to be a British province".[29] Now, there is hardly anything impracticable about this suggestion. If it was possible in Mysore, why was it not so in the Punjab? One serious flaw of the existing administrative structure was its dual character arising from the association of Englishmen with local governors in all provinces except Multan. F. Currie's proposal was aimed at the streamlining of the administration by the removal of this defect. But Lord Dalhousie having, according to Ramsay Muir, a ferocious logicality of mind, had no love for such half-measures or compromise solutions. Therefore, the defect lay not so much in the scheme suggested by Currie as in the approach the Governor-General brought to bear upon the problem. When his suggestion was rejected, Curie did not even demur, but on the contrary, like an obedient civil servant or because he himself had no genuine faith in the suggestion, he whole-heartedly fell in line with the views of his master.

On the basis of what has been said above regarding his anxiety to treat the issue of the Multan revolt on the plane of international law, regardless of the subordinate status of the Lahore Darbar under the terms of the Treaty of December 1846 and his categorical rejection of the ideas of a buffer state and direct administration by the British, it may be reasonable to presume that almost from the very beginning of the disturbance at Multan, Lord Dalhousie had a strong inclination to annex the Punjab. Even if the rebellion of Sher Singh had not come to pass, there is a strong probability, almost a certainty, that he would have made the annexation all the same. We have already seen that as soon as Major-General Whish began to bombard the fort of Multan,

Dalhousie declared that their right to do what they pleased with Punjab was established beyond any doubt. Nevertheless, the spread of disturbances greatly facilitated the execution of his plans. He was not responsible for the origin of the policy of postponing operations till the next winter for that was initiated by Lord Gough, the Commander-in-Chief on military grounds, but there is no doubt that he saw at least after some time, great advantage in delayed action, and secretly wished the disturbance to spread. "The rebellion of Raja Sher Singh followed by his army, the rebellion of S. Chuttur Singh with the Darbar army under his command, the state of the troops and of the Sikh population everywhere", he informed the Resident on 8th October 1848, "have brought matters to that crisis I have been for months looking for".[30] And he wasted no time in declaring that they were "now not on the eve of, but in the midst of war with Sikh nation and the kingdom of the Punjab".[31] The fact is that although he had practically made up his mind by June or July when he discussed with the Resident the question of annexation in detail, he was in need of providing a greater justification for his projected action than the one furnished by the localised revolt of Dewan Mul Raj and the inability of the Lahore Darbar to deal with it. It was with this object in view that he jumped at F. Currie's information that there were signs of a widespread conspiracy against the British in the Punjab, and without waiting for the verification of the same, forthwith sent the Resident's letter home.[32] His reaction may be summed up in his own words: "That despatch is important, and if fully followed up, decides the question".[33] Again, he felt greatly dismayed at the prospect of the Multan trouble fizzling out by itself. He remarked that if it actually happened, their policy "would be greatly more doubtful and perplexing". "The punishment of the criminal would be secured either way, not so the reparation we have declared our intention of exacting",[34] he lamented. Therefore, when on 14th September, Raja Sher Singh rose in rebellion in sympathy with his much harassed father, Chatar Singh, the Governor of Hazara, the Governor-General was most happy.

Having got, what he had all along desired, an excuse for the invasion of the Punjab he thundered: "The result of this made movement to the people and dynasty of the Sikhs can be no longer a matter of discussion or of doubt"[35], or "The Sikhs have forced me, for this government, again to draw the sword, and I beg you to interpret my words in their clearest and most emphatic meaning when I say that being compelled to it, I have drawn the sword and have thrown away the scabbard, both in relation to the war immediately before us, and to the stern policy which that war must precede and establish". Elsewhere at a Barrackpore ball given on the eve of his departure for the Punjab frontier in September, 1848, he had exclaimed, "unwarned by precedent, uninfluenced by example, the Sikh nation has called for war and on my word, Sirs, they shall have it with a vengeance".[36] Here is an all too obvious attempt on the part of the Governor-General to give to the ensuing Punjab operations the name of war, so that later on he might on this score run away with annexation as a trophy of conquest. Of course, he was assisted in this by the declared anti-British aims of the insurrectionists. The attempt, however, immediately landed the Resident at Lahore in an anomalous position and he wrote to the Governor-General: "Now if that be the case, I with my assistants am in an anomalous position, as superintending and aiding the administration of the Lahore state... ".[37] Lord Dalhousie had to recognise the force of this argument and to agree that no formal declaration of war should be made. Rather, in order to allay people's genuine fears, a Proclamation was issued on 18th November, 1848 by the Resident with the approval of the Governor-General saying that the British army "has entered the Lahore territories not as an enemy to the constituted Government, but to restore order and obedience".[38] Raja Sher Singh and his father were declared rebels against the Maharaja's government.

We have seen above at some length the circumstances in which the policy of the so-called middle course or moderation was ruled out, and the decision finalised to annex the Punjab to the British dominion. The question now arises:

What were the factors which weighed with Lord Dalhousie in arriving at the conclusion that he adopted? Among the influences working on his mind, the foremost place is occupied by considerations of security.

The basis of his arguments was the violation of treaties by the Lahore Darbar. "If the grossest violation of treaties—if the repeated aggression, by which its national security is threatened, and the interests of its people are sacrificed—can ever confer upon a nation the right of bringing into necessary subjection the power that has so injured it and is ready to injure it again", he reported to the Court of Directors, "then has the British Government now acquired an absolute and undoubted right to dispose, as it will, of the Punjab, which it has conquered".[39] In the same report he claimed that whereas "The British Government has rigidly observed the obligations which the treaty imposed", and "has fully acted up to the spirit and letter of its contract", "there is not one of the main provisions of the agreement which they (the Sikhs) have not either entirely evaded or grossly violated". The Proclamation of March 29, 1849 listing the charges against the Lahore Darbar put at the top the charge of breach of faith, which, after mentioning the British faithfulness and the Sikh faithlessness, made reference to the further delinquency that "of their annual tribute no portion whatever has at any time been paid and large loans advanced to them by the Government of India have never been repaid".[40]

The first charge has been challenged by a number of writers, such as John Sullivan, John M. Ludlow, Major Evans Bell and Dr. Ganda Singh. There is a list of thirty-four leading chiefs in the Blue Book, who with their relatives and dependents, took no part in the rebellion.[41] Twenty-eight of these were Sikhs, two were Mohammadans and four Hindus. A careful analysis of the several lists and documents proves that the majority of those who signed the treaties were not involved in the hostilities against the British. Of the 16 Sirdars, who signed the treaties, only five joined in the rebellion.[42] Of the eight members of the Regency Council, six remained faithful throughout; one was suspected; one only Raja Sher Singh, took the field against the British. The Resident remained in the capital of the Punjab undisturbed throughout the rebellion; his orders were fully and faithfully carried out by the officers of the Lahore Darbar, who gave him the fullest cooperation in the suppression of the rebellion. Particularly were applauded the services of General Cortlandt, General Gulab Singh Povindea, Col. Alla Singh, Diwan Dina Nath, Sheikh Emam-ud-din, Misr Sahib Dayal and Diwan Jawahar Mal. General Whish in his final despatch of the 23rd January 1849, after the fall of Multan, expressed his thanks to General Cortlandt who commanded the regular regiments and artillery of the Darbar at the siege of Multan. The Governor-General himself sent his thanks to the General for the same services, as an officer of the Maharaja of Lahore, through the Resident.[43] It was with the help of General Gulab Singh, the Governor of Peshawar and his son, Col. Alla Singh, that "Maj. Lawrence most gallantly remained at his post until the middle of October, 1848, when the troops broke into open rebellion". The Assistant Resident "repeatedly praised their exertions" "to preserve good order in the district of Peshawar and to keep the troops steady to their allegiance".[44]

Similarly, Raja Dina Nath's mission to the Hazara Province in September 1848 and his conduct after his return from there evoked much praise from the Resident who thus wrote to the Governor-General: "His presence in that part of the country had the effect of assuring the inhabitants, and he certainly appears to have used his influence, in every way, to defeat the machinations of Sirdar Chuttur Singh". Since his return he appears to have entered zealously and earnestly into the measures adopted for punishing the rebels, by the confiscation of their jagirs and the attachment of their houses and property, and for counteracting the plots of the insurgents".[45] Sheikh Emam-ud-din and Diwan Jawahar Mal rendered valuable services by driving the rebels out of the district of Jhang. Misr Sahib Dayal, "an able and highly intelligent person of considerable experience and knowledge of the country" was on account of "his approved fidelity to the interests of the young Maharaja and the British Government" selected by the Resident in November 1848 to accompany Lord Gough as "the chief officer on the part of the Darbar".[46] At an earlier period he had crushed the "menace" posed by Bhai Maharaj Singh who, in communication with Diwan Mul Raj, was scouring the country and summoning the Sikhs to join in a religious war.[47] It has been estimated by Major Bell that "at least 20,000 subjects of the Lahore State enrolled in its service, fought on the side of the Government and assisted in suppressing the rebellion".[48] The same story of co-operation and help on the part of the Lahore Darbar is revealed by the perusal of the *Akhbar-i-Darbar-i-Lahore* and the *Akhbar-i-Multan*, which form the subject of a paper published in the *Proceedings of the Indian Historical Records Commission* for 1944.[49] For instance may be noted the news item for 28th August 1848, which reads as follows:-

> "As desired by the Resident, the Lahore Darbar issued Parwanas to their military and civil officers to send reinforcements to Herbert Edwardes at Multan and to pay the salaries of the men under his command".

It is thus wrong to believe with Dalhousie that the Lahore Darbar "gave no effective and substantial help" during the emergency.

It is significant that the Resident at Lahore, too, sent a favourable report about the Darbar to the Governor-General. On August 15, 1848 he wrote to Lord Dalhousie: "The conduct of the Darbar collectively and individually has been entirely satisfactory in everything connected with this outbreak, and indeed in all other respects for the last two months".[50]

Similarly, as regards the financial delinquency, the charge levelled by the Governor-General does not seem to be well-founded. It is wrong to say that no portion of the money due to the British was paid by the Lahore Darbar, for there is a written report of the Resident dated 23rd February 1848, saying that,[51] "The Darbar have paid into this treasury gold to the value of Rs. 13,56,837. By this payment they have reduced their debt to the British Government from upwards of forty lakhs of rupees to less than twenty-Seven". If a financial equilibrium had not been restored, and the regular payment of the tribute not commenced, when the rebellion of 1848 once more threw everything into confusion, it was no fault of the Council of Regency. Not only had the British authorities accepted the trust with their eyes open to the disordered state of the finances but also the Resident—opposed by the Council of Regency and supported by the Governor-General—had introduced extensive changes into the fiscal system, leading, as had been anticipated, to a very serious loss of revenue, which he fully admits in his reports to the Governor-General on August 28 and December 16, 1847 and January 12, 1848.[52] The Resident himself explains the attitude of the Darbar towards the fiscal reforms introduced by the British. He says:

> "The settlement was of course most summary and its details have yet to be filled up. Its working must be most carefully watched. The Darbar was averse to its introduction, but yielded, as they always do; and contented themselves, with the exception of Raja Deena Nath, with standing aloof from its execution leaving the whole matter to the Resident and his Assistants. Raja Deena Nath sees the financial embarrassment of the state and feels that the more we interfere with details, especially where the revenue is concerned, the less will be the Darbar's responsibility for financial difficulties and deficiencies".[53]

On the basis of the loyal and cooperative behaviour of the Lahore Darbar, of which a general idea has been given above, it is the definite opinion of John Sullivan, John Ludlow, Major Bell and Dr. Ganda Singh that the violation of the treaties was committed by the British and not by the Lahore Darbar. This will be evident from the following statements of their views:

"Though the state of Lahore had remained faithful to the engagements with the British Government, that Government had violated its own engagements with the Lahore State". Sullivan, *Kooh-i-Noor*, p. 66.

"Lord Dalhousie has, as such, violated treaties, abused a sacred trust....... and made an acquisition as unjust as it was imprudent.

Major Bell, *Retrospects and Prospects of Indian Policy.*, 179.

"It was in fact the British—the Governor-General and the Resident—who faithlessly and blatantly violated the treaty by which they were bound to preserve the peace of the country and protect the Maharaja".

Ganda Singh, *Private Correspondence, Intro.*, 157.

In particular, these critics of Lord Dalhousie's policy have held the British guilty of breach of guardianship of the boy-Maharaja. "This is perhaps the first instance on record in which a guardian has visited his own misdeeds upon his ward", say J. Sullivan. "The British Government was the self-Constituted guardian of the Rajah and the regent of his kingdom; a rebellion was provoked by the agents of the guardian, it was acknowledged by the guardian to be a rebellion against the government of his ward, and the guardian punished that ward by confiscating his dominions and his diamonds to his own use".

(*Are we Bound by our Treaties?*)

John M. Ludlow writes: "Dhuleep Singh was an infant; his minority was only to end in 1854. We were his declared protectors. On our last advance into his country, we had proclaimed that we came to punish insurgents and to put down, all armed opposition to constituted authority'. We fulfilled that pledge by annexing his whole country within six months. In other words, we protected our ward by taking his whole territory from him".

British India, ii, 166-7.

Similar sentiments have been voiced by Evans Bell on the question of wardship.

According to the critics, the annexation of the Punjab by Dalhousie was an act of burglary or a breach of faith. But Lord Dalhousie, it appears, approached the problem differently. His main preoccupation was the security of the British Empire in India and the safety of the frontier. He therefore considered the question of the treaty observance in a sense deeper than the formal. He explains the object of his policy thus:

"That which we desire to see-that which we must have-as indispensably necessary for the future prosperity of the territories we already possess is peace throughout our bounds. That which we desire to secure in the Punjab is a friendly and well-governed neighbour, and a frontier without alarms, and which does not demand a perpetual garrison of 50,000 men".[54] With this object in view, he dismisses the loyalty of the Council and Sardars by saying: "Of what advantage is it to us that the Council and Sirdars are friendly, if they have not the ability to control their army, which is hostile".[55] He elaborates the point: "If the Sikh Army and the Sikh people are eager to seize, and have the power of seizing, on every opportunity of violating the peace which we desire to render permanent, of what value to us, as a state, is the impotent fidelity of the Sirdars ?"[56] He was well aware of the popular sentiment for the boy-prince, Daleep Singh, as also of the obligations of the Government of India as his guardian but he could not allow any such thing to override the interests of the state he represented. He says "I sincerely lament the necessity by which we are compelled to depose from his throne a successor of Maharaja Ranjit Singh; but when I am fairly convinced that the safety of our own state requires us to enforce subjection of the Sikh nation, I cannot abandon that necessary measure, merely because the effectual subjection of the nation involves in itself the deposition of their Prince. I cannot permit myself to be turned away from fulfilling the duty, which I owe to the security and prosperity of millions of British subjects, by a feeling of misplaced and mistimed compassion for the fate of a child"...[57]

The problem basic to his view of the security of British possessions in India was how to deal with the Khalsa patriotism, which had rallied from the reverses of the first Anglo-Sikh War under the influence of the ever-tightening hold of the British over the Punjab. This patriotism permeated the vast majority of the Sikhs including their army and was on the look-out for an opportunity to rise and make a bid for the emancipation of the country from the British control. The desired opportunity was provided, as soon as some of the leading chiefs like Chatar Singh and Raja Sher Singh consented to lead the national struggle. The attention of the Governor-General was drawn forcibly to it immediately after the Multan outbreak. The murder of Van Agnew and Anderson by the rebel Diwan's men was no doubt a serious matter for the British. It was not merely the loss of two precious human lives but a great affront to the imperialistic prestige of the British in India, which must be avenged. But it was not so much this matter—because it could be settled by the punishment of the culprits—as the ready desertion of the Sikh escort with the murdered officials to the side of Diwan Mul Raj and the subsequent equally ready reply of the Lahore Darbar that they could not send any portion of their army against the rebels of Multan as they could not trust it, that impinged on Lord Dalhousie's mind. He explained his reactions to F. Currie on 13th July 1848: "We know positively that every man in their army is a traitor though he dare not do a treasonable act—some of them do commit the deed—all wait for a safe opportunity to do it.

The insurrection shows itself in another part, and the leader of it is received with open arms, apparently by high and low, through the principal Doab in the Punjab".[58] Again, ".......if the army, in spite of discipline, in spite of pension and pay, is thus traitrous to a man, if both soldiers and Sikhs of every degree thus catch at every opportunity of ejecting or destroying us, although we are protecting and aiding them, and if as is the case, not one shilling of the treaty-subsidy is paid, are we to overlook this gross national offence, are we to content ourselves with hanging Mul Raj, taking reimbursement of our own expense and enough to reward and reimburse Bahawal Khan, then forgive the rest and go on till the 5th September 1854, sacrificing 22 lacs per annum, bearing all the labour, all the anxiety and then retire with the certainty that we have a state on our frontier whose Government is as incompetent and whose army is as uncontrollable as were the army and Government which we found there in Feby: 1846? Are we to do this or are we to say, we have tried you enough, we have borne with you enough, we have dry-nursed and bolstered you up enough; your army and people are and ever will be hostile to us, all our generosity is thrown away upon you, you injure us and either will not or cannot give us redress, we will bear with you no longer, your power is at end and your country shall be ours".[59]

Later on, answering the general charge that his policy of delay had caused the development of a mere local revolt into a conflagration, he writes: "Whether the immediate commencement at that time of the siege of Multan would or would not have averted the war that has occurred, can never now be determined. But this, at least, is certain, that if the short delay which took place in punishing the murder of two British Officers at Multan, could produce an universal rising against us throughout all the Punjab, the very fact itself betokens the existence of a deep and widespread feeling of hostility against us, which could not long have been repressed. The worst that can be alleged against the delay is that it precipitated the crisis; and opened, somewhat earlier, to the Sikhs that opportunity for renewal of war which, sooner or later, so bitter a spirit of hostility must have created for itself".[60]

But what was for Lord Dalhousie the inveterate and inextinguishable hostility of the Sikhs was in reality the Khalsa nationalism aiming at freedom from the British domination. The Governor-General was so firmly convinced of the ultimate purpose of this movement that he would return again and again to this theme in his correspondence, whether private or official. The reports from the Resident and his Assistants scattered over the Punjab, having a bearing on the subject and his own fears based on them were indisputably confirmed after the rebellion of Chatar Singh and his son, Raja Sher Singh. "The disbanded soldiers and the people flocked to the army, in thousands, from the Manjha, and proclamations were issued calling upon all to make war upon the British".[61] The proclamation issued by Raja Sher Singh on 20th September 1848 establishes beyond any doubt that this was no rebellion against the Maharaja or the Regency Council but a revolution directed against the British. This general rising of the Sikh troops and the people for the specific purpose of overthrowing the British power in the Punjab was buttressed with an alliance made with Amir Dost Mohammad on the basis of cession of Peshawar to him. Dalhousie's mind was now finally made up on the question of annexation; and he declared himself against all compromises.[62] The need for acting on grounds of security was now overwhelming.

As early as August 1848, the Home Government had left to the Government of India "ample discretion as to ordering our future relations with the Government of Lahore".[63] Taking advantage of this and without getting the prior sanction of the Home Government, the Governor-General annexed the Punjab by Proclamation on 29th March 1849.

Immediately after this, Dalhousie wrote a long letter to the Court of Directors making out a strong case of annexation.[64] After what had happened, he claimed an absolute right to dispose of the Punjab any way the British liked and urged upon the Home Government that "that right must now be fully exercised". He averred that not only the Sikh "troops and people have risen in arms" but also "not content with making war themselves upon the British, the Sikhs have laboured to induce other states and sovereigns in India to attack us also". "There are," he went on, "in the possession of the Government many letters which have been addressed by the Sikh chiefs to the neighbouring powers, Musalman, Hindu and Sikh, earnestly invoking their assistance; and the burthen of every letter is the necessity of destroying and expelling the British". He continued: "The bitterness of their enmity has carried them yet further still. No one ever thought to see the day when the Sikhs would court the alliance of the Afghans, and would actually purchase their assistance by a heavy sacrifice. Yet their hatred to the British name has induced them to do even this. They invited Amir Dost Mohammed Khan from Kabul to their aid. They promised him, as the reward of his assistance, the Province of Peshawar and lands which the King of Kabul formerly held, a possession, which the Sikhs themselves valued beyond price; which for years they had struggled to obtain; and which they gained and held, only by vast expenditure of treasure and with the best blood of their race". He cited as an example of the depth of the Sikh anti-British feelings: "So inveterate has their hostility to us proved to be that the securing of Afghan cooperation against the British has been sufficient to induce the Sikhs to forget their strongest national animosity, and has, in their eyes, compensated even for Afghan cruelty to their people and for Mohammadan insults to their religion". He concluded: "I hold that it is no longer open to this Government to determine the question of the future relations of the Punjab with British India, by considerations of what is desirable or convenient or even expedient". And further: "I hold that the course of recent events has rendered the question one of national safety and that regard for the security of our own territories and the interests of our own subjects must compel us, in self-defence, to relinquish the policy which would maintain the independence of the Sikh nation in the Punjab". He ends with the recommendation: "I have thus fully laid before you the grounds on which I have formed the conclusion that having regard to events, which recently occurred, it is indispensable to the security of the British territories and to the interests of our people that you should put an end to the independence of the Sikh nation and reduce it to entire subjection". Before closing the letter Lord Dalhousie assured the Directors of his *bona fides*: "While deeply sensible of the responsibility I have assumed. I have an undoubting conviction of the expediency, the justice and the necessity of my act", and "What I have done. I have done with a clear conscience and in the honest belief that it was imperatively demanded of me by duty to the State".

Obviously, it seems to be the firm conviction of Lord Dalhousie that to give a further lease of life to Khalsa nationalism with its strong determination to wrest full freedom from the British intruders and in alliance with an enemy of the British, Amir Dost Mohammad Khan of Kabul, would not only keep the frontier in a state of perpetual disturbance but would also spell a serious danger to the safety of the empire in India.[65] Therefore, he argued that if otherwise practicable, annexation would be the best solution of the problem. And as regards the aspect of practicability, he thus wrote to the Court of Directors: "Although I have more than once stated to you that the Government of India did not desire, and ought not to desire, the conquest of the Punjab, I do not wish, by any means, to convey to you the impression that I regard the Punjab as a possession which it would be seriously difficult for us to maintain or which would be financially unprofitable".[65a] He apprehended no difficulty because the Sikhs were only "a small proportion of the population of the Punjab". "A large proportion of the inhabitants, and especially the Mohammedan people, peaceful in their habits and occupation, will hail the introduction of our rule with pleasure", he assured. On the financial ground all his apprehensions had been removed by Sir F. Currie's assurance, a few months earlier, that the resources of the Lahore State were adequate to meet all the expenses of occupation.[66] He therefore confidently observed: "The revenues are very considerable in the aggregate. A large proportion has hitherto been diverted from the public treasury in jaghirs to the chiefs. A considerable amount will now be recovered from the jaghirs of those who have been engaged in hostilities against us". He had "no hesitation in expressing a confident belief that the Punjab will, at no distant time, be not only a secure, but a profitable possession".[67]

Major Evans Bell has found fault with the entire reasoning of Lord Dalhousie in this respect. His objections are: (i) Equivocal use by the Governor-General of the terms "the Sikh people" or "nation" and "the people of the Punjab"; (ii) "The people of the Punjab in general were not hostile as Lord Dalhousie acknowledged;" (iii) the security fears of Lord Dalhousie were exaggerated because, "the Sikh army and the turbulent portion of the Sikh people had been effectually subjected and deprived of the means of making war. Reduced in numbers, subdued to orderly discipline, the Sikh army never could have regained its insolent pre-eminence in the state, as the embodied representative of the Sikh religion and commonwealth—the Khalsa Panth. And its conspicuous humiliation was sure to operate in a very wholesome manner upon the Sikh population, not only in the Punjab but also throughout Sirhind, the Jullundur Doab and the feudatory states on both sides of the Sutlej. Deprived of all supremacy and influence over many of these minor states, whose resources were now transferred to the British Government and proved of material assistance during the campaign of 1849, weakened by the loss of Jullundur and Cashmere—the former in our possession, the latter placed on her flank as a jealous rival—the Punjab State, even if freed from the British occupation, could hardly be considered independent after the Treaties of 1846. Certainly, her independence was not of such a character as to afford reasonable grounds of apprehension for "the tranquillity of India" or "for the security of our own territories".[68]

Now let us examine these objections. Firstly, it has been said that the equivocal use of some terms such as Sikh people or nation and the people of the Punjab has created confusion and is not only improper but also incorrect. Certainly, it is incorrect, because the people of the Punjab were not Sikhs alone, but it must be dismissed as a minor objection, as nowhere the meaning of the Governor-General is ambiguous. The confusion seems to be in the mind of Bell and not Dalhousie. Secondly, it has been said that the people of the Punjab in general were not hostile, the Muslim inhabitants being a notable exception; and this fact was acknowledged by Dalhousie himself. It is true so far as it goes. But the question is: Could Muslims or others, whatever their number, be equated, in the then situation, with the dominant Sikh sect, long accustomed to political supremacy, which held the key to the peace of the Punjab in their hands? Lord Dalhousie emphatically declared: "There never will be peace in the Punjab, so long as its people are allowed to retain the means and the opportunity of making war. Here never can be now any guarantee for the tranquillity of India, until we shall have effected the entire subjection of the Sikh people and destroyed its power as an independent nation".[69] This also meets the third objection raised by Bell, who, in fact, advocates the view of continuing Lord Hardinge's system, irrespective of the recent events. A thorough-going and imperialistically-minded man like Lord Dalhousie could not regard as satisfactory, from the point of view of defence, the political system that had failed to prevent the resurgence of Khalsa nationalism.

It may be pointed out that Lord Dalhousie's views were shared by many other eminent British statesmen. The chief opponent of annexation, Henry Lawrence, too, admitted the justice of the measure, his objection being only to its expediency.[70] Lord Hardinge, the architect of the Lahore settlement of 1846, admitted both.[71] Henry's younger brother, John met Dalhousie at Ferozepur a little before the final decision and advised him in emphatic terms: "No delay! The Khalsa must not be allowed again to raise its head".[72] Thrice he uttered the words "Annex it now". Major Edwardes calls the annexation "providential". He has expressed his belief in these words:[73] "If the most favourable circumstances had succeeded and on the 4th of September, 1854, the Governor-General, in fulfilment of treaties permitted to remain in force", had withdrawn the British troops and handed over the Punjab to its Youthful Sovereign" with a revenue improved by peace, an exchequer replenished by honesty and economy, and army improved by discipline," no one can believe "that the peace of the frontier would have lasted for a year or a Second Sikh War have been avoided".[74] None can exactly say what would have happened in, before or after 1854, if the annexation had not been made in 1849. But one thing is certain that Lord Dalhousie and many others like him at the time felt that they could not safely take risk with the security of their empire by postponing or foregoing the action that was taken. The Home Government also gave unanimous approval to the policy of the Government of India. Even Major Bell has admitted that "it has not excited the same disgust as the annexations of Nagpur, Jhansi and Oudh".[75] His explanation is that "it looked like a conquest", so that "the iniquity of the transaction was shrouded by the smoke of battle". This seems to be nearer the truth. The Sikhs has made, in their love of freedom, a bold bid for throwing off the British yoke. To subdue them the British had plunged into action a huge army which had to fight several hard-contested battles to win victory. So it was like a conquest, though not a conquest in the strict sense of the term, as their anomalous position in the Punjab had compelled the British to use the mask of fighting for the Maharaja.

We have seen above the main considerations that governed the decision of Lord Dalhousie in annexing the Punjab. The annexation may well be called the inevitable culmination of the long-pursued British policy towards the Punjab state. Equally inevitable was that the feelings of the Khalsa should have been aroused by the British designs. The Anglo-Sikh war of 1845-46 was in fact a defensive action on the part of the Khalsa to save their country from the British. They were defeated. But it turned out to be only a partial reverse because their defeat had been brought about more through the treachery of their leaders than through superior military might. Hence a process of national resurgence commenced soon after, which was considerably aided by the British efforts to tighten their grip increasingly over their country. A powerful bid was made in 1848-49 to throw the enemy out of their land. It was with this strong organised patriotic upsurge that Lord Dalhousie came into clash, and his decision of annexation may be viewed as a measure to provide against this factor. In taking this decision, however, the Governor-General was greatly helped by the general trend of the East India Company's policy, since 1841, in favour of leaving or setting aside no rightful opportunity to add to the revenue or the territory of the Government of India".[76]

REFERENCES

1. Ganda Singh, *Private Correspondence Relating to the Anglo-Sikh Wars,* Amritsar—Patiala, 1955 (henceforth *Private Correspondence*) p. 27—Hardinge to F. Currie dated May 20, 1847.
2. *The Career of Major Broadfoot,* London, 1888, pp. 269, 270.
3. Ganda Singh, *Private Correspondence,* p. 19.
4. *Ibid.,* p. 26—Hardinge to F. Currie, April 24, 1847.
5. A.B. Keith, *Constitutional History of India,* p. 213.
6. Dodwel, *Cambridge History of India,* Vol. V, p. 586.
7. Napier, Sri W., *Gen. Sir C. Napier,* Vol. IV, p. 188.
8. Garratt and Thomson, *Rise and Fulfilment of British Rule in India,* p. 340—Sleeman to James Hogg, January 12, 1853.

9. *Private Correspondence*, p. 73. Dalhousie to F. Currie dated 13th July, 1848; Bosworth Smith, *op. cit.*, Vol. I, p. 241.
10. *Private Correspondence*, p. 55.
11. *Ibid.*, p. 59—Dalhousie to Currie, 28th May, 1848.
12. *Ibid.*
13. *Punjab Papers*, 1849, p. 660.
14. Major Bell, *Annexation of the Punjab*, p. 11.
15. *Private Correspondence*, p. 72—Dalhousie to Currie, 13th July, 1848.
16. *Ibid.*, p. 74—Dalhousie to Currie, 13th July, 1848.
17. *Ibid.*, p. 94.
18. *Ibid.*, p. 67.
19. *Ibid.*, p. 73.
20. *Ibid.*
21. *Ibid.*, p. 153.
22. Edwin Arnold, *Administration of Lord Dalhousie*, Vol. I, p. 205—Dalhousie's letter to the Court of Directors.
23. *Private Correspondence*, p. 139.
24. Pearson Hesketh, *Hero of Delhi*, p. 148.
25. Bell, *Annexation of the Punjab*, p. 82.
26. Edwardes and Merivale, *Life of Sir Henry Lawrence*, p. 434; Innes, *Sir Henry Lawrence*, pp. 109-11; Rait, *Life and Campaigns of L. Gough*, London, 1913, pp. 214-216.
27. *Ibid.*
28. *Private Correspondence*, p. 130—Dalhousie to Currie, December 9, 1848.
29. *Ibid.*, p. 71.
30. *Ibid.*, p. 100—Dalhousie to Currie, 8 October, 1848
31. *Ibid.*
32. *Ibid.*, p. 87—Dalhousie to Currie, August 19, 1848.
33. *Ibid.*
34. *Ibid.*, p. 74—Dalhousie to Currie, July 13, 1848.
35. *Ibid.*, p. 100—Dalhousie to Currie, October 8, 1848.
36. Khilnani, *The Punjab under the Lawrences*, p. 99.

37. Marshman, *History of India,* Vol. III, p. 321; *Private Correspondence,* p. 103—Currie to Dalhousie, October 12, 1848.
38. Bell, *op. cit.,* pp. 90-91.
39. Edwin Arnold, *op. cit.,* Vol. I, p. 214.
40. *Ibid.,* pp. 202-204; Latif, *History of the Punjab,* pp. 572-573.
41. Bell, *op. cit.,* p. 65.
42. *Ibid.,* p. 66.
43. *Punjab Papers,* 1849, p. 586.
44. Bell, *op. cit.,* 68.
45. *Punjab Papers,* p. 379.
46. Bell, *op. cit.,* p. 71.
47. *Ibid.,* p. 71.
48. *Ibid.,* p. 76.
49. *Volume XXI,* pp. 43-46.
50. *Punjab Papers,* 1849, p. 289.
51. *Ibid.,* pp. 110-111.
52. *Ibid.,* pp. 23, 24, 56, 57, 93, 99, 104, 105; Bell, *op. cit.,* p. 74.
53. *Punjab Papers,* 1849, p. 128.
54. Edwin Arnold, *op. cit.,* p. 212—Dalhousie to Court of Directors. Edwardes expresses a similar opinion. "There was not in our Residency a stauncher advocate for clinging to the last shadow of the Treaty than myself, yet I own it would be affectation not to consider the present simultaneous risings, as an expression of national hostility. Our treaty was not alone with Maharaja Dulleep Singh, it was with the whole Sikh people. The Commons have as much right to break the treaty as the Throne". *Private Correspondence,* p. 275—Edwardes to Currie, September 19, 1848.
55. Edwin Arnold, *op. cit.,* p. 212.
56. *Ibid.*
57. *Ibid.,* p. 217.
58. *Private Correspondence,* p. 72.
59. *Ibid.,* p. 73.
60. Edwin Arnold, *op. cit.,* 207.
61. *Ibid.*

62. *Private Correspondence,* pp. 87, 112—Dalhousie to Currie, Oct., 18, 1848.
63. *Ibid.*
64. Edwin Arnold, *op. cit.,* pp. 205-219.
65. It may he pointed out that it was not the Sikh Alliance with Kabul which decided Dalhousie's mind on the question of annexation. That only confirmed him in his decision which had been made by him towards the end of June or in early July 1848 when he got hold of a bundle of intercepted Sikh letter, *Punjab Papers,* 1849, p. 235.

65a. *Ibid.,* p. 218.
66. *Private Correspondence,* p. 73.
67. *Punjab Papers,* 1849, pp. 664-665.
68. Bell, *op. cit.,* pp. 79, 80.
69. *Punjab Papers,* 1849, p. 662.
70. Bosworth Smith, *op. cit.,* Vol. I, p. 249; Gibbon, p. 156; Edwardes and Merivale, *op. cit.,* p. 437.
71. *Private Correspondence,* p. 49. Edwardes and Merivale, *op. cit.,* p. 439.
72. Bosworth Smith, *op. cit.,* Vol. I, 250; Edwardes and Merivale, *op. cit.,* p. 439.
73. Edwardes, Sir Herbert, *A Year on the Punjab Frontier in 1848-49,* pp. 145-146. He had begun to advocate annexation right from September 1848 when the general rising became a reality.
74. General Thackwell expresses a similar view: "That the Sikhs will ever love our rule or lose that patriotic spirit which now consumes them is most improbable". *Narrative of the Second Sikh War, London,* 1851, p. 281.
75. Bell, *op. cit.,* p. 8.
76. The general trend of the E. I. Coy.'s policy on the issue of annexation of Indian states comes out very clearly from the following statements of eminent writers:

    Col. Sleeman: 'Few old officers of experience, with my feelings and opinions on this subject, now remain in India; and the influence of ...a school characterised by impatience at the existence of any native state, and its strong and often insane advocacy of their absorption by honest means, if possible—but still their absorption...too great over the rising generation, whose hopes and aspirations they tend so much to encourage".

He also complained: "That there is no pretext, however weak, that is not sufficient in their estimation, for the purpose of annexation; and no war, however cruel, that is not justifiable, if it has only this object in view".

Col. Sleeman's representation to Dalhousie on Punjab annexation submitted in the month of September 1848.

The Cambridge History of India, Vol. V, p. 586.

"Reviewing Lord Dalhousie's administration in so far it affected the Indian states, it is clear that the policy of absorbing them in cases of failure of direct heirs was not of his making, but was inherited by him and whether right or wrong, was at that time, the avowed policy of the Company, whose one anxiety was to consolidate its possessions".

Sir Charles Napier, *The Life and Opinions of Gen. Sir C. J. Napier*, ed. by Sir W. Napier, Vol. IV, p. 188.

"Were I emperor of India for twelve years, she should be traversed by railways and have her rivers bridged.....no Indian prince should exist. The Nizam should be no more heard of ... Nepal would be ours".

East India Company's conviction was that no honourable possibility of acquiring territory should be passed over.

A.B. Keith, *Constitutional History of India*, p. 213.

Index

□□□